THE POLYGRAPH IN COURT

By

ROBERT J. FERGUSON, JR., AARC

Member American Polygraph Association
Polygraphist Licensed and Certified
by the State of Texas
Chief Examiner Texas Industrial Security, Inc.
Fort Worth, Texas

and

ALLAN L. MILLER, BBA, E.T.S.U.

Founder-President
Texas Industrial Security, Inc.
Fort Worth, Texas
Member Texas Association of Polygraph Examiners
Affiliate Member American Polygraph Association
Licensed and Certified by the State of Texas

CHARLES C THOMAS · PUBLISHER
Springfield · Illinois · U.S.A.

61694

Published and Distributed Throughout the World by

CHARLES C THOMAS • PUBLISHER

BANNERSTONE HOUSE

301-327 East Lawrence Avenue, Springfield, Illinois, U.S.A.

© *1973, by* CHARLES C THOMAS • PUBLISHER

ISBN 0-398-02679-3

Library of Congress Catalog Card Number: 72-88443

With THOMAS BOOKS *careful attention is given to all details of manufacturing and design. It is the Publisher's desire to present books that are satisfactory as to their physical qualities and artistic possibilities and appropriate for their particular use.* THOMAS BOOKS *will be true to those laws of quality that assure a good name and good will.*

Printed in the United States of America

N-1

This work is humbly dedicated to men like John E. Reid, Leonard Harrelson, Lynn Marcy, Alex Greggory, Charles Zimmerman along with other members of the American Polygraph Association, who have expended lifelong efforts toward the enhancement, enrichment, establishment, and recognition of polygraphy as the most objective means for accurate truth verification; and to those great champions of justice, the brilliant trial lawyers, such as the outstanding F. Lee Bailey, Edward Bennett Williams, Melvin Belli, Percy Foreman, John Tobin, James Russ, and so many others, whose knowledge, skill and expertise have been the inspiration for this book.

FOREWORD

DID YOU EVER HAVE an innocent client convicted of a serious crime? Maybe you can not answer that question. After all, lawyers are not at the scene of the crime. They do not have any inside knowledge other than what their clients tell them and what they can determine and infer from the evidence. But lawyers, prosecutors and defense attorneys alike can go one step further. The defense attorney or prosecutor can go that one step further by requiring that his client or key witnesses submit to a polygraph examination.

If you have never asked a client to take a polygraph examination maybe you need to ask yourself why. It is certainly not the expense, because as an investigative tool it is one of the least expensive. Perhaps you do not want to know whether or not your client is guilty or innocent. To know that you represent an innocent man only increases the pressure and the awareness of the responsibility that goes with proper legal representation.

If you care about your clients, and if you are willing to take that one additional step, then you will find this an interesting and important book.

I have had an innocent client convicted of a crime he did not commit. I have had that client submit to a polygraph analysis which showed he was innocent. I have used the same information from the polygraph test to investigate the crime to the point where I felt that I knew who did commit the crime. The heart of my defense was that my client had voluntarily submitted to and been cleared by a competent polygraph examination. I failed in my effort to have the court consider this most important piece of evidence. As I look back on that first attempt to introduce and qualify the polygraph examiner and his test results, I realize how important and useful this book could have been to me.

In writing this foreword I attempt to point out the areas in this book that are of assistance to a defense lawyer or prosecutor.

I think first of all you will find a convincing underlying philosophical perspective presented by the authors that rests upon the assumption that it would be a better world to live in if everyone told the truth. This is an interesting position that many of us might well reject. But the authors start from this assumption and proceed to argue that there is a way to detect the truth, and because a better world would result from the knowledge of the truth, the acceptance of the scientific advances in polygraph analysis will make this a better place in which to live.

The authors equate truth with justice. Criminal defense lawyers do not operate on this same equation. Justice can be done even though a guilty man goes free. This is best exemplified in one of the largest areas of the practice of criminal law, the motion to suppress evidence based on the violation of a defendant's Fourth, Fifth or Sixth Amendment rights. An important piece of evidence may be suppressed because the police used illegal means in obtaining it. The government's case may completely fold as a result of the granting of a motion to suppress evidence. Justice would have been done even though a guilty man would have gone free and the truth would not have been revealed to a jury.

While there is a concept of justice that does not totally equate with truth, I think no one should claim that justice is done when an innocent man is convicted. Yes, all the procedures may have been followed. He may have had an adequate defense. But, if an innocent man is convicted we should not accept this as justice.

Polygraph tests help determine the truth. But before they can fully help us to achieve justice, they must be recognized by the courts. In Chapter 2 the authors reproduce a thorough and thoughtout legal brief for the admissibility of the results of a polygraph test. The authorities are cited in detail, and numerous cases not ordinarily available by the normal methods of research are presented. The argument speaks for itself, and without elaboration I would only add that as a first step toward an attempted presentation of polygraph test results in court, an attorney would do well by adopting this brief.

It is not enough to have a good legal argument for the admissibility of the polygraph results. Resistance by the courts to the admissibility of this evidence is astonishingly high. I do not pretend to know all the psychological reasons behind this resistance to an important new scientific advance. But these barriers of history, prejudice and ignorance will not be overcome simply by good legal arguments. If you plan to produce a polygraph expert in court, be prepared to present more than a legal argument. Be prepared to explain what the polygraph is about.

Chapter 4 is where you will start. To qualify the polygraphist in court, you can follow no better example than given in this book. If you do not have a qualified polygraph analyst who can answer the questions set forth in Chapter 4 do not make the attempt. The criteria of expertise for a polygraphist are much higher than those expected of any other expert. If we compare the standards that have been imposed for admissibility of the polyghaphist's expert testimony against the standards required of psychiatrists, we realize how inconsistent our courts have been in the standards they have set for the admissibility of expert testimony. All lawyers relish the idea of cross-examining a psychiatrist. Nothing is easier or more fun. I wonder if our prosecutors and defense lawyers would so relish the idea of cross-examining a competent polygraphist.

This book does more than give you the legal brief to support the admission of your expert's testimony and give you the proper direct examination for the admissibility of that evidence. It gives the layman a thorough working knowledge of polygraph tests. Part II of this book goes beyond what one usually finds available in a discussion of polygraphy. The validity of polygraph tests is argued in terms of basic recognized emotional responses to deception. You will recognize in reading these chapters a direct correlation between your own emotional responses which the polygraph instrument records. These same responses are explained in physiological and psychological terms. But the point is clear; we do respond to the conscious telling of a lie. We do respond emotionally. Where lies are told because of a *desire* not to get caught, it is not surprising that this desire or emotion is reflected physiologically in a way that can be detected by monitors of physiological responses. The *Polygraph in Court* starts from the simplest most recognized assumption that when we are under stress, we respond in ways that affect our heartbeat, respiration and perspiration. And these are measureable physiological responses to the psychological fact that one knows when he is not telling the truth.

How then does the polygraph analyst read what is basically a registry of physiological responses to psychological stimuli? The authors provide excellent examples of exactly what the analyst is doing. You will not learn how to be a polygraph analyst. You will learn how the polygraph chart is read and you will be able to answer many of those perplexing questions that are raised about polygraph analysis. What if someone makes himself "emotionally respond" to a question? How can you tell a highly nervous person from a liar? What if someone is very frightened when they go into a polygraph test? Will this ruin the test? Can the calculating liar beat the test? You will be able to see how the polygraph analyst answers these questions by looking at the very charts he would look at. You will see the fluctuations, by seconds, to the physiological responses correlated to certain questions. You will, I think, be impressed with the presentation.

The only thing that this book does not offer by way of a complete exposition of a polygraph analysis is a movie or a viewing of a polygraph test in operation. I have seen the authors conduct such tests on vieedo taped closed circuit television. The firsthand observation of the tests being given and of the responses and the analysis of the charts probably is the most impressive evidence I can imagine of the reliability of polygraphy. Robert Ferguson, Jr., with an hour at his instrument has saved me many hundreds of hours in fruitless investigation and pursuit of my client's dreams, fantasies or just plain lies.

If the courts are never convinced as to the admissibility of these tests, then lawyers should be. Nothing can save you more time in investigative work. Nothing can be more valuable to you than talking honestly with your client. Even if you never sought to introduce the results of one of these tests, you should take it upon yourself in fulfilling your duty to your client in adequate representation of his cause to use these tests. You also owe it to yourself to understand this important scientific advance. This book will help you fulfill those duties.

R. DAVID BROILES
with the law firm of
Hooper, Kerry, Chappell and Broiles
Fort Worth, Texas

FOREWORD

T HIS BOOK, *THE POLYGRAPH IN COURT*, will hasten the day when the instrument and its associated techniques will be recognized by the judicial system on the same basis as other expert testimony and scientific evidence. That day is long overdue.

Judicial precedents supporting the admissibility of the polygraph are overwhelming. Expert testimony and scientific evidence now routinely accepted by the courts include, among others, latent fingerprint evidence, firearms identification, tool mark evidence, traces of hair, fiber and other materials from weapons and instruments of attack, document examination and identification, traces of blood, fingernail scrapings, traces of dusts, soils, metals, glass, ash, poisons and drugs, and other materials.

One needs only to examine the requirements for admission to membership in the American Polygraph Association to recognize the professional stature of the polygraph examiner today. It is interesting to note that the polygraph is used extensively in Medical Schools throughout the country in their Departments of Psychiatry to implement their study of the emotions.

As early as 1959, a survey revealed that police departments in more than 200 American cities and the state police in 48 states were making use of the polygraph.* The survey further indicated the extent to which the polygraph is being employed in the Armed Forces, including the U. S. Air Force, the U. S. Marines and the Military Police. Parenthetically, the polygraph training program at the Provost Marshal General's School at Camp Gordon, Georgia, is conceded to be among the best and most comprehensive programs of its kind in the entire United States.

In another area where the polygraph is used extensively and on an expanding scale, it is significant that the conservative *Wall*

---

*Goodnick, Louis: *A Survey of Police Use of the Polygraph,* a Master's Thesis, New York University, New York, 1959.

Street Journal featured on the front page of its October 1961 issue an article on the increasing use of the polygraph by business and industry in the screening of personnel. On the roster of known users of the polygraph were major companies in steel production, copper refining, automobile manufacturing, meat packing, food processing, electronics manufacturing, mail order retailing and wholesale drug concerns.

The authors have presented the case for admissibility in a convincing and thoroughly professional manner. *THE POLYGRAPH IN COURT* is a welcome addition to the literature of criminal justice administration. Because of its inherent interest to the polygraph profession, the law enforcement field, practicing attorneys, including the prosecution and defense, and the judiciary, it should experience a wide distribution.

V. A. Leonard, BS, MA, Ph.D.
Honorary Life Member
American Polygraph Association
Denton, Texas

PREFACE

RESEARCH in any endeavor partakes of infinities and, in turn, widens our capacities. The higher we mount the steps of knowledge, the more magnificant are the prospects it stretches out before us, and rewards of effort commence to substitute facts for appearances.

The Polygraph in Court is the first legal, psychological, and physiological correlation, under one cover, of modern polygraphy based on actual live court cases and testing situations.

Supported by the records, writings and illustrations of recognized authorities in their respective fields, this work also presents functional psychological and physiological ingredients responsible for the unchallenged accuracy and acute reliability of the polygraph technique.

It is our sincere hope that intelligent men of every profession will materially benefit from the contents contained herein.

ROBERT J. FERGUSON JR.
ALLAN L. MILLER

INTRODUCTION

T HIS TEXT aims to present a rather comprehensive view of the facts and principles embodied in modern polygraphy, correlating these with analytic, descriptive, structural, legal and psychophysiological counterparts.

For truth verification to prevail during all phases of pretrial, posttrial, presentencing, and postconviction situations, it becomes almost paramount that attorneys, judges and jurors realize when they are indulging in subjective speculation, frequently based on uncorroborated hearsay, and then objectively do something about it.

In this most modern twentieth century, there are far too many persons, subsequently proven innocent, regularly being accused, indicted, convicted, sentenced and incarcerated.

By the same token, there are far too many criminals who described their crimes in minute detail, led police to bodies of their victims, and who have frankly admitted enslaving young people to hard narcotics, walking free on adjudged legal technicalities having little relationship to the fact that they did commit the crime.

In this twentieth century there is far more deliberate, unbridled perjury in our trials than ever before. And yet, appellate courts, for the most part, have consistently ignored the most accurate and reliable method of ascertaining the truth thus far developed.

That the infamous Frye decision in 1923, even though the prosecutor, jury and judge were later shown to have convicted an innocent man, could to this day be one of the main barriers against polygraph's admissibility into trial evidence seems incredibly inconceivable.

When Dr. William Marston tested Frye in 1923 he did so using a crude systolic blood pressure apparatus.

That was not polygraphy. That apparatus had not even the faintest resemblance to the polygraph technique, nor did that apparatus record with hardly more than a small portion of the sensitivity of modern polygraph instruments. Yet because of the court's ruling in this one "wrongful incident," a lot of truth verification and a great deal of justice has since been thwarted.

While relevant precedent may be a necessary controlling attribute, irrelevant precedent should never be compounded to the detriment of the times.

Is there too much injustice because we have come to regard justice as that which is established, and thus all our established laws will be regarded as just, without being examined, just because they are established?

The polygraph examiner is primarily concerned about ascertaining the "whole" or something less than the "whole" in truth or deception, not getting involved in speculative theories or unfounded hypothesis. In this particular we are referring to what takes place inside, and comes from, the human body, not the dog, cat, mouse or rubber tree plant.

In *The Polygraph in Court* we have endeavored to illustrate, on the basis of medical and physiological documentation, exactly how a verbal stimulus during polygraphy goes through the ear, brain, autonomic nervous system, to organ destination, and thence into development of individual cardiovascular, respiratory and galvanic, skin response tracings on a moving chart.

Coordinatingly, we are specifying consciousness and awareness of right or wrong, truth or deception, as the material ingredients of the polygraph technique. In order to properly correlate these factors we have dramatically inserted the mental generalities of knowing, feeling, and willing as purposive factors dependent upon conscious nervous processes in the brain. We might paraphrase to say that a conscious agency is, therefore, presumed to account for the character and quality of our conscious states.

Physiological psychology, as contained in polygraph examination, objectively considers consciousness as either the direct result or the correlate of brain and nervous system activity. Needless to say, polygraph chart tracings do not come from unconscious origins but, of course, deviations from "physiological norm" may come from sensitivity or other mental associations.

We know that before the brain can digest a stimulus it must be seen, heard, or felt. In some isolated instances it may even be sensed or anticipated. The stimulus in polygraphy is the question asked by the polygraphist. Herein, then, we are initially referring to sound. The question goes through predetermined pathways to one or more brain centers in the cerebral cortex. There it is digested and enters the realm of consciousness and meaning. It appears that the brain is the medium or agent for consciousness and not its cause, for consciousness may be nonmaterial or even spiritual in its nature and yet dependent upon the brain to manifest itself.

Accordingly, we see the activity of the nervous tissue, with the brain as its starting point, acquaint itself with the facts of histology, anatomy and physiology of the nervous system in response to certain auditory stimuli inserted by the polygraphist.

Also interwoven throughout this text are three other material ingredients which permit a broader understanding of the merger of psychophysiological knowns into heretofore polygraph unknowns. These are (1) observation, (2) introspection, and (3) mental awareness. Different degrees of each of these three may be figuratively ascertained only when the merger is reduced to a common unit. This, in polygraph examination, is accomplished through a process of elimination. The final analysis is termed "results." It is the content side of consciousness which furnishes the facts for scientific physiological recordings produced on the polygraph chart.

For some time there has been much misconception circulating amidst the uninformed with respect to "beating the lie detector test." Even some psychological experimenters using galvanometers under poorly controlled laboratory conditions arrived at the unsubstantiated conclusion that such a test was inconclusive because the "instruments used" could not detect the difference between subject "work" and "emotion." We feel the chapter entitled "The Physiology of Subject Movement" shoots holes clear through such ridiculous assertions.

During the past fifteen years we have been extremely pleased to note an increasing interest by judges, lawyers, psychologists and psychiatrists in the results obtained through competent application of polygraphy. While polygraphy certainly is not infallible, nor is it a panacea for all the courts' ills, common sense dictates its invaluable contribution to truth verification in so many areas.

For whatever it is worth, *The Polygraph in Court* is designed to help eliminate costly and unnecessary trials. Its purpose is to show that through polygraphy there is a much higher degree of accuracy not only in assisting to bring the guilty to the bar of justice but also for protection of the innocent.

Is it not true that prosecuting attorneys, with all the power at their disposal, are supposed to do everything within that power to protect the innocent?

To every judge, juror, prosecuting and defense attorney, who are only men and women, also vehemently swayed by personal and political desires and prejudices, we can only say that justice is the great interest of man on earth. It is the ligament which holds civilized beings and civilized nations together. Wherever her temple stands, so long as it is duly honored, there is a foundation for general security, general happiness, and the improvement and progress of our country.

R.J.F.
A.L.M.

ACKNOWLEDGMENTS

Our sincere appreciation to those persons listed below for their true professional expertise, interest, material contributions, review and editing labors which helped us during the long months of manuscript preparation and research to compile, write and put this volume together. We feel this book belongs to them just as much as it does to us.

F. Lee Bailey, attorney at law, Boston, Massachusetts. We encourage everyone to read his book, *The Defense Never Rests,* Stein and Day Publishers, New York, 1971.

John E. Reid, Chicago, Illinois. There is probably no other living person who knows as much about polygraphy.

Lynn P. Marcy, polygraphist emeritus, Dearborn, Michigan.

Leonard Harrelson, president, Keeler Polygraph Institute, Chicago, Illinois.

Fred L. Hunter, polygraphist, John E. Reid & Associates, Chicago, Illinois.

Charles Zimmerman, polygraphist emeritus, Auburndale, Massachusetts.

Melvin J. Williams, Chief Warrant Officer, Army C.I.D. (retired), Minneapolis, Minnesota.

Earl Tighe, Public Defender, Redwood Falls, Minnesota.

Ira E. Scott, Coordinator, School of Polygraphy, Law Enforcement Training Division, Texas A & M University, College Station, Texas.

Joe S. Gonzalez, specialist in criminal-narcotic polygraphy, El Paso, Texas Police Department.

Robert C. Cummins, a polygraphist dedicated to professionalism, John E. Reid & Associates, Chicago, Illinois.

Ronald Decker, Director and Chief Instructor, Army School of Polygraphy, Fort Gordon, Georgia.

Natale Laurendi, polygraphist emeritus, District Attorney's office, New York City.

Sgt. Gene Danish, polygraphist, San Antonio, Texas, Police Department.

W. W. Baker, polygraphist, Texas Department of Public Safety.

Noble Brymer, Lieut., polygraphist, Nashville, Tennessee, Police Department.

Warren Holmes, polygraphist-criminologist, Holmes Polygraph Service, Miami, Florida.

Chris Gugas, Sr., polygraphist emeritus, former president American Polygraph Assoc., Hollywood, California.

Richard O. Arther, polygraphist emeritus, Director, National Training Center of Lie Detection, New York City.

Edward M. Wier, M.D., Children's Clinic, Fort Worth, Texas.

J. V. Basmajian, M.D., Director, Department of Anatomy, Queen's University, Kingston, Ontario, Canada.

William B. Emmal, attorney at law, Fairbanks, Alaska.

Joseph P. Parker, attorney at law, Fort Worth, Texas.

G. H. Lawrence, M.D., Assistant Professor, Neuropsychiatric Department, St. Louis University School of Medicine, St. Louis, Missouri.

Russell L. Vinson, D.O., Physician and Surgeon, Haltom City, Texas.

Wallace, Craig, attorney at law, Fort Worth, Texas.

The Hon. Olin E. Teague, Congressman, Texas.

Cleve Backster, the Backster School of Polygraphy, New York City.

Bob Phillips, Eastland, Texas, for his brilliant creative efforts put forth on the dust jacket of this book.

J. J. Heger, president, C. H. Stoelting Co., Chicago, Illinois.

Richard W. Inman, president, Associated Research, Inc., Chicago, Illinois.

J. D. Williams, A.A.R.C., National Security Director, The Zale Corporation, Dallas, Texas.

Dee E. Wheeler, polygraphist emeritus, Fort Worth, Texas, Crime Laboratory.

F. T. Lindsey, branch manager, Truth Verification, Inc., Fort Worth, Texas. His initial assistance was tremendous.

Richard Earl Williams, Executive Vice President, Texas Industrial Security, Inc., Ft. Worth, Texas.

Roy R. Steele, licensed polygraphist, Texas Industrial Security, Inc.; member Texas Association of Polygraph Examiners.

Benjamin Malinowski, former senior instructor (retired) at the U.S. Army Military Police Polygraph School, Fort Gordon, Georgia, now in Atlanta, Georgia.

Robert Brisentine, polygraphist, C.I.D. Agency Liaison and polygraph control officer.

Walter A. Van de Werken, polygraphist, lecturer, C. H. Stoelting Co., Chicago, Illinois.

Michael O'Rourke, attorney at law, Hennepin County, Minnesota, Legal Advice Agency.

Alfred and Martin Rosen, attorneys at law, New York City.

Milton A. Berman, polygraphist, Louisville, Kentucky.

The Hon. John H. Dimond, Assoc. Justice (retired) Alaska Supreme Court, Juneau, Alaska.

No amount of thanks could ever suffice for the help, encouragement and the writing of the Forewords by attorney R. David Broiles, with the law firm of Hooper, Kerry, Chappell & Broiles, 200 Ft. Worth Club Bldg., Ft. Worth, Texas, and the brilliant psychologist-author, Dr. V. A. Leonard of Denton, Texas.

Special recognition must go to Payne Thomas, Charles C Thomas, Publisher, Springfield, Illinois, who first saw the nucleus of this manuscript back in 1968 and never lost faith.

If per chance we have not properly credited assisting sources here or elsewhere, such is purely by accident or oversight, certainly not intentional.

Should this volume serve to spread some knowledge and a better understanding of the polygraph profession, the long months of manuscript preparation shall not have been totally in vain.

R.J.F.
A.L.M.

CONTENTS

THE POLYGRAPH IN COURT

PART I

Chapter 1

WHAT IT'S ALL ABOUT

AFTER RESEARCHING several thousand criminal cases quietly buried in police, district attorney and prison records, we gradually become more aware of how poor investigation, unconcern and legal complacency permits false "positive" identification, arrest, indictment and conviction of the innocent, all under the guise of "probable cause."

So, let's start with what happens in some police investigations.

A prominent citizen is robbed on one of the streets of a metropolitan city. He reports to the police and demands immediate action.

The police want to show him they are on the ball. He is questioned for a description of the assailant.

Our prominent citizen is emotionally upset and, no doubt, somewhat frightened. When robbed, the light was far from good. His inner tensions run high.

"How big was he? How tall was he? What was his color?"

The citizen searches his mind.

"About the same as that fellow over there?" the officer asks, pointing to one of the detectives.

"No, a little smaller."

"About like that other fellow?"

"Something like him."

"All right. Five feet eight inches," the officer says. "Now, how about weight? About like this fellow?"

"No, more like that other chap."

"Weight one hundred and sixty-five."

Then they take the citizen into a rogue's gallery where they bring out several volumes of photographs, and where they consult charts labeled "modus operandi," and so forth.

Suddenly one of the officers exclaims, "Say, I've got an idea. Pete Backus got out of the pen last month and this is exactly the kind of a job he'd pull off. He used to haunt this area and this is like his MO."

"By George, that's right," another officer chimes in. To the citizen he knowingly smiles. "Look here, I think we've got this thing solved. I think we know your man."

He flips through a mug book and points to the picture of Pete Backus.

The man starts to shake his head.

"Now wait a minute," the officer says. "Let's not be hasty about this. You may have to change your opinion. I think if you could see this man you'd recognize him as the robber. Remember that this picture was taken four or five years ago and that pictures sometimes don't look too much like a man. Now, just don't go off on a tangent on this thing. Study that picture carefully. Look at it in a better light."

The citizen keeps studying the picture. He doesn't think it's the man. The officer asks him why not, asks him to point out any particular where the picture doesn't fit.

Eventually the citizen makes what is called a "partial identification."

Then he goes home. Two weeks pass, then a grinning detective calls at his front door. "I think we've got your man. Come on down with me and identify him."

At headquarters the citizen witnesses a lineup with five men in it. The man in the middle is Pete Backus. The citizen immediately feels a flash of recognition. He's seen that man before. His face is familiar. It was in connection with the holdup. He nods emphatically. "That's the man."

How much of that identification is predicated upon a recollection of a face of the man who held him up, and how much of it upon the fact that he studied the photograph of Pete Backus so carefully that he became familiar with a photographic likeness?

We don't know. Police officers don't know. No one knows. The witness himself doesn't know.

Police officers do know that some people make positive identifications of individuals who couldn't by any stretch of the imagination have participated in the crime.*

When professors of science, or any art based on scientific principle, swear they can distinguish between the whole truth and something less than the whole truth and back their assertions academically and physiologically, would it not be too much for persons like judges to say the witness cannot thus distinguish and on that ground refuse to hear his opinions at all?

By such a course of action, a judge would undertake of his own sufficiency to determine how far a particular science, not possessed by him, can carry human knowledge, and to determine it in opposition to the practitioners of that science.

Prior to his untimely death on March 11, 1970, Erle Stanley Gardner, famous attorney, author, American, philosophically remarked: "Why does a man become a slave to the very thing he hoped would set him free?"

Leaving behind him literary legacies and legal legends that will live forever, he turned his *Court of Last Resort* (a court of public opinion) over to the American Polygraph Association's Case Review Committee with these last words:

> In my experience of using the polygraph to ascertain the truth of a matter, whether it be ferreting out of the guilty, or for protection of the innocent, I have come to realize that scientific interrogation is too important a part of our present civilization to be either plowed under, on the one hand, or permitted to die on the vine, on the other hand.

The problem of facing realities cannot be mitigated unless there is a realization of the mental and emotional stress induced by environmental changes. Justice is not and cannot be a concept devoid of the human element. Where there is respect for the dignity of human beings, and regard for the truth, the machinery of the administration of justice will function efficiently.

Ignorance, failure to understand, ill will, or the desire for arbitrary power which originates in the experiences of individuals

---

*Gardner, Erle Stanley: *The Court of Last Resort*. William Sloane Associates, New York, 1952, pp. 250-253.

may cause its breakdown. Separate man from the administration of justice, and there is nothing.

Similarly, for attorneys and judges to endorse the prosecution and conviction of defendants, in the face of scientific evidence to the contrary, becomes no less grevious an act than touching once again a torch to human flesh, all the name of justice.

Modern court procedures must embrace the recognized status of modern conditions of mechanics, psychology, physiology, sociology, medicine, philosophy, history, and all the other available sciences. The failure to do so only further serves to question the ability of the courts to efficiently administer justice.

No government is better than its concept of justice. If our kind of democracy hopes to survive, the machinery of justice must afford equal protection to all and be swift in its operation. Whenever there is a separation between truth and justice, neither is safe.

One of the healthiest aspects of a democracy is the continuous inquiry of its citizens into the operation of government. The machinery of justice reflects the moral climate of the citizenry. The ethics and morals of the representatives of the people—be they judges, legislators, "politicians," attorneys, police, clergymen, union leaders, or teachers—will be no higher than the ethics and morals of the people they represent.

We must not blind ourselves to truth.*

Justice is truth in action, inclusive of all virtues, older than sects and schools and, like charity, more ancient than mankind. Every man seeks for truth, but only God knows who has found it. The triumphs of truth are the most glorious, chiefly because they are the most bloodless of all victories, deriving their lustre from the total number of the saved, not slain.

But, in recent years, what has been happening in America, as well as to our once highly cherished and once reverently regarded system of justice?

Why do we indulge and permit excesses and outrages? Why do so many, even now, continue to perpetrate and sanction them? Rome fell when its citizens became so obsessed with greed and

---

*Dienstein, William: *Are You Guilty*. Thomas, Springfield, 1954, pp. 18, 149.

personal ambition that they lost sight of the long range goal—the good of the nation as a whole (without which there can be no fulfillment of individual interests) .

In many ways we are experiencing symptoms of a similar moral breakdown. We are slowly losing perspective of the proper role of government in relation to the individual and are abandoning genuine rights for the sake of instant satisfaction of needs and desires. Too many of us confuse the desire *for* something with the right *to* something. There are certain rights in a free democracy which are the function of government to guarantee and protect. Among these is the right to life, liberty and the pursuit of happiness. But there are other so-called rights, about which we hear a great deal lately, which are not really rights at all. They have taken on an aura of credence as "rights" because of the myths surrounding them.

In the process of perpetrating these myths, genuine rights— such as the right of the majority to freedom from fear, to protection by the law, and to the freedom to choose—have been so twisted and degraded that not only has its true meaning been obscured, but the acts committed in its name have made a mockery of its original intention. It is becoming increasingly fashionable today to justify almost anything by calling it a "right."

It is time to take another look at the mythical rights on the alter of which we are slowly sacrificing our legitimate rights. Liberty does not mean license from the law. The right to dissent means protest within the bounds of law, not mob rule. The right to the pursuit of happiness means equal opportunity, not guaranteed income and equal shares.

The philosophy of equal shares is contrary to a man's fundamental right to place a value on his work. A man's work is an expression of himself. When you deprive him of the means by which to judge the quality of his efforts, namely, proportionate reward, you take away not only the dignity and incentive of work but also pride in achievement. The philosophy that goes with the demand for guaranteed income is not only impractical, it is a direct denial of principles which have made this the richest nation in the world—the right to competition, free enterprise and reward based on merit.

Present crime rates are a grave threat and of great concern. But a greater danger lies in a complacent attitude and false sense of security in the face of the root cause of widespread lawlessness —a breakdown of the moral fiber. The internal chaos generated in the individual will become manifest in society as a whole. We are seeing visible signs of this everywhere.

It is manifest in the student unrest in the universities . . . in their demands for "student power," in the use of subversive tactics to achieve such goals as seizing the role of administrators and wanting to teach rather than learn, and in their choice of heroes who, if given the opportunity, would destroy this country. Their parents pay tuition and board while they court communism and play at guerrilla warfare, without conception or concern for the consequences.

It is a sad spectacle that many persons have become so immune to genuine values that they can take their own hypocritical attempt to play at being little men so seriously that they become a threat to themselves and to their country; when they can succeed in deluding themselves to the extent that annihilation of all authority seems a worthwhile goal and the swaggering demagogic posture of contempt for work, family, the home and society, a fulfilling life.

It is an irony and a tragedy that the affluent permissive environment, out of which many of these so-called revolutionaries came, has backfired; that instead of contributing to the development of character and a sense of responsibility, it has led them to seek a life of continuous ease and escapism; a life in which the gap—the human need for socially worthy meanings—is pathetically filled by latching on to utopian, bizarre ideals which, because they are so unrealistic, allow them to remain perpetual children. The danger to the country is that in their naivete such persons become easy victims for the corrupters and the real revolutionaries.

To require the status quo as an object for destruction in order to achieve a sense of identity is a pitiful dependency on just that status quo. Those who rely solely on deviation to make their message meaningful are in effect saying that without the status quo, they are nothing.

This is true of the black power movement with its need for exaggeration and belligerence. It is true of the hippies who require offensive manners, indolence, beads, beards, and filth to feel "turned on" and withdrawal into the unreal world of drugs to "really live." It is true of just plain hoodlums who must have crime to get their kicks, and it is true of those who need to degrade all authority in any establishment to feel moral.*

The militants, radicals, and criminals can be identified and dealt with accordingly. But it is difficult to recognize and pinpoint concessions that slowly and imperceptably undermine our system of justice, as well as the principles of freedom, and literally tear the heart out of our kind of democracy.

The dissatisfaction with rampant crime—whether or not society correctly understands all the reasons for it—is a tremendous impetus.

If ever there was a time in the courts or the legislature, those who are selling truth, reliability, an improvement in the criminal system, something to shortcut it, something to eliminate unnecessary and costly trials, and give more assurance to the people should be heard.

Some day there will be a guarantee that the innocent people who obey the law remain on the outside rather than the inside, and the idea will be received with more warmth, a great deal more warmth, than was ever the case in the past.

Although the people are unhappy with the state of law and order, there has been so little attention paid to the accuracy of our criminal process that we stand just as good a chance today as we did in the past of putting an innocent man in prison due to misidentification or of turning a guilty one loose because of the suppression of some evidence illegally obtained.

It is time for the profession of defending criminals to take a long hard look at its obligations. It is time for the bar to clear up all questions as to whether or not a lawyer has the duty to find

---

*Hon Teague, Olin E., Congressman, Texas, in The House of Representatives, Wednesday, September 4, 1968.

out if his client is telling the truth, or whether he deliberately ought to avoid putting that question and simply raise a reasonable doubt, if he can do so, as a matter of course.

Nobody profits by putting a guilty man on the street. We cannot imagine—except for those who are mercenary enough to enjoy the fees notwithstanding the result—that many lawyers of good integrity really sleep well at night knowing a sadistic murderer has been put back in society because they were able to find a loophole in the law.

For years, cases were tried in the dark. Surprise was the name of the game. The defense never knew who the prosecutor's witnesses were until they appeared on the witness stand. Nearly every case went to trial unprepared, by the deliberate intent of the law, even though lawyers knew such as unethical according to their own cannons. But, with surprise coming out and some planning, some understanding going in, there were very few cases that the lawyers involved in could not settle as to truth if they chose to do so.

In that, even 90 percent of those cases now put to trial by jury for the purpose of ascertaining the truth—and it's a poor vehicle for that purpose, really—could possibly be eliminated.

Most disturbing to the falsely accused is the cold hard fact that there is no guarantee of acquittal in our legal procedures. No where in the Constitution or Bill of Rights is there a guarantee that if one obeys the law he will be left alone and his liberty will remain intact. Much worse, if a person goes through the game of Russian roulette that our jury trials too often involve, a mistake can be made.

There is no reason why jurors cannot make mistakes, because the cases put to them, if they are triable at all, are usually close and contentious cases, where credibility becomes a very narrow question. The drawing of inferences, if the evidence is circumstantial, is equally close. The opportunities for error are myriad and, indeed, many are made. It is suspect that 50 percent of all these mistakes fall on each side of the line, but the point is that once an error is made, it is not correctible by any process of law.

It is entirely legal to convict and execute an innocent man

provided he gets a "fair" trial. He is not entitled to the accuracy or reliability available through science; he is entitled only to due process. Should he sit in prison and find no error in his trial record, he may not file a suit claiming he is innocent. That is not grounds for release.

Now, is this not a gaping defect in our system that has existed far too long? It is archaic, even barbaric.

What have judges, prosecutors and defense lawyers whose job it is to marshal the truth, if they can, really done? They invariably rely on ancient theory—and it's far older than the scientific art of polygraphy—that if you get two good lawyers producing evidence and putting it through the crucible of cross-examination, the fire generated by the controversy will burn away the slag, and only the hard and pure core of truth will remain. This is good talk, something we feed children when they learn the Pledge of Allegiance to the flag; but no honest lawyer will tell you that this is an effective method of guaranteeing a truthful outcome.

The notion of proof is a misnomer which does not exist. Proof occurs in theory when a jury finds one way or another. If they are mistaken, the fact is none the less proof. All that we have is evidence—information that goes through a filter called the trial judge and then may be considered by the triers of fact. They can disregard it, believe all of it, part of it, or none of it and act upon it as they may see fit, and no one will ever be able to ask them why they did or did not accept some piece of information in determining the outcome of the case. Cross-examination may be helpful in many areas, but it is no guarantee of anything.

Uninformed judges have, for the most part, turned their backs on polygraphy since the Frye case in 1923 primarily, we feel, because they felt it would supplant the jury. They hope that no kind of scientific evidence will supplant the jury unless its scientific certainty arises so high that there is no point in permitting it to be evaluated.

The only kind of evidence heretofore available that even comes close to fitting this category is the blood test used in paternity cases.

Polygraphy, however, falls into a much more anomalous position. It has also been considered conclusive, as a matter of policy, in many jurisdictions. There are many law enforcement departments where a man under suspect who is cleared by a competent polygraphist will no longer be a suspect. As the famous trial and defense lawyer, F. Lee Bailey, noted in his talk before the 1968 American Polygraph Association convention at Silver Spring, Maryland, "Polygraphy—that is the finest kind of clearance anyone can get."

In these United States if one is indicted and tried he can never win more than half of what he had before. The stigma of acquittal is a damnation that comes very close to that of imprisonment. The people will say, because they have been allowed to think this way for years, "He did it or they wouldn't have tried him for it; the lawyer got him off." The counsel gets great credit when, indeed, nothing more than the truth was shown.

The person who avoids trial through polygraphy enjoys as good a reputation as the one charged with paternity enjoys when he is cleared by a blood test, which shoots right through the trial system and locks up the case with a fixed result.

Defense lawyers should recognize that it does not serve a particularly useful purpose to always stand on constitutional rights and attempt to procure acquittal in every case. More importantly, they should never use such tactics in a jury trial without homing in on the question now only they have access, because no one makes them read a "Miranda" warning before they interrogate their own clients.

The burden that rests on the shoulders of a defense lawyer who knows his client is innocent is a terrible one. It requires that he deliberately inject into trial records error—that is to say, realize that the judge is disregarding a precedent foremost in the defense's mind and remain silent about it. On its face that might sound unethical until one realizes that if it is corrected and an error-free trial is run which results in an inaccurate verdict, a jury can be mistaken. It can take the word of some glib liar and disregard the testimony of an inarticulate, uneducated, unintelligent, but honest man who may be the defendant—whose credibility seldom is worth very much simply because he is the defendant.

The defense doesn't want to be in the position of telling the innocent man who is on his way to prison, "Chum, that's the end of the line. There's nothing to appeal. There is nothing more I can do." Disregarding truth, he must try to get a reversal on technical grounds and go through the same ball game again and perhaps with the same results ad infinitum.

This is not a satisfactory system. Prosecutors opposed to polygraph admissibility, or its use in a judicial proceeding, have been cutting their throats for years in order to win individual cases. The ethics of the matter are clear. Although a defense lawyer has a right and sometimes a duty to raise every defense for a man he knows to be guilty, there is no right, and everyone in law enforcement has contrary duty when there is even a suspicion that the defendant may be innocent. The prosecutor is there to protect him as well as society.

If polygraphy was used more, judges would appreciate the true facts as many of the nation's leading lawyers already know them to be.

Juries will not slavishly follow the polygraph as though it were the last word in every question of credibility. They will evaluate it just as they would an x-ray skiagraph or an electroencephalogram. Polygraphy would be nothing more than another aid to their determination as to what the facts are. Pretty soon the word would get out that at least the people brought to trial had turned down an opportunity to avoid the trial, which is the happiest result. Defense and prosecutors should sit down and agree on where the weaknesses are, if indeed any are claimed. We all know that much more rests on the ability of the polygraphist than on the instrument being used. Such could become tantamount to a handbook of the rules of evidence, useless to the nonlawyer but very valuable to someone who, on the spur of the moment, can use it as a tool, or as a scalpel to a doctor—just a knife to us, but to him the means to change hearts in a human being.

If these things could be agreed upon by responsible lawyers and the polygraph technique utilized in a responsible fashion, it would jack the accuracy of our criminal justice system well into the high nineties among the cases that now go awry. And, perhaps 90 percent of those cases could be straightened out.

We ought to straighten them all. The day will always be with us when one innocent man will go to jail, and the day will always be with us when several guilty men will go free for technical reasons, even if not for reasons of inaccuracy or a jury mistake. But in modern times, when we have walked on the moon and are shooting for Mars, we believe it unforgivable that society has so long disregarded the polygraph with open eyes, although under the table it is painfully and sometimes felicitously aware of the tremendous significance and value of this science which it supports *sotto voce* from its official circles.

A lot more truth wouldn't hurt the country.

At every level, once asserted, it is up to the prosecutor to pick up the ball. However, in so many previous instances, they have fought polygraph's admissibility where they could just as easily have said, "All right, this guy has cleared polygraphy by four different experts who came up with the same results. I'm satisfied they all can't be mistaken, so he didn't do it." If the prosecutor would then dismiss the case and let the people understand he is willing to do that for every citizen, polygraphy would rise in public esteem and the truth about its fairness, objectivity and high reliability would come out.

Society is much better served if, in the final analysis, despite all the grand protection of the system and the dignity with which we attempt to conduct our trials and cause our convictions when they do result, we find out who the guilty people are and punish them in some sensible way, not necessarily the way we do today. We need to find out who the innocent are and stand up and say, "Your Honor, this man did not do it. I want society to know it. I want his friends and his boss to know it. He is entitled to go back, and we admit a mistake has been made—it was an unfortunate mistake—but this is the business." He should be compensated by our legislature for whatever he has lost.

Weeded out that way, there are few cases that would need to be thrown into the chance book of trial, which too often are.

We believe the salient affects of such a procedure, a willingness to put more emphasis on truth—a fictional goal we too quickly turn away from—would have a tremendous effect on law and order.

Most of the people that commit crimes didn't expect to get caught. If they did, they expected that by hiring a magician, not a lawyer—and there aren't any of those, but people don't know it —they would get off; they would beat the rap. They have heard that it is easier now, through the assertion of technicalities, to per-haps win an acquittal, even though there is evidence of guilt avail-able. This certainly does little to discourage crime or to encourage adherence to the rules.*

But, by the same token, the man in the ghetto is rapidly dis-illusioned when, as a poor man, he's hauled in, accused, vilified, and perhaps convicted or at least put to trial, when his only crime was being poor and not very bright and unable to intelligently defend himself. He doesn't go back to his community with the kind of respect for law and order that is going to help him tell his brethren and his children that you can rely on our system and on the police if you behave yourself, and you won't be inconveni-enced or punished.

This is what is needed. Is our system of law and justice a whopping failure? In many, many cases it has not done what all of us hoped it would do. This is not so much to grant a fair trial as it is to guarantee accurate results in all but a very few unavoid-able cases. We need the prognostician, a realistic prognostician, for the benefit of anybody who is laboring at the crossroads as to whether he is going to try to make his money by sticking a pistol in a man's face in a bank, or by working in the bank and trying to get up through the ranks, and handle money licitly instead of illicitly. We must give him a little guidance down the line.

Behind the scenes, every day since the infamous Frye case in 1923, polygraphy has protected the falsely accused and ferreted out the guilty in law enforcement, government and private in-dustry. Yet, this unique art still suffers from appellate as well as legislative precedent compounded upon precedent.

---

*Subject matters of similarity may be found in a speech by F. Lee Bailey before the 1968 American Polygraph Association Convention, Silver Spring, Maryland.

When the most objective means of truth verification is consistently strangled by lawyers and the judiciary, costly and unnecessary trials take place, protection of the innocent is denied, and the criminal monsters continue to gorge themselves at the expense of society as a whole.

However, a few legal breakthroughs are indications that sooner or later progressively minded judges who are really sincere in their attempts to "judge" rightfully on the plain of truth, are seen as follows:

The first time polygraph test results were admitted as evidence in Illinois in a felony case was February 18, 1953. The Hon. Charles S. Dougherty, Justice of the Criminal Court, Cook County, admitted testimony over objection of the prosecutor that a defendant was telling the truth. The defendant was freed. Also recorded are three other felony cases in Pittsburgh, Pennsylvania, where judges in the Common Pleas Courts allowed test results into evidence over objection of opposing counsel. None of these were appealed.*

There are several decisions upholding admissibility of polygraphic evidence where the test was made pursuant to an agreement and stipulation. In 1948 the California District Court of Appeals, in the case of *People v. Houser** held the defendant bound by an agreement he had made to permit polygraphic results to be admitted as evidence. The court said: "It would be difficult to hold that the defendant should now be permitted on this appeal to take advantage of any claim that (the examiner) was not an expert . . . and that such evidence was inadmissible, merely because it happened to indicate that he was not telling the truth. . . ."

Polygraphy has made a noteworthy contribution in the solution of bastardy cases. Blood tests on the child and alleged father can only be used to exclude the father if his blood type is different from that of the child. However, if the defendant's blood type is the same as the child's this evidence means that the defendant is

---

*Reid, John E., *The Lie Detector in Court*, De Paul Law Review, Vol. 4, No. 1, Autumn-Winter 1954.

*83 Ca. App. 2d 686. 193 P.2d 937 (1948). *Also see* 331 Mich. 606, 50 N.W.2d 172 (1951).

only one of thousands of men who, by having the same type blood, could be the father. Polygraphy on the mother can reveal the fact that the mother has had sexual intercourse with other men during the period of possible conception.

In the *American Bar Association Journal,* Vol. 50, No. 12, December 1964, Roger Alton Pfaff, Presiding Judge, Consolidated Domestic Relations and Conciliation Court, Los Angeles County, California (now retired) wrote: "Since March, 1962, Los Angeles Superior Court has been utilizing the polygraph in domestic relations cases, first in child custody, and later in paternity cases. Attorneys were so satisfied with the results that now they, not the judge, suggest use of polygraphy."

On the basis of a study made of 312 consecutive paternity cases handled at the Chicago laboratories of John E. Reid & Associates, 93 percent of 589 tested parties admitted to the polygraphist that they had committed perjury when testifying in court.

This suggests that any jury/judge without polygraphy has an almost impossible task in deciding what is the truth.

Dr. G. H. Lawrence, Assistant Professor, Neuropsychiatric Department, St. Louis University School of Medicine, wrote of his first contact with polygraphy in the March 1966 issue of Security World magazine: "It became immediately apparent then, and still is, that polygraphy obtains information that cannot be obtained from any other source such as background investigation, psychometric testing or psychiatric examination. . . ."

For years the federal government was the largest user, but now nearly every progressively minded law enforcement agency along with literally thousands of private firms are utilizing polygraph's high reliability every hour of the working day. If the polygraph falsely accused, defamed, physically harmed, brought about successful litigation against it (which it has not) no one could afford to use it.

All competent polygraphists report that the freedoms and reputations of up to 85 percent of persons tested on suspected criminal involvement are protected.

Defendant was indicted for rape. An agreement was made between the defense and prosecution for polygraphy with each side to rely on the results. Polygraphy indicated defendant to be telling the truth. The prosecution obtained an order of nolle prosse of the indictment. Thereafter, defendant was again indicted on the same charge, was tried in the circuit court and was convicted.

On appeal, the District Court of Florida reversed the judgment and remanded with instructions to quash the indictment, holding, inter alia, that the original agreement to abide by the polygraph results was valid and enforceable.*

That polygraph admissibility is seriously being considered from various important angles by the judiciary is seen in the following article which appeared in the July 1971 issue of the *New Jersey Law Journal:*

> CRIMINAL LAW—EVIDENCE—LIE DETECTORS—Court may consider on behalf of defendant results of post-conviction polygraph report as to facts not considered by trial jury or material to their deliberations in arriving at determination concerning sentence.

The foregoing was digested from an opinion by McFarland, J.D.C., rendered June 11, 1971. *Hudson Co. Ct. State v. Watson.*

Defendant was convicted after a jury trial of contributing to the delinquency of a minor. Thereafter, the prosecutor submitted an affidavit of the complaining witness stating that the defendant had threatened her life. This affidavit was submitted in support of a motion to revoke defendant's release in custody of the probation department. Defendant denied the threat and offered to submit to polygraphy. The examination was held and in the opinion of the examiner the defendant was telling the truth.

The attorney for defendant moved formally for judicial acceptance of the result of the polygraph test in postconviction matters before the court. The prosecutor who has never consented to the use of the test objected, contending such is contrary to law.

The sole question for the court was whether it should accept the polygraph report in its presentence consideration.

HELD: After trial, expert testimony based on a polygraph test examination will be admitted for consideration on behalf of the defendant who voluntarily takes a test to show facts not decided

---

*Butler v. State of Fla. (Fla. App.) 228 So.2d 421, 36 ALR 3d 1274 ALR 3d covers the point. *See* 36 ALR 3d 1280 which discloses enforceability of agreement by state officials to drop prosecution if accussed successfully passes polygraph test.

by the trial jury or material to their deliberation, for example, to show his attitude, or obedience to instructions of the court, and to disprove accusations that he has not been tried for.

Sentencing is a heavy responsibility for the court. The state and the defendant no longer have the adversary rights they had in the course of the trial. The duty of the court is to have the best available information concerning every aspect of defendant's life.

During April 1963, the results of a polygraph test proved more persuasive than positive eyewitness identification during an aggravated robbery trial when District Judge Dana Nicholson, Hennepin County, Minnesota, listened to polygraph test results following stipulation. Results declared the defendant innocent. So did Judge Nicholson. In April of 1969, following polygraph's admissibility over objection of the prosecution, again with Judge Nicholson presiding, a jury found a defendant not guilty of lurking in order to commit theft.*

During early February 1970, a Phoenix, Arizona, Superior Court Jury found Willie T. Lockett guilty of robbery and assault with a deadly weapon. Judge Howard F. Thompson was not satisfied. He ordered polygraphy, which indicated conclusive innocence. Judge Thompson vacated the jury's verdict and set Lockett free.

In another break with precedent, polygraphic results were admitted over objection of the prosecution during a burglary trial before Superior Court Judge Denver S. Pekinpah, Fresno County, California, Superior Court. This was on February 24, 1971. The judge rejected the contention of Deputy Prosecutor Stephen Carlton that to break the rule would, in effect, "eliminate the jury system."

On March 20, 1971, a Denver, Colorado, man was acquitted in Denver County Court on charges of assaulting a deputy sheriff after the results of a polygraph test were admitted into evidence over objection of the prosecution. Judge William Burnett presided.

During June of 1971, a police brutality suit was filed against

---

*State of Minn. v. Andrew Ferrando, Criminal Case File No. 53350, April 7, 1969; see Ferguson, Robert J., Jr.: *The Scientific Informer*, Thomas, Springfeld. 1971, p. 219.

the city of Westland, Michigan, in the aftermath of a unique court ruling by Southfield District Judge S. James Clarkson. The judge permitted introduction of polygraph test results on defendant Robert J. Ridley over objection of the prosecution which resulted in an acquittal on disorderly conduct charges. Judge Clarkson said he ruled to admit because of the quality of the examiner, the type of questions asked, and because "more and more we are becoming aware of the quality of the instruments."

In June of 1971, Municipal Judge Neil A. Riley, Hennepin County, Minnesota, relied on polygraphy to vacate the conviction of a Minneapolis woman for a telephoned bomb threat.

On December 10, 1971, over objection of the prosecution, Federal Judge Earl R. Larson, United States District Court House, Minneapolis, Minnesota, in the case of *United States vs Guidarelli* (4-70 Crim. 199, Motion For Reduction of Sentence) permitted lengthy polygraph testimony by Robert J. Ferguson, Jr., with respect to defendant's "intent" to evade income taxes claimed due by the government in 1965 and 1966. Judge Larson also permitted the question formulation put to the defendant and the fifteen polygraph charts conducted on the defendant into record.

The Supreme Court of the United States decided in 1967 (385 U.S. 493) that polygraph examinations used for internal, administrative hearing purposes were proper.

In answer to the 1964-65 Moss Subcommittee hearings questionaire, numerous of the nineteen Federal agencies acknowledging use of polygraphy concluded their reports with, ". . . utilized to gain information not otherwise attainable by other investigative techniques," and, ". . . in connection with matters extensively investigated but difficult to resolve."

In recent years one will be hard put to discover where any person who has been cleared by polygraphy was convicted and imprisoned.

Recent union and legislative attempts at abolition of polygraphy were as senseless as allowing it to go unlicensed. If any polygraph legislation is ever promulgated at the federal level it should pointedly be directed towards creation of uniform licensing laws in all states with severe penalty for violations thereof. So, if prohibitive polygraph legislation can be enacted for the benefit of special interest groups, then truly this nation is in dire need of stronger men in positions of elected and appointed leadership.

The "accuracy" of polygraphy has long been complimented by the unceasing challenges of its critics. These are the same persons who wage the never ending fight to prohibit law enforcement from using modern scientific devices and techniques to bring the guilty to the bar of justice.

Radically claiming that polygraphy is only 80 percent "accurate," the uninformed or misinformed critic fails to take into consideration scientific acknowledgment that no other method of truth verification comes close to even an 80 percent reliability figure.

This is the time for polygraphy. Its integrity as a method, as a scientific technique, has risen steadily and, although perhaps not well noticed by the courts, there is now ability to put experts from the professions knowledgeable in this acutely reliable art on the witness stand. They can assure the trial judge that he can regard with a high degree of reliance the test within its own sphere and for the benefits which may flow forth in the sorely needed search for truth.

Chapter 2

AN ARGUMENT FOR POLYGRAPH'S
ADMISSIBILITY

In THE statement of facts herein we shall assume a defendant has been found guilty of an offense, has been sentenced, and is now before the court on appeal. In the meantime he has twice volunteered for polygraphy and has been declared innocent at the conclusion of both tests.

Defendant previously presented motions to the trial judge that the complainant subject himself to polygraphy, and that defendant himself be subjected to an impartial test by a polygraphist designated by the court. Both motions were denied and exceptions were duly saved.* At trial, pursuant to an agreement between counsel and the court, a written offer of proof was submitted at the conclusion of the evidence. The offer of proof consisted of the testimony of various experts relating to the scientific validity and reliability of polygraphy; two experts offered testimony pertaining to the results of tests made on the defendant and his witness which indicated truthfulness in both instances.

Upon this offer of proof, the trial judge made the following ruling:

> the Court will accept the testimony of these witnesses only in relation to their qualifications, based upon the subject matter of the type of work they do—that if they were here present, they would so testify. But the Court sustains the objection as to the result of any polygraphic test upon the instant subjects relating to this particular case.

Defendant's exception was duly noted.

---

*This chapter has been based on the appellate record of Commonwealth v. Angelo Fatalo, No. 12956, before the Supreme Judicial Court for the Commonwealth of Massachusetts, Middlesex County, May Sitting 1963, F. Lee Bailey for appellant. *Also see* Bailey's 1971 expertise in the case of United States v. Captain Ernest Medina, U.S. Army jurisdiction, polygraph admissibility voir dire in absence of jury, *re:* the 1968 My Lai, Vietnam massacre.

SUMMARY OF ARGUMENT

I. The criteria for ascertaining the admissibility of polygraph test results was enunciated in 1923 as "general scientific acceptability"; the rationale and rule of the Frye case has been consistently followed by the authorities in various jurisdictions; a valid scientific test of credibility would be an asset to the judicial process; "General scientific acceptability" does not mean a universality of scientific approval such as would justify judicial notice, but only a substantial body of scientific opinion in support, before scientific evidence should be ruled "admissible." The polygraph test should be evaluated just as other types of scientific evidence are evaluated and treated similarly by the courts.

II. The polygraph is vastly improved over the systolic blood pressure test offered in 1923, and rejected in the first reported decision on lie detection. Legal authorities are critical of the unreasonably high standard of reliability imposed on the polygraph test as a prerequisite to admissibility. The polygraph test is statistically reliable and accurate in better than 96 percent of cases tested. The polygraph test is as reliable, comparatively, as other scientific devices, instruments and techniques presently recognized as the basis of admissible expert opinion; as against the uncorroborated eyewitness testimony upon which defendant was convicted, the polygraph test is much more reliable. Polygraph test results are admissible, by the overwhelming weight of authority, where a proper foundation is laid; a proper foundation was laid in this case; the test results offered in this case should have been admitted.

III. The overwhelming weight of authority holds that polygraph test results are admissible where the parties stipulate thereto in advance of trial; admissibility upon stipulation is recognized not because stipulations are binding, but because courts have found that polygraph test results have a definite probative value.

IV. When the prosecutor refuses to enter into a stipulation, despite the reasonable request of defendant for a fair and impartial polygraph test, the opinion of an examiner selected by defendant should, upon the showing of a proper foundation, be received in evidence.

V. The court below should have granted defendant's motion for an impartial polygraph test, upon a showing that the prosecutor refused to stipulate.

VI. The court should have granted defendant's motion for a polygraph test of complainant, to show that complainant was lying; or, in the alternative, complainant's refusal to take such a test should have been admissible to impeach him.

VII. Public policy does not militate against the admissibility of polygraph tests to the limited extent sought in this appeal. The refusal to recognize the validity of a scientific phenomenon supported by scientists is improper, constitutes overreaching from the bench, and would serve to lower the prestige and esteem of the judiciary in the public eye. On the whole case, it must be recognized that defendant is probably innocent and he should be given a new trial.

ARGUMENT I

THE TRIAL JUDGE SHOULD HAVE RULED THAT THE SCIENTIFIC RELIABILITY OF THE POLYGRAPHIC DECEPTION TEST WAS ESTABLISHED BY DEFENDANT'S EVIDENCE THEREOF AND SHOULD HAVE ADMITTED THE RESULTS OF THOSE TESTS EMBRACED IN THE OFFER OF PROOF.

The case at bar presents to this court for the first time the question of the admissibility in evidence of the results of a polygraph test. If the trial judge should have admitted the results, his error was substantial and there is a serious question as to the guilt of the defendant. If not, the conviction stands and the defendant must serve a prison sentence and bear the stigma of a felon for the rest of his life.

The question embodied in this appeal, although of first impression in this state, is of course by no means new. In fact, the first reported opinion relating to the "lie detector" was recorded almost fifty years ago in *Frye v. United States,* 293 F. 1013 (1923). The court in the Frye case, a prosecution for murder, held that the results of a systolic blood pressure test administered by William Marston were properly excluded when offered to corroborate Frye's denial of guilt. The test given Frye was at best a crude forerunner of the modern polygraph test, and yet justice was thwarted by the exclusion: Frye served three years of a life sentence before his innocence was demonstrated by the confession of a third person. N.Y. Judicial Council, Fourteenth Annual Report 265 (1948). Thus an interesting question is posed: Was science right, in correctly corroborating the innocent defendant, or was the law right, in excluding the offer of science from its legal trial machinery, whose avowed *raison d'etre* is to seek factual truth? The law, in this case at least, appears to have misfired.

The Frye case is worthy of some deep consideration in the case at bar for several reasons. First, because it is probable that both science (as per Marston's opinion) and the law (as per the rationale of the appellate court) were right, each in its own way; for although Frye was in fact telling the truth, the decision excluding scientific evidence was certainly predicated upon sound legal reasoning and evidentiary principles.

Second, the result in the Frye case dramatically points up the danger in the hyperconservative tradition of the law; although it is wise to proceed cautiously to embrace new scientific methods of judicial proof, it is equally wise to scrutinize most particularly any offered method of reaching truth before casting it aside, else innocent men may suffer and the prestige of the courts will suffer in equal degree. Third, the Frye case (and the many subsequent cases which have echoed its holding) is the case upon which the defendant most heavily relies in presenting this appeal; for if it is followed, the convictions must be reversed.

It would, of course, be possible to cite many cases wherein the polygraph test has been considered and to dissect and analyze each one. But it is doubtful that this would be helpful to the court in deciding the case at bar. In the first place, the principle of stare decisis is inherently retrospective and is of questionable value where scientific evidence is concerned; for science progresses from day to day. What a reviewing court may have found yesterday as to a given scientific technique or device cannot be said to control today's decision, for some advance may require a different result. As it was put by Mr. Justice Holmes in 1895:

An ideal system of law should draw its postulates and its legislative justification from science. As it is now, we rely on tradition, or vague sentiment, or the fact that we never thought of any other way of doing things, as our only warrant for rules which we enforce with as much confidence as if they embodied revealed wisdom. . . .*

Second, there is little in the cases of precedential value, for (with some exceptions) the decisions by and large echo one another in exactly the manner condemned by Mr. Justice Holmes, above.

> With reference to the prevailing general rule that polygraph test results are inadmissible, nearly all of the cases parrot the language of the Frye case of 1923. . . .†

Since it is certain that this court has no desire to "parrot" a case decided some fifty years ago, the question of the present status of the polygraph test must be approached directly and logically, bearing in mind the evidence in the record and the principles of law to be used in determining just what that evidence means.

In order to place the question at bar in its proper framework, it is first necessary to ask whether it is even desirable to utilize in our trial system a scientific aid in evaluating credibility. Dean Wigmore, in considering this question in 1923, responded as follows: "If ever there is devised a psychological test for the evaluation of witnesses, the law will run to meet it."*

Dean Wicker, thirty years later, wrote the following:

> If and when convincing evidence is produced that reasonably reliable scientific methods of exposing falsehoods either in or out of the courtroom are available, these methods should be promptly utilized by the legal profession. Lawyers, judges and law professors know that there is today in our courtroom entirely too much intentional perjury and that it is usually difficult, and often impossible, for even an experienced trial lawyer to expose on cross-examination many of the lies of false-swearing witnesses. The legal profession can no longer assume a complacent attitude concerning our present methods of exposing mendacity.†

Although the law plainly did not "run to meet" the test

Speeches. Little, Brown, Boston, 1918.

†Wicker, Wm., *The Polygraphic Truth Test and the Law of Evidence*. 22 TENN. L. REV. 711 (1953).

*Wigmore, Evidence, 875 (2d ed. 1923).

†Wicker, *op. cit.*, p. 712.

offered to it in Frye, it must nonetheless be conceded that Wigmore was right. No honest lawyer or judge could help but agree that any instrument, device or technique which could increase the power of the courts to compel truthfulness, and discover and expose to the trier of fact testimonial mendacity, must be received with open arms. The next question, therefore, is this:

> "If it appears that some scientific method of determining truthfulness is available, what standard of reliability must it meet before it is to be received in evidence, to be weighed by the trier of fact?"

Inasmuch as there are many types of scientific evidence admitted in evidence as a matter of routine in the several jurisdictions of the United States, the reports are not without instances of judicial expression as to the criteria of admissibility. Dean Wigmore has suggested the following:

> . . . since the additions made possible to our unaided senses are due to the use of instruments constructed on knowledge of scientific laws, it is plain that the correctness of the data then obtained must depend on the correctness of the instrument in construction and the ability of the technical witness to use it. Hence, the following three fundamental propositions apply to testimony based on the use of all such instruments:
> A. The type of apparatus purporting to be constructed on scientific principles must be accepted as dependable for the proposed purpose by the profession concerned in that branch of science or its related art. This can be evidenced by qualified expert testimony; or, if notorious, it will be judicially noticed by the judge without evidence.
> B. The particular apparatus used by the witness must be one constructed according to an accepted type and must be in good condition for accurate work. This may be evidenced by a qualified expert.
> C. The witness using the apparatus as the source of his testimony must be one qualified for its use by training and experience.*

Professor McCormick, in his *Handbook on the Law of Evidence* (West Publishing Co., 1954) makes the following comment on the criteria of admissibility of scientific evidence:

> We face at the outset the question, to what extent must the device, technique or theory be shown to have won scientific acceptance before the results or conclusions based thereon can be used in evidence? The

---

*Wigmore, Science of Judicial Proof, 450 (3rd ed. 1937) .

court which first faced the question of admissibility of the results of a "lie detector" examination announced as the test whether the supporting theory had gained general acceptance among "psychological and physiological authorities." The court held that this test was not met and rejected the evidence, and this particular kind of evidence has been rejected with like reasoning by other courts ever since. By contrast, another court quite recently, considering the admissibility of the results of the use of the Harger breath test for measuring intoxication seemingly rejected this criterion of general scientific acceptance, and said: "Dr. Beerstecher (a biochemist) testified that the instrument in question is accurate and he gave his reasons for it. He admitted that there are others who disagree with its accuracy. The objection to this testimony, therefore, goes to its weight and not to its admissiblity."

It seems that the practice approved in the second case is the one followed in respect to expert testimony and scientific evidence generally. "General scientific acceptance" is a proper condition upon the court's taking judicial notice of scientific facts, but not a criterion for the admissibility of scientific evidence. (p. 363)

Professor Richardson, in his recent and excellent treatise *Modern Scientific Evidence* (W. H. Anderson Co., Cincinatti, 1961) states the following (6.2, 6.3):

Through the years our courts have been called upon to recognize scientific discoveries and pass upon their legitimate function, if any, in judicial proceedings. In principle, the admission of scientific processes as legal evidence should properly be based upon the theory that the evolution in practical affairs of life, whereby the progressive and scientific tendencies of the age are manifest in every other department of human endeavor, cannot be ignored in legal procedure. And, that the law, in its efforts to enforce justice by demonstrating a fact in issue, will allow evidence of those scientific processes which are the work of educated and skillful men in their various fields of technical experience, and apply them to the demonstration of a fact, leaving the weight and effect to be given to the effort and its results entirely to the jury or other fact-finding agency.

Thus, it will be seen that in order to be in a position to lay a foundation for the admission of scientific findings the proponent must (1) be able to prove scientific acceptance, if not judicially noticed, of the particular scientific procedure by which the data is adduced, (2) show that the test was properly controlled or the device was functioning properly and (3) that the operator or technician was the one possessing requisite skill by reason of training or experience.

With the above-quoted basic premises as to the criteria of admissibility to use as a frame of reference, it is now appropriate to turn to a study of those kinds of scientific evidence which have won judicial acceptance in order that their "general scientific acceptance" and standard of reliability may be used for comparison to the polygraph test. Accordingly, several of the more commonly known types will be discussed.

Blood Grouping Tests to Determine Paternity

There are three possible phases of admissibility concerning scientific evidence, to wit: (1) Inadmissible, (2) admissible, to be weighed by the trier of fact, and (3) conclusive. This latter phase is rarely attained by any type of scientific evidence (nor is it sought here with reference to polygraphy), but paternity blood tests are an exception. Whereas at one time blood grouping tests excluding the defendant as a possible parent were admissible for their weight, to be disregarded as the jury might choose (*Berry v. Chaplin*, 74 Cal. App. 652, 169 P.2d 442; *Harding v. Harding*, 22 N.Y.S.2d 810; *State v. Clark*, 144 Ohio St. 305, 58 N.E.2d 773), such tests are now generally recognized as conclusive, thus precluding any guesswork by the jury in the name of "credibility evaluation." The first jurisdiction to recognize the need for total acceptance of science in this area was Maine, whose Supreme Judicial Court said in 1949:

> If the jury may disregard the fact of nonpaternity shown here so clearly by men trained and skilled in science, the purpose and intent of the Legislature, that the light of science be brought to bear upon a case such as this, are given no practical effect.*

A similar result was reached ten years later in *Comm. v. D'Avella*, 339 Mass. 642, 162 N.E.2d 19. Thus in this instance, at least, scientific fact has become judicial fact with no dimunition. The inference arises that the courts are interested in the increased efficiency and accuracy of factual determination which science can furnish and will yield to science absolutely in a proper case.

---

*Jordan v. Mace, 144 Me. 351, 354, 69 A.2d 670, 672.

Firearms Identification

It is now well-settled law in virtually every jurisdiction that a properly qualified "ballistics" expert may give his opinion to the jury as to whether or not a certain bullet was fired by a specific gun, or whether a certain cartridge case was imprinted by a particular firing pin. *Comm. v. Giacomazza,* 311 Mass, 456, 42 N.E. 2d 506 (1942). *Comm. v. Millen,* 290 Mass. 406, 195 N.E. 541 (1935). The Millen case is especially noteworthy in any consideration of the question at bar here, for it was the science of ballistics which saved Berrett and Molway, identified just as positively and just as erroneously as the defendant herein has been, from an unjust conviction for murder. Although the case is not in the appellate reports its notoriety is sufficient to bear citation. The testimony of Captain Van Amburgh, State Police Ballistics Expert, was sufficient to render meaningless the testimony of five positive eyewitnesses. Had it not been for scientific evidence, our trial system might well have misfired so egregiously as to put two innocent men in the electric chair.

Firearms identification evidence has been admissible at least since 1902. As an example, in *Comm. v. Best,* 180 Mass. 492, 62 N.E. 748, Mr. Justice Holmes hesitated not even momentarily in holding that a test bullet was perfectly competent evidence to prove that the murder bullet came from defendant's Winchester rifle. In view of the precedent then set, it is interesting to consider the decision in *People v. Berkman,* 307 Ill. 492, 139 N.E. 91 (1923) which was reported twenty-one years after the Best case was in print. In Berkman, the trial judge had admitted over the objection of the defendant the testimony of one Dickson, a police ballistics expert. Dickson testified that in his opinion certain bullets came from a specific pistol. In reversing the conviction for prejudicial error, the Supreme Court of Illinois said, per Duncan, J.:

> He even stated positively that he knew that that bullet came out of the barrel of that revolver, because the rifling marks on the bullet fitted into the rifling of the revolver in question, and that the markings on that particular bullet were peculiar, because they came clear up on the steel of the bullet (sic). There is no evidence in the case,

by which this officer claims to be an expert, that shows that he knew anything about how Colt automatic revolvers (sic) are made, and how they are rifled. There is no testimony in the record showing that the revolver in question was rifled in a manner different from all others of its model, and "we feel very sure" that no such evidence could be produced. The evidence of this officer is "clearly" absurd, besides not being based on any known rule that would make it admissible. If the real facts were brought out, it (sic) would undoubtedly show that all Colt revolvers of the same model and the same caliber are rifled precisely in the same manner, and the statement that one can know that a certain bullet was fired out of a 32 caliber revolver, where there are hundreds and perhaps thousands rifled in precisely the same manner and of precisely the same character, is "preposterous." (Emphasis supplied.)

It would appear that in this clash between science and the law, science lost; in other words, a scientific technique that had been well established was dashed to pieces in an appellate tribunal "simply because the judges decreed it out of existence." In this case, as in many of the cases where the polygraph has been concerned, a court has gone far beyond its powers and abused its privilege on passing upon the sufficiency of a scientific achievement by overruling science on its own ground. It is one thing to say that for one reason or another, grounded on legal principle, scientific evidence must be excluded; it is quite another for a court to inform science that it does not exist. The stubborn ignorance of the drafter of the Berkman opinion, who pompously contributed his own ballistics expertise to buttress his opinion, would no doubt be enlightened to discover that there never has existed an "automatic revolver," Colt or otherwise.

The exposition of Judge Duncan in Berkman is unfortunately paralleled by Judge Irving Kaufman, an otherwise learned and well-known jurist, in *United States v. Stromberg*, 179 F. Supp. 279 (1959). In rejecting polygraphic evidence, he stated the following:

But a machine cannot be examined or cross-examined; its testimony as interpreted by an expert is, in that sense, the most glaring and blatant hearsay. Though the defendants cite in their brief certain articles which they contend establish the scientific accuracy of the polygraph tests, I am not prepared to rule that the jury system is as yet outmoded. I still prefer the collective judgment of twelve men and women who have sat through many weeks of trial and heard all the evidence on the guilt or innocence of a defendant.

It is highly doubtful that Judge Kaufman troubled himself to read the "certain articles" cited in Defendants' brief, or he would have had less concern with the testimony of machines or the abolition of the jury system. Here is a perfect instance of a judge who dared not even take a look at what could be a marvelous aid to accurate verdicts, but chose instead to turn on the defensive and snarl at a scientific offering which he apparently regards as dangerous to his own job security.

Just as modern society must shake its head at the Berkman decision, it will in the not too distant future be forced to cast the same derisive look at Stromberg. When judges, who must by definition be the most objective and open-minded persons on the face of the earth, snuff out by outrageous fiat truths which are essential to the heart of the system they represent, they shirk responsibility. The deliberate blindness exhibited by Judges Duncan and Kaufman could, if exercised with any frequency, destroy our entire system of justice.

Chemical Tests for Intoxication

One of the more recent developments in the field of scientific evidence relates to the testing of alcoholic absorption by the human body to determine intoxication. The first reported case dealing with this matter is *State v. Duguid,* 50 Ariz. 276, 72 P.2d 435 (1937). The evidence was held properly admitted, as it was a few years later in *Comm. v. Capalbo,* 308 Mass. 376, 32 N.E.2d 225 (1941). In Donigan, Chemical Tests and the Law, Northwestern University Traffic Institute, 1957, the author points out that chemical tests for intoxication have enjoyed wide judicial approval:

> In keeping pace with modern science, the courts realize that chemical tests to determine blood alcohol concentration are of definite probative value in showing to what degree a person's mental and physical faculties have been affected by the use of alcoholic beverages. Accordingly, they have demonstrated a willingness to approve the ad-

missibility of this type of scientific evidence when the tests have been conducted properly and an adequate foundation is laid for their introduction. (p. 14)

The Supreme Court of Michigan, in approaching the question of admissibility of chemical intoxication test results, used as a criterion "general acceptance by the medical profession."*

It is noted that medical science does not absolutely endorse the "drunkometer," "alcometer," "breathalizer," "intoximeter," or any other of the several devices used to measure alcoholic absorption by sampling the breath. But universal acceptance is not necessary, for as has been pointed out above, "general scientific acceptance" is the proper criterion of judicial notice, not admissibility. Where there is a lack of unanimity in the medical profession whether intoxication can be determined by breath, the scientific disagreement affects only the weight and not the admissibility of the evidence.* The same principle should be applied to polygraphy.

Dermal Nitrate Test

For purposes of comparison and analogy alone, brief mention of the so-called paraffin test is appropriate. As evidence tending to show that a person has fired a gun recently, it has been accepted in some cases (*Comm. v. Westwood,* 342 Pa. 289, 188 A. 304 (1936) and rejected in others (*Brooks v. People,* (Colo. 1959) 339 P.2d 993). One court, in setting the criterion for admissibility, ruled that the dermal nitrate test was "not so inherently unreliable as to be inadmissible."† This rather loose standard is interesting, in view of the universality of approval which seems to have been demanded in the case of polygraphy. In fact, the dermal nitrate test is notoriously unreliable and is often eschewed by investigators who know that defense counsel will make capital of a negative result, which may occur even where the subject has fired a gun all day long.

*People v. Morse, 325 Mich, 270, 38 N.E.2d 322 (1949).

*State v. Olivas, 77 Ariz. 118, 267 P.2d 893 (1954); People v. Bobczyk, 343 Ill. App. 504, 99 N.E.2d 567 (1951); Toms v. State (Okla. 1952) 293 P.2d 812.

†Henson v. State, Tex Cr. App. (1953) 266 S.W.2d 864.

ARGUMENT II

THE STATUS OF THE POLYGRAPH TODAY.

There is no mention in any of the reported cases in this state of the polygraph. Accordingly, there is no precedent to bind this court; but there is wealth of material in articles, books, and decisions in other jurisdictions to be considered and reviewed.

As has been conceded above, the rationale in the Frye case is not objectionable. The standard there enunciated, which has since become rather famous, is as follows:

> Just when a scientific principle or discovery crosses the line between the experimental and demonstrable stages is difficult to define. Somewhere in this twilight zone the evidential force of the principle must be recognized, and while courts will go a long way in admitting expert testimony deduced from a well-recognized principle or discovery, the thing from which the deduction is made must be sufficiently established to have gained general scientific acceptance in the field in which it belongs.
>
> We think the systolic blood pressure deception test has not gained such standing and scientific recognition among physiological and psychological authorities as would justify the courts in admitting expert testimony deduced from the discovery, development, and experiments thus far made.*

It is doubtful that the Frye court meant, by coining the term "general scientific acceptability," a standard equal to that usually reserved for judicial notice, for it is specifically indicated that "admissibility" must be accorded when scientific principle or discovery is "somewhere in the twilight zone" between the experimental and demonstrable stages. This is without question the appropriate phase of development for judicial recognition.

The careful reasoning and consideration of the Frye court in passing upon the question presented to it is noteworthy, in view of the arbitrary and summary rejective language appearing in later cases passing on polygraphy; phrases written by judges who wouldn't know a lie detector if they stumbled upon it and who no doubt never took the trouble to investigate its true accuracy. Further, the findings of the Frye court related not to the polygraph as we know it but to the Marston systolic blood pressure

---

*Frye v. United States, 293 F. 1013, 1014.

test. The contrast in the two was described by Lynn P. Marcy, a polygraph examiner and instructor well known to the profession, as follows:

> The basic decision in this matter was returned in the 1923 case of *Frye v. United States,* where the court properly held that the lie detector test had not yet demonstrated that scientific recognition and acceptance which would merit the acceptance of such testimony. This case has been parroted by the courts down through the years, despite the fact that the proposed "lie detector test" in the 1923 case was the Marston systolic blood pressure test, which was merely an intermittent recording of the examinee's systolic blood pressure during interrogation using a standard blood pressure cuff and stethoscope, and a subsequent plotting of the recordings on graph paper for diagnosis. From the scientific standpoint, this crude early technique can't hold a candle to the instrumentation and techniques in use today, yet there has been no judicial notice of the great validity and widespread acceptance of the contemporary polygraph examination. The answer to this apparent reluctance on the part of the courts has been supplied by the courts themselves at least as far back as 1938. In the case of the *People v. Forte,* the New York appellate court affirmed the lower court decision concerning "lie detection" results "in the absence of testimony indicating the attainment of scientific recognition for the technique."*

And, by way of comment, it is appropriate to note that the "lie detection" rejected in *People v. Forte,* 279 N.Y. 204, 18 N.E.2d 31 (1938), referred to the "pathometer" test of the late Father Summers of Fordham University; the "pathometer" measures only galvanic skin response, which is but one of the many (numerous) physiological recordings produced by modern polygraph instruments. Further, the assignment of error in Forte did not relate to the exclusion of test results, but to the denial of defendant's motion that he be allowed to reopen the evidence so that he might take the "pathometer" test. The court did not rule that the results of such a test are inadmissible as a matter of law, but only that no foundation had been laid in the trial court and judicial notice of the accuracy of such tests could not be taken.

It is probable that counsel in the Forte case had been banking

---

*SCIENTIFIC INVESTIGATION IN CRIMINAL JUSTICE. Boston University Law-Medicine Research Institute, 1961, pp. 114-115.

on the decision in *People v. Kenney,* 167 Misc. 51, 3 N.Y.S.2d
348 (1938), where the results of the Summers pathometer test
were accepted over the objection of the prosecution. However, in
Kenney a very thorough and strong foundation was laid by the
witness (Father Summers); this is the "only reported case" on lie
detection where such a foundation was laid, and thus the only
case which has real precedental value to the case at bar.

Legal scholars are an usual source of inquiry in determining
the status of a given development, because of the intensive study
applied by them to particular areas of the law. Therefore, it is
necessary to examine what has been said in texts by those who
have made some actual and sincere investigation of polygraphy.

Dean Wicker of the University of Tennessee College of Law,
in his review of the collected cases in 1953 makes the following
observation:

> With reference to the general rule that polygraph test results are in-
> admissible, nearly all of the cases parrot the language of the Frye
> case of 1923 and give as the principal reason for excluding test re-
> sults that they have not yet gained such standing and recognition
> among physiological and psychological authorities as would justify
> the courts in admitting expert testimony deduced from the discovery,
> development, and experiments thus far made. This statement is un-
> doubtedly an accurate description of the status of lie detector tech-
> niques in 1923. It is probably also accurate for the 1930's and early
> 1940's. However, it apparently does not portray present day standards,
> nor the developments likely to be projected within the next decade
> or two.*

Professor McCormick, in his treatise on evidence,† speaks out
with conspicuous indignance on the refusal of the courts to take
an objective look at polygraphy:

> One reason usually given for these general pronouncements is that
> the tests have not yet won sufficient acceptance of their validity.
> Frequently the opinions seem to demand a universality of scientific
> approval, which as pointed out above, has no basis in the standard
> applied to other kinds of expert testimony in scientific matters. If
> we thus deflate the requirement to the normal standard which simply
> demands that the theory or device be accepted by a substantial body

---

Op. cit., p. 721.
†*Op. cit.,* p. 174.

of scientific opinion, there can be little doubt that the lie-detector technique meets this requirement.

In the light of these findings, it is believed that the courts' wholesale exclusion of lie-detector results, for want of scientific acceptability and proved reliability, is not supported by the facts. Many courts can easily recede from this position, in a case where the foregoing facts as to acceptance and reliability are adequately proven by the expert himself as a foundation for his testimony giving the test-results. In most of the cases where the results were held inadmissible no such foundation was laid, and the decisions may be explained on that ground, since the scientific facts were not so indisputable and readily verifiable as to enable the court to take judicial notice of them. The day for judicial notice will dawn after another decade of such explanations by expert witnesses.

Whereas Professor McCormick anticipated that by 1963 the courts would have accorded polygraph tests such status that judicial notice might be taken of their accuracy, we are even now still troubled with the question of admissibility, which should have been settled long ago.

Just where it is that courts get their information that polygraphy is not scientifically recognized is puzzling, for there is substantial evidence to the contrary which is consistently ignored.

In the first reported survey on deception testing and the law,* it was noted that only seven of thirty-eight leading psychologists queried expressed lack of faith in polygraphy. A more recent and comprehensive survey† also reports wide scientific acceptance.

The principal question of course is not "scientific acceptance" as such, but this: "Is there real efficacy and reliability in polygraphy—will it help to resolve issues of credibility which so frequently face our courts?"

From available statistics, it would seem that the conclusion is unavoidable that the polygraph is an efficient means of distinguishing mendacity from truth.

Dr. LeMoyne Snyder, one of the most eminent men in medico-

---

*McCormick, *Deception Tests and the Law of Evidence,* 15 CALIF. L. REV. 484 (1927).

†Cureton, *A Consensus as to the Validity of Polygraph Procedures,* 22 TENN. L. REV. 728 (1953).

legal circles today approached the question of test reliability in 1943 in the following language:*

> The next question is apt to be, "Is the machine infallible?" That question is exactly like asking whether a clinical thermometer, stethoscope, x-ray machine or compound microscope is infallible. A trained scientist may be mistaken in what he sees or hears by any of these devices. Like the thermometer and stethoscope the polygraph is simply an instrument for noting or recording physiological processes and it is possible for the operator to be mistaken in his interpretation of the recording. Even in the best of clinics the interpretation is not 100 percent accurate, but that does not imply that the machine should not be used. The same can be said for the polygraph.

Defendant in the instant case was convicted solely on the uncorroborated testimony identifying him as the assailant. Erroneous identifications are notoriously unreliable and have been found to be the most frequent cause of wrongful convictions.* Against this dangerous evidence, defendant sought to introduce the much more accurate scientific findings of a trained polygraph examiner and was prevented from so doing. On the question of the comparative reliability of the two types of evidence, which comparison must certainly be considered in determining whether defendant was fairly convicted, the following observation is pertinent; it was made by a trained psychologist with substantial experience in polygraphy:

> It is, of course, established by psychologists that eyewitness testimony is not highly reliable as legal evidence. Much more reliable is the conviction which is anchored in the measurable reactivity of the autonomic and visceral responses of the human body such as the polygraph is able to record. Both observation of an event and oral testimony about it are often at variance with internalized impressions.*

Beyond all of the writings quoted herein, which of themselves should be sufficient indication of "reliability" to satisfy this court that test results should be admissible, there is the very substantial foundation laid by the offer of proof. In this respect the defend-

---

*15 Rocky Mtn. L. Rev. 162, 164.

*Borchard: *Convicting the Innocent.* Garden City Publishing, New York, 1932, p. 367.

*Trovillo, *Scientific Proof of Credibility,* 22 Tenn. L. Rev. 743, 744.

ant's case is unique, for nowhere in any of the reports is it indicated that evidence of this sort was adduced by the proponent of polygraph test results.

A litigant who is faced with a trial wherein he knows that lying or mistaken witnesses will wrongly accuse him of a crime, and who has at his disposal the opinion of a competent polygraphist whose tests indicate that the litigant is telling the truth must, if he intends to make use of this evidence, turn to past judicial decisions in order to determine what conditions are prerequisite to admissibility. A study of the overwhelming majority of those decisions indicates that polygraphy would be admissible upon a showing of scientific acceptability.†

From these decisions the litigant must conclude that if there is in fact a general scientific recognition of the polygraph test, and if such fact is introduced into the record in a proper fashion, his test results will be ruled admissible. He must then determine, assuming that recognition exists, the proper manner of laying the foundation.

It has been suggested by Professor McCormick* that such a foundation might be introduced by the testimony of the polygraph expert himself. In any other field of scientific endeavor this method would no doubt be adequate, but in view of the obvious hesitation of the courts to allow evidence which bears so closely on the principal function of the jury, such a measure would be risky.

Ever since Frye, judges have asked for some assurance from physiological and psychological authorities as a basis for ruling test results admissible. Accordingly, it would appear that some testimony from men in these professions is desirable, if not essential, to a proper foundation. For whereas the establishment

---

†Frye v. United States, 293 F. 1013 (1923); State v. Bohner, 210 Wis. 651, 246 N.W. 314 (1933); People v. Forte, 279 N.Y. 204, 18 N.E.2d 31 (1938); People v. Becker, 300 Mich. 562, 2 N.W.2d 503 (1942); State v. Cole, 354 Mo. 181, 188 S.W.2d 43 (1945); State v. Lowry, 163 Kans. 622, 185 P.2d 147 (1947); People v. Wochnick, 98 Cal. App.2d 124, 219 P.2d 70 (1950); Henderson v. State, (Okla. Crim. Ct. App. 1951) 230 P.2d 495; State v. Kolander, (Minn. 1952) 52 N.W.2d 458; Boeche v. State, 151 Neb. 368, 37 N.W.2d 593 (1949).

*HANDBOOK ON THE LAW OF EVIDENCE, *supra,* 174, p. 372.

of a scientific achievement may be suspect when predicated solely upon the testimony of those strictly concerned with it, testimony of those from related fields who have judicial recognition and can lend the integrity of their respective professions to buttress the asserted scientific phenomenon affords a judge much greater assurance that that phenomenon is real and reliable. Further, inasmuch as the issue here in question relates physiological reactions to mental processes, the testimony of a psychiatrist as to the interrelation of physiological and psychological processes and their probable effect upon the accuracy of the technique could shed valuable light. The testimony of a police officer, with long experience in the use of polygraphy from a prosecutor's standpoint, ought to be persuasive, especially where the test results are offered on behalf of a defendant. And finally, it would seem that testimony from one who is not only a doctor, criminologist and polygraph expert but an attorney as well should be invaluable in determining the status of such tests. And if witnesses such as those described above are *not* sufficient to establish the necessary foundation, it becomes apparent that the courts are talking about an impossible standard and do not wish to deal with scientific deception "in any event."

The trial judge in this case, with the assent of the prosecutor, was good enough to recognize that the expense of producing all of the available experts whom the defendant desired to call would be prohibitive; and that any decision as to admissibility ought to be made in this court, because of the gravity and breadth of the question involved and the fact that an erroneous ruling on this question could not be corrected if it went against the state. Hence the testimony offered is in the form of a written offer of proof. This, however, ought not to diminish to any extent its probative force, since substantially similar testimony has been given by each witness in this state at one time or another.

In view of the numerous fallacies extant concerning polygraphy, mention of the principal points cumulatively established should be helpful:

1. The act of knowingly making a false assertion of fact by an individual causes certain physiological changes in the human body.

2. Among these changes, which are involuntary and beyond conscious control, are certain definite and consistent changes in pulse rate, blood pressure, respiration and electroconductivity of the endocrine system.

3. The polygraph instrument measures and records physiological phenomena with substantial precision.

4. While attached by its various devices to the body of a human being to whom certain questions are being put, the instrument measures and records those physiological responses described above and relates them to the combined stimulus of the question and the attempt, if any, at deception.

5. The absence of response to stimuli indicates that the testee has answered truthfully; the presence of response containing deception criteria indicates the testee is withholding information.

6. Where responses indicate that information is being withheld, the polygram does not reveal just what that information is, but only that it is sufficiently psychologically substantial to physiologically disturb the subject who is consciously withholding it.

7. Polygraphy has proved to be of great value in criminal matters because it enables the innocent, or truthful, individuals to be eliminated from suspicion.

8. The accuracy of polygraphy, within the limitations described above, is directly proportional to the skill of the examiner using it; and statistically, a skilled examiner will make an erroneous diagnosis in less than perhaps 2 percent of his examinations.

9. Polygraphy, in the proper hands, is sound in theoretical principle and upon empirical experience as well.

10. It is not true that nervousness, pathologic or psychopathic mendacity, rationalization or drugs are likely to contribute to an erroneous diagnosis since the technique today is equipped to combat these factors.

If the foundation, standing as it does without rebuttal or contradiction, is insufficient to establish the foundation so often sought by reviewing courts, a serious question arises as to whether or not such a foundation can be established under any circumstances. We are prepared to submit in writing, or personally, a number of expert witnesses whose testimony may be rebutted but in no way medically or physiologically contradicted. The witnesses whose testimony is offered are eminent, each in his field, beyond reproach. It would be very difficult to infer that men such as these would act so irresponsibly as to knowingly support admissibility of a hazardous and erratic device. Rather than rule that this foundation is inadequate, it would be much more appropriate to simply declare that the courts would prefer to get along without instrumental truth and close the matter.

On the basis of the writings, statistics and opinions of the evidentiary experts quoted, and on the basis of the testimony in the record, this court should rule that this defendant *has* given sufficient proof to be entitled at least to have the trier of fact consider the polygraphic evidence for whatever weight he or they may choose to give it.

ARGUMENT III

THIS COURT SHOULD RULE THAT THE OPINION OF A POLYGRAPH EXAMINER IS ADMISSIBLE ON A STIPULATION BY THE PARTIES.

Whereas in this state, and some others, there is no reported case where sufficient foundation has been laid to cause an appellate tribunal to rule that polygraphic evidence is admissible over objection, there is considerable authority holding such evidence admissible on stipulation.*

In only two cases where a stipulation was made was the evidence held inadmissible. In *LeFavre v. State,* 243 Wis. 416, 8 N.W.2d 288 (1943) the court held the test results inadmissible where the trial judge had excluded an examiner's written report because the testimony of the examiner was not offered and the report was hearsay. However, the Wisconsin court then pointed out that despite the exclusion it had the "word of the District Attorney" that the results were favorable to the defendant, which it regarded as "very significant," and reversed the conviction anyway. In *State v. Trimble,* 68 N.M. 406, 362 P.2d 788 (1961) the

---

*People v. Houser, 85 Cal. App.2d 686, 193 P.2d 937, (1948) ; State v. McNamara, 252 Iowa 19, 104 N.W.2d 568 (1960) ; State v. Lowry, 163 Kans. 622, 185 P.2d 147 (1947) ; Comm. v. McKinley, 181 Pa. Super. 610, 123 A.2d 735 (1956) ; Colbert v. Comm., 306 S.W.2d 825, 71 A.L.R.2d 442 (Ky. 1957) ; State v. Arnwine, 67 N.J. Super. 483, 171 A.2d 124 (1961) ; State v. Valdez, 371 P.2d 894 (Ariz. 1962) .

New Mexico court summarily ruled that test results were not admissible despite a stipulation and made no discussion of the great weight of authority contra.

The Valdez case is worthy of close attention, for it contains what appears to be the deepest and most comprehensive study of the polygraph test thus far made by a court of last resort. Although that court indicated by way of dictum that test results were not to be admissible generally, it found that the reliability of the technique was substantial. After reviewing the statistics on accuracy, Vice Chief Justice Udall observed (at p. 900) :

> Although much remains to be done to perfect the lie detector as a means of determining credibility we think it has been developed to a state in which its results are probative enough to warrant admissibility upon stipulation.

The Valdez case must be distinguished from the case at bar in one important respect; in that case there was no foundation evidence furnished by psychologists whose advice has too often been described as the best barometer of irresponsible subjectivity. The opinion is predicated wholly upon writings and not to any degree upon evidence at the trial.

In addition, it is apparent on close inspection that the Valdez court went far beyond the simple question of admissibility by stipulation. Almost any rule of evidence can be relaxed where the parties agree to relax them, whether the subject be a writing, real evidence, or an oral stipulation as to the testimony of an absent witness. Just as the failure to object will cure almost any error of admissibility (except where the evidentiary principle involved is deemed to be a matter of substantive law, such as the parol evidence rule), stipulation will obviate the rules. Here, however, the court did not examine only the stipulation and its binding effect, but the authenticity of the subject matter stipulated to. Therefore, curious as the decision may be in the light of legal principle, it demonstrates a definite stride toward recognition of the polygraph. The language of the court in its holding endorses not the process of stipulation so much as the reliability of the evidence stipulated to, and the decision is therefore highly significant. In the case at bar, this court has only to cover the remaining few inches to actual admissibility in order to place the polygraph test in its proper judicial status.

In each of the stipulation cases (and in some which are unreported trial court decisions, see (1943 *Wis. L. Rev.* 435, 26 *J. Crim. L. & C.* 262 [1935-6]) a rather curious element is present. The parties agree that a test shall be administered, that a certain examiner is qualified to administer it, and that his opinion shall be admissible; however, both parties invariably reserve the right to cross-examine and attack if the result is unfavorable. Usually a stipulation settles the evidence as to the issue in question, and neither party attacks what he has agreed to. The question then arises, "just what are the parties stipulating to where the polygraph is concerned?"

It would appear that they are in fact giving a sort of limited recognition to the accuracy of the technique, and to the skill of the examiner, each having the caution to permit himself an exit if the results are against him. This situation is in and of itself some indication of the reliability of the polygraph, or no responsible attorney would ever consent to such an agreement. Stipulations are made because attorneys believe their clients, and feel that the polygraph will demonstrate the worth of that belief.

ARGUMENT IV

WHERE A PROSECUTOR REFUSES TO STIPULATE, TESTIMONY OF DEFENDANT'S EXPERT SHOULD BE RECEIVED.

It is plain that the ruling in Valdez is based not upon contractual principles such as are involved in the process of stipulation, but because the polygraph test has "some probative value." The requirement that there be a stipulation is no more than an effort on the part of the Arizona court to see to it that future evidentiary polygraph tests are subject to certain controls, and that polygraph examiners do not begin to appear for each party with conflicting results. It is also manifest that in each of the cases cited upholding admissibility on stipulation, the results were "against" the defendant. This is the more dangerous side of the polygraph technique, because it is equivocal. In these cases it was only shown that the defendant had not told the "complete truth"; this does not necessarily mean that he was guilty as charged, or that he had done the act suggested by the questions. In this case, however, the test results are unequivocal, and they are consistent only with the defendant's innocence.

Under our system of criminal justice, courts are not so concerned with those guilty who might escape punishment as they are with those innocent who might be wrongfully punished, and properly so. Many defendants have escaped conviction because the state could not satisfy its burden of proof, or because despite very incriminating circumstances there remained in the mind of the trier of fact a reasonable doubt. Therefore, if equivocal polygraph test results are admissible against a defendant, even on stipulation, unequivocal test results in his favor ought not to be excluded under any circumstances.

If the rule were to emerge as admissibility on stipulation and only on stipulation, a defendant who has little other than a polygraph test to demonstrate his innocence is at the mercy of the prosecutor. And where because of public sentiment, to which elective officials are surely responsive, or for some other reason, a prosecutor forgets that his first duty is to justice and not to conviction and therefore refuses to stipulate, thus depriving defendant of good, probative evidence, defendant will be deprived of substantial rights. Therefore, even if this court were to accord completely with the Valdez case, it nonetheless ought to be the rule that where a written request for a stipulated examination is refused by the prosecutor, defendant may select his own expert and introduce the test results at trial if he wishes to do so.

In this case, it is difficult to imagine what more the defendant might have done by way of inviting the prosecutor to full participation in a polygraph test. When first arrested, and before he ever consulted counsel, defendant asked that he be given a polygraph test. He was refused. After indictment was returned, and defendant was incarcerated on high bail, his counsel sought an opportunity to have him tested by motion, and the prosecutor opposed it. He opposed it even though counsel offered in open court "to have the District Attorney's own man run the test, the state police officer, or have him present, or have him join me in the selection of an examiner. . . ." Prior to the second trial, defendant made a motion for an impartial examination to be conducted by an examiner selected by the court; this the prosecutor opposed. The state should not now be heard to complain that the test results should not be received in the absence of stipulation.

In each case of vigorous opposition to any connection between this defendant and a polygraph, the district attorney has argued unreliability of the technique. In view of this position it is difficult to understand the reports appearing almost daily in the newspapers that in one serious criminal matter or another some suspect has been "cleared" by a polygraph test.

It is most unfortunate that officials did not see fit to allow this defendant to voluntarily submit to such a wonderful exclusionary device, or he need never have been prosecuted. It would appear that this defendant is being denied the equal protection of the laws, if the polygraph test has become so integral a part of the prosecuting process that it can clear suspects without a trial. The inference is inescapable that police officers and district attorneys who announce to the public whom they serve that certain individuals are "cleared" by polygraphy in serious criminal matters are publicly endorsing the test as conclusive—every bit as conclusive as the blood test for paternity.

ARGUMENT V

THE COURT BELOW ERRED IN DENYING DEFENDANT'S MOTION FOR AN IMPARTIAL POLYGRAPH TEST.

Defendant, after failing to obtain the cooperation of the prosecutor, filed a written motion asking that the court appoint an impartial polygraphist to test defendant so that the results might be offered at trial. The motion was denied, and an exception duly saved. It is submitted that this was error. In view of the holding in Valdez, where the probative value of polygraphy was recognized, the motion was consistent with defendant's right to present at trial evidence favorable to him. As was stated by Professor McCormick (*Handbook on the Law of Evidence,* p. 373) :

> . . . by rule of court or by decisional recognition of powers traditional to the common-law judge, it should be declared that on appli-

cation of either party on notice a reasonable time before trial, or on the judge's own motion, a test of a party or a witness may be provided for, with the results to be admissible in evidence if the expert can reach a conclusion satisfactory to himself as to truth or deception. If the person to be tested refuses to undergo the test, there is an end of the matter except that if he is a party his refusal may be proved against him.

ARGUMENT VI

THE COURT BELOW SHOULD HAVE GRANTED DEFENDANT'S MOTION THAT COMPLAINANT BE SUBJECTED TO A POLYGRAPH TEST, OR THAT HIS REFUSAL BE ADMISSIBLE TO IMPEACH HIM.

Consistent with the practice urged by McCormick, and because a complainant in a criminal case is a "party" in the sense that he pits his credibility against the defendant, it would not be an unfair burden to ask that such witness demonstrate that he at least believes what he is saying. If such witness refuses to be tested, it is manifest that the prosecutor ought to take a long look at his case, else he be prosecuting on false evidence; and if he elect to continue, the jury ought to be informed of the witness' refusal in every case where the defendant himself has been willing to submit.

ARGUMENT VII

POLICY CONSIDERATIONS DO NOT MILITATE AGAINST THE LIMITED RECOGNITION URGED BY DEFENDANT IN THIS CASE.

There will no doubt come from many the old hue and cry that our trial system is about to be replaced by a battery of polygraphs, that men will be governed by machines, and that legal integrity is about to be destroyed if polygraphy is to be given a whit of recognition. These contentions can be answered quietly and logically.

First, it is doubtful that the testimony of a polygraphist will usurp the function of any jury. His opinion may well help them to arrive at the truth, which is their sworn duty in any event. They are helped by experts of all kinds, some of whom (such as psychiatrists) appear frequently on both sides of a given case contradicting one another completely. It is unlikely that this will ever come to pass where polygraph examiners are concerned, since competent experts will in almost all cases come to consistent conclusions; and further, perhaps unique to this field, the so-called paid expert who prostitutes his profession for the party who bids highest will be greatly deterred from giving a dishonest opinion, since no polygraph expert could very well refuse a test himself if the honesty of his testimony were challenged.

The suggestion that juries will follow blindly after polygraph test results is an unfounded fear. Juries are all too capable of disregarding any evidence to which they do not take a shine.

There is nothing in this case or this brief to suggest that the polygraph might be admitted in civil matters, or that the failure of a defendant to submit to a test should be admitted to impeach him, or that test results could support a conviction where the other evidence alone would be insufficient.

Defendant asks "only" that this court rule that polygraph test results may be admitted on behalf of a criminal defendant, where it is shown that he has demonstrated his willingness to submit to an impartial test prior to trial.

No attention has been paid to the "hearsay" objection occasionally asserted against polygraphy since such a position is wholly without merit. The evidence is the examiner's opinion, that is subject to cross-examination and contradiction just as is any other expert testimony.

No doubt adverse and summary judicial deprecation of polygraphy has been principally responsible for the failure of the field to attract more educated men and more research than it has. This is most unfortunate, for had normal scientific development not been thus discouraged our trial system might today enjoy greater efficiency and a lot less lying.

In order to affirm this conviction, this court will have to emulate the Illinois Court of 1923 and overrule the scientists. The fallacy of such an approach was condemned long ago.

It is obvious that the day for admissibility of polygraphy is near at hand. Professor McCormick and Dean Wicker quite apparently thought it would have dawned some years past as they wrote so long ago. This is an appropriate case; the foundation offered has been more than adequate; and on all the evidence there is every reason to suspect that the defendant is innocent. Unless this conviction is reversed, justice can never be done.

Many years ago in this country women were executed as witches upon the testimony of children that "spells" had been cast by the defendants. This was not a very scientific procedure. The fires at the stake are out now and this country is beginning to live down official murder such as was then perpetrated. To endorse the conviction of this defendant in the face of all of the evidence that he is not guilty would be no less grievous an act than touching once again a torch to human flesh, all in the name of justice.

*   *   *

The order of proof to support the foregoing would normally contain the names and qualifications of the experts called in by the defense who are knowledgeable about polygraphy, its history, reliability and use, as well as the relative subject matters about which each expert would testify.

Chapter 3

TRUTH VERIFICATION VS. OUTDATED PRECEDENT

T HE ONLY SCIENCE that comes close to "exactness," if it can be called a science, is the classification, comparison and identification of fingerprints. Even so, exactness in fingerprints lessens in reliability, or no ability at all, when there is not enough of a print available to legally qualify it for identification purposes in court, or when there is nothing with which to compare a latent print.

It took nearly thirty years of individual, professional and legislative perserverance before fingerprints and ballistics, which are totally objective, were admitted into evidence.

And yet, for many years, the courts have had little qualm about admitting the testimony of psychologists and psychiatrists whose highly opinionated testimony has been fairly well established to be about 50 percent pure subjectivity, loaded with experimental hypothesis and contradictions.

The adversaries of polygraphy can no longer hide behind the "invasion of privacy cry." After several hundred thousand polygraph tests the layman, as well as the scientist, has come to realize there is no validity to such claims. This is further supported by the absence of litigation against polygraphy in government, law enforcement and private industry.

Likewise, the scientific world has unequivocally verified that modern polygraph instruments are reliable and valid for the purpose of recording physiological changes which take place within the human body. As a result, there are few objection avenues left to overcome before polygraphy in the hands of competent practioners becomes admissible into evidence.

One objection still put forth, mostly by prosecutors, frequently follows thus:

In 1971, at the close of a voir dire hearing during which

several polygraph experts testified, as the defense laid the foundation and criteria necessary for admissibility of test results, the prosecutor argued:

"May it please the court, this is not an easy act to follow, for someone with my inexperience and youth. But I think, your Honor, my understanding of the law, as has the defense also indicated, is that the general basis for exclusion of polygraph results have been since the decision in the United States case back in 1923: the general lack of scientific acceptability and standardization.

"Now, we have had considerable testimony for almost two days concerning the statistical accuracy of the polygraph instrument, various scientific practical problems in its operation, the existence and use of various techniques, and various auxilliary policies as well. For example, the effect of the admission of polygraph results, the effects it might have upon the use of an instrument in the investigative stage by police agencies. Recognizing that a defendant can neither be practically nor legally compelled to take a test, the difficulties in permitting him to shop around, if you will, to find a polygraph result which will clear him and then only bring that fact to the attention of the authorities may be insurmountable. There is difficulty in having untrained experts being permitted to testify, at least in the absence of licensing regulation by a state.

"However, I think another and more serious objection in this particular case is the tendency of jurors to treat polygraph results as absolutely conclusive.

"Consider for a moment, if you will, the vigor with which the defense has conducted his hearing and the practically unshakable confidence that every one of these witnesses had in the complete reliability of the polygraph instrument. I would submit to your Honor that no one, indeed, no one in this courtroom probably much less a jury of twelve ordinary citizens, could fail to be anything but overwhelmed.

"I would suggest that the very argument of reliability carries with it the seeds of the most serious objection. If a jury were permitted to sit here and listen to these experts, I cannot believe they would go back into that room and do anything other than render a verdict consistent with the results that may be presented to them.

(Authors' insert: A jury does the same thing with or without polygraphy).

"Furthermore, I think that in this area of polygraphy we are dealing with the subjective interpretations of one man. Notwithstanding the protestations of the witnesses, the attempt by defense counsel to analogize these to other methods of scientific experiments, I would suggest the fundamental difference between the firearms identification, blood tests in paternity suits, is that the entire skill of the polygraphist lies solely in his interpretive ability.

(Authors' insert: A qualified, competent polygraphist utilizes his question formulation and his instrument to obtain the physiological recordings. His ability and education, plus experience, permits him to separate truth from deception which the recordings contain. So also the blood analyst, the ballistics expert, must use his own revealing instruments along with collateral substances and be qualified to operate them properly; they must have ability, education, training and experience in order to determine blood types, or match the rifling marks of a gun barrel with marks found on a spent bullet).

"We have heard evidence here that the instrument is very simple, but the entire skill lies in the ability of the polygraphist to be able to subjectively interpret the recordings. In other areas of science, nowhere do you get the extent of the subjective inferences that must be drawn as you do in the case of the polygraph examiner.

(Authors' insert: All recordings produced by any physiological recording instrument, device or invention must be interpreted and evaluated by the person so operating or conducting and an opinion, prognosis, diagnosis, result rendered).

"I would suggest to the court that by admitting polygraphic results we would, in effect, be replacing that which has traditionally been twelve subjective judgments by jurors, members of the community, with that of one subjective judgment rendered by a polygraphist. Indeed, I do not know if it is so unrealistic to view the polygraph instrument as replacing the twelve man jury. I suggest this danger could become particularly acute in a perjury case.

"The defense has suggested that perhaps this is a most appropriate case because we are dealing with people where there is a conflict in testimony. But, the argument cuts both ways: We are involved in a perjury case; guilt or innocence can be phrased—did the defendant lie?—the People, your Honor, have brought an information which charges that this particular defendant lied. This information is presented to the jury. The jury is told: 'your function in determining guilt or innocence is to decide, nothing more, did the defendant lie?' Then we have this expert come in with his result and the only thing he can testify to is that the defendant lied or the defendant did not lie.

"The prosecution believes that a polygraphist's opinion, if presented to a jury, would be tantamount to an opinion of guilt or innocence, which has traditionally been offensive.

"I would suggest to this court that because of the danger in letting one subjective opinion preempt the function of twelve men, the People would submit it as inappropriate for this court at this time to receive such evidence. The People would respectfully request that the defendant's offer of such evidence be denied.

The court: Any rebuttal by the defense?

Defense: No. It just occurs to me that if polygraph examiners are so consistently right in their opinions, supported by objective physiological chart tracings which clearly differentiate between truth and deception, the fact that their opinions might influence laymen jurors to agree with them for protection of the falsely accused, is hardly a disaster.

The foregoing almost staggers the practical sensibility of professional and scientific-minded men. Obviously the prosecution had no knowledge of even the basics comprising the art of polygraphy and apparently had never made an attempt to study the subject matter in any detail.

As a result, only outdated precedent compounded upon outdated precedent prevailed.

One professionally oriented subjective opinion based on objective truth verification, physiologically, is worth more to the falsely accused than any fifty subjective opinions of laymen jurors who are too frequently confused by legal jargon, massively worded instructions to the jury, and a play of words by a prosecutor who could care less that an innocent man might be convicted through lack of knowledge and plain ignorance on the part of gullible jurors.

For, it has been said, most aptly, jurors are just human beings, also swayed by vehement personal prejudices and opinions.

Retrospectively, we now take a look at relevant portions of an opinion relating to polygraphy issued by the Supreme Court of Alaska which, in a manner of speaking, talks out of two sides of its mouth at the same time. It is a sad state of affairs when supposedly learned men find it necessary to hide behind outdated precedent which factually has nothing to do with an issue at bar, or rely on so-called experts who have never trained to be a polygraphist and who have never conducted a live polygraph test.

THE SUPREME COURT OF THE STATE OF ALASKA

THOMAS PULASKIS,	)	
	)	
Appellant,	)	File No. 1108
	)	
v.	)	O P I N I O N
	)	
STATE OF ALASKA,	)	(No. 649 — November 9, 1970)
	)	
Appellee.	)	
	)	

Appeal from the Superior Court of the State of Alaska, Third Judicial District, Anchorage, Edward V. Davis, Judge.

Appearances: R. Collin Middleton, Ketchikan for Appellant. Benjamin O. Wlaters, Jr., Assistant District Attorney, Harold W. Tobey, District Attorney, and G. Kent Edwards, Attorney General, for Appellee.

Before: Boney, Chief Justice, Dimond, Rabinowitz, and Connor, Justices; Fitzgerald, Superior Court Judge.
Rabinowitz, Justice.

In this appeal, appellant asks us to reverse his conviction of the crime of larceny. The principal ground advanced by appellant is that it was plain error on the trial court's part to have admitted into evidence the results of polygraph examinations which were given to him prior to trial. Appellant further claims that he should have been granted a judgment of acquittal because the prosecution failed to produce sufficient corroborative evidence of the testimony of its chief witness, an alleged accomplice. Appellant also argues that the entry of judgment of acquittal was required because the prosecution failed to prove that the victim of the larceny owned the property alleged to have been stolen. We affirm the judgment and commitment entered by the superior court.

In his second specification of error, appellant asserts that the state's evidence was legally insufficient to corroborate the testimony of the accomplice, Renee La Cour. Appellant argues that apart from the inadmissible results of the lie detector tests, which were administered to appellant, the corroborative evidence did not sufficiently connect appellant with the commission of the larceny (R. Perkins, *Criminal Law* 195-96 [1957]; 2 R. Anderson, *Wharton's Criminal Law & Procedure* 497 [1957]). In support of this argument, appellant relies upon the decision of the Ninth Circuit in *Ing v. United States* (278 F.2d 362 [9th Cir. 1960]).

One year after Ing was decided, this court in *Oxenberg v. State* (362 P.2d 893 [Alaska 1961]) rejected sub silentio Ing's analysis of Alaska's accomplice corroboration statute. . . .We have consistently adhered to Oxenberg's criteria.* Our most recent reliance upon Oxenberg is found in *Dimmick v. State* (473 P.2d 616 [Alaska 1970]).

This brings us to the crux of this appeal. Appellant argues that it was plain error for the trial court to have admitted testimony and a written report concerning the results of lie detector tests given him. While represented by counsel, appellant, prior to

---

*Merrill v. State, 423 P.2d 686, 700 (Alaska 1967); Thomas v. State, 391 P.2d 18, 23 (Alaska 1964); Braham v. State, 376 P.2d 714 (Alaska 1962); Mahle v. State, 371 P.2d 21, 26 (Alaska 1962).

trial, consented to take a polygraph examination.† Pursuant to his consent, appellant was subjected to two polygraph examinations. During the impanelling of the trial jury, appellant's counsel inquired of the entire prospective panel whether anyone had ever taken a lie detector test. One prospective juror answered in the affirmative and in the presence of the panel, appellant's counsel then elicited an opinion from the juror that he did not believe polygraph machines to be infallible* Counsel for appellant then asked the entire panel if they had done any reading on the subject of polygraph machines. One prospective juror answered in the affirmative and in the presence of the entire panel related that she was left with "a very unfavorable impression" of polygraph machines on the basis of her reading. In his opening statement to the jury, appellant's trial counsel stated that the polygraph examinations in question were not of value.

As part of its case in chief, the prosecution called Sergeant Anderson of the Anchorage Police Department. Without objection from defense counsel, Sergeant Anderson was accepted as a qualified polygraph examiner. Anderson then testified, again without objection, as to the circumstances surrounding his administration of two separate polygraph examinations to appellant. Anderson testified that in his opinion the examinations revealed that deceptive answers were given to four crucial questions. No objection was made to this opinion evidence nor was any motion subsequently made to strike any portion of Sergeant Anderson's testimony. Instead, during the state's direct examination of the witness, counsel for appellant explicitly stated that he had no objection to the introduction into evidence of Sergeant Anderson's written report of appellant's polygraph examinations. Appellant's counsel also cross-examined Sergeant Anderson to a considerable

---

†Our holding renders unnecessary any decision whether evidence of the results of lie detector tests can be looked to as corroborative of an accomplice's testimony. Counsel for appellant in this appeal did not represent appellant at any stage of the proceedings in the lower court.

*Appellant's counsel asked this same juror during voir dire: Could you follow the court's instructions which I'm sure Judge Davis will give regarding lie detectors and divorce from your mind any previous knowledge that you may have acquired either firsthand or secondhand by books and talking to people. . . .

extent concerning the general inadmissibility of polygraph results in the courts.

Prior to the conclusion of the trial, appellant's counsel requested the following instruction which was subsequently given by the trial court in its charge to the jury:

> The results of a test by a polygraph machine, commonly called a lie detector, have been admitted by stipulation by the State and the Defendant. The polygraph is a scientific instrument which records certain physiological phenomenon, such as changes in the pulse rate, blood pressure, and respiration. The polygraph machine has not yet achieved scientific reliability and is not an instrument that automatically and unerringly discloses a lie by the person being tested.

In *Gafford v. State,* we said by way of dicta, "The general rule is that the results of polygraph tests are not admissible in evidence."* In the case at bar, the manner in which the issue of polygraph reliability has been raised calls for a more detailed discussion of the subject.

The polygraph machine ordinarily consists of a cardiograph which registers pulse rate, a sphygmograph which measures blood pressure, a pneumograph which measures respiration, and usually a galvanometer which measures electrodermal responses.* The theory for using the polygraph to detect lies is that the act of lying causes conscious conflict in the mind of the examinee, which produces an emotion of fear or anxiety, manifested by fluctuations in pulse rate, blood pressure, breathing, and perspiration.†

As we said in Gafford, the general rule precludes admission of the results of polygraph tests. The authority usually cited as the

---

*440 P.2d 405, 410 Alaska, (1968), *cert. denied,* 392 U.S. 1120 (1969).

*Henderson v. State, 94 Okla. Crim. 45, 230 P.2d 495, 501 (Crim. App. 1951); Kleinfeld, *The Detection of Deception-A Resume,* 8 Fed. B.J. 153 (1947). Laboratory experimenters generally regard galvanic skin response as the best indicator of deception, but field examiners generally do not; possible galvanic skin response is the only indicator sensitive enough for laboratory experiments on subjects who do not care much whether they succeed in deceiving the experimenter, but is too sensitive for the intensely emotional circumstances of real life interrogations. Thackray and Orne, *A Comparison of Physiological Indices in Detection of Deception,* 4 Psychophysiology 329 (1968).

†Skolnick, *Scientific Theory and Scientific Evidence: An Analysis of Lie Detection,* 70 Yale L.J. 694, 699-700 (1961).

first reported American case holding such evidence inadmissible is *Frye v. United States.* . . .

Judicial antipathy towards the admissibility of polygraph evidence continues. Inadmissibility is the general rule, though some jurisdictions make an exception if the polygraph evidence was received at trial pursuant to stipulation. The decisions reflect a high degree of sensitivity to the numerous potential sources of error in the ascertainment of deception through polygraph examination.

The central problem regarding admissibility is not that polygraph evidence has been proven unreliable,* but that polygraph proponents have not yet developed persuasive data demonstrating its reliability. Little worthwhile experimentation has been done to determine the reliability of polygraph evidence.†

This is not to say that the worth of polygraph evidence cannot ever be proved to the satisfaction of this court. Two approaches which courts might find persuasive are (1) surveys of the opinions of experts familiar with polygraphs as to their usefulness in detection of deception, and (2) experiments yielding meaningful data on the accuracy of polygraph examiner's opinions as to the veracity of the examinees.* On the basis of our study of the rele-

---

*Typical of this judicial concern is the court's opinion in Henderson v. State, 94 Okla. Crim. 45, 230 P.2d 495, 501-02 (Crim. App. 1951). In that case the court refers to Professor Inbau's conclusions as to the factors responsible for errors in polygraph examinations. Professor Inbau's factors fall in five broad categories: (1) emotional tension; (2) physiological abnormalities; (3) mental abnormalities; (4) unresponsiveness in a lying or guilty subject; and (5) unobserved muscular movements which produce ambiguities or misleading indications in the blood pressure tracing.

†Levitt, *Scientific Evaluation of the Lie Detector*, 40 Iowa L. Rev. 440 (1955).

(Authors' insert: Professor Inbau's five factors are as antiquated and lacking in validity as some appellate court decisions denying polygraph's admissibility. So also are the opinions of Levitt noted above.)

*For data to be meaningful, it must disclose how frequently polygraph examiners are correct and how frequently they are incorrect when they report that subjects are lying or telling the truth. Since a greater proportion of examiners' opinions are probably correct when they are permitted to abstain from giving opinions when they are at all uncertain, the data should reveal in what proportion of cases surveyed the examiners were unable to state opinions. Experiments will be difficult to design in such a way that their results will be generalizable to criminal

vant literature, we are not prepared to say whether polygraph examiners' opinions are reliable. Judicial acceptance of polygraph tests must await the results of more persuasive experimental proof of reliability.

On the basis of our study of the judicial authority and academic literature in this area, we conclude that the results of polygraph examinations should not be received in evidence over objection. Even if no objection has been tendered, the trial court ordinarily should reject such evidence. A stipulation for admission does not increase the reliability of polygraph results and therefore should not lead to any deviation from the exclusionary policy.

This does not mean that we find polygraph tests so demonstrably unreliable as to require a finding of plain error even in the circumstances of the record in the case at bar. In this particular case, we conclude that appellant waived any objection to Sergeant Anderson's opinion testimony and also waived any objection to the written report of the results of the polygraph examinations.* It appears that counsel's strategy was to permit the polygraph examiner's opinion to be received into evidence because he thought his client would be benefitted by the jury's knowledge of his consent to be tested more than he would be harmed by the results of the tests. In his final argument appellant's counsel told the jury that the defense did not have any objection to Sergeant Anderson's opinion testimony concerning the results of appellant's polygraph examinations. Explaining why he did not object to Sergeant Anderson's testimony, defense counsel argued, "It's very simple, guilty people don't voluntarily take lie detection tests nor do they testify."

Ciminal Rule 47 (b) provides that "Plain error or defects affecting substantial rights may be noticed although they were not

---

investigation, and scientific research to obtain meaningful data will be difficult to perform on actual cases of criminal investigation. The attempted solution of these problems must be left to those who are competent in the techniques of social science. Once we are provided with meaningful data on the accuracy of polygraph examiners' opinions, we may reconsider the difficult decision as to whether they are sufficiently reliable to be admitted as evidence and are otherwise objectionable.

*Cadzow v. State, 471 P.2d 404 (Alaska 1970) .

brought to the attention of the court." The plain error rule is in-
applicable where failure to object at the trial court level amount-
ed to an intelligent waiver of a known right.* In *Rank v. State†*
appellant argued that admission of testimony that he refused to
take a lie detector test was plain error; we rejected this contention
on the ground that his attorney's extensive cross-examination on
the subject manifested an intelligent waiver of a known right. In
light of the relevant portions of the record in the case at bar
which we have referred to, we think that Pulakis' counsel's actions throughout the course of the trial below present a more
compelling factual situation for finding an intelligent waiver of a
known right than existed in Rank.

In *Gafford v. State* we held that appellant could not raise on
appeal the trial court's error in failing to instruct the jury to disregard a reference to a lie detector test where counsel below informed the court that defendant chose not to request such an instruction. In the case at bar, we think the course of conduct of appellant's trial counsel comes within the ambit of the Gafford rule
and precludes appellant from raising any issue pertaining to Sergeant Anderson's opinion testimony, as well as the written report
of the polygraph examinations.

As we have pointed out earlier, the strategy adopted by appellant's trial counsel was centered around allowing, not excluding, the polygraph evidence. Counsel for appellant questioned the
prospective jurors intensively on the subject of polygraph examinations, and he elicited responses favorable to appellant's position. In his opening statement and closing argument, trial counsel minimized the importance of the evidence. No objection was
made to the qualifications of the expert witness or to the admissibility of the testimony. In fact, counsel stated explicity that
there was no objection to the admission of the written report of
the expert witness. On cross-examination, appellant's counsel obtained significant admissions from the expert about the unreliability of the polygraph test. Highly favorable jury instructions
were requested and were given by the court.

---

*Hammonds v. State, 442 P.2d 39, 43 (Alaska 1968).
†373 P.2d 734, 735-36 (Alaska 1962).

We think that this entire pattern of events demonstrates a clear, intelligent waiver of any privilege to exclude this evidence.

Affirmed.

* * *

Other than Erle Stanley Gardner, Edward Bennett Williams, Maurice Rosen, A. I. Rosner, amongst perhaps a very few others, one of the most knowledgeable legal advocates of polygraphy, particularly where it is used for protection of the innocent, is the modern counterpart of Clarence Darrow, F. Lee Bailey, Boston, Massachusetts.

During the voir dire testimony of expert witnesses on polygraphy, out of presence of the jury, before the Honorable James P. Churchill, Circuit Judge, at Pontiac, Michigan, commencing June 23, 1970,* this brilliant attorney and polygraph authority placed himself on the witness stand in behalf of the defendant and, first being duly sworn, testified as follows (after stating his experience, training and qualifications) : "In 1961, a month or so after my admission to the Bar, because of my experience with the polygraph, I was called into the middle of a first degree murder case wherein, by unintentional stipulation on the part of the defense, a polygraph examiner had taken the stand and testified that the accused, in the course of an examination, had given deceptive responses about whether or not he had killed his wife. His wife's death was admitted by the defense.

"I was called in for the sole initial purpose of cross-examining that witness who was a nonqualified examiner according to the testimony, practiced part time, and was a kind of charlatan about whom the court had shown some concern. The chief defense counsel suffered a heart attack in the process and I finished the case for him and the defendant was acquitted.

"In my experience it was fairly simple to show the jury why the man had not the qualifications nor the expertise to be credible, why his testimony was defective, and why it should be regarded at best as inconclusive.

"Since that time I have made constant use of the polygraph

---

*State of Michigan v. Peter N. Lazaros, CR-6237, in the Circuit Court for the County of Oakland; Robert C. Goussy, Thomas Carlson, Asst. Attorneys General; F. Lee Bailey, C. Michael Kimber, for the Respondent.

for several purposes. First, to inform me as defense counsel whether or not to rely on a client's assertions and adopt the strategy that the defendant was innocent or whether to fall back on his constitutional protections because he was something less than innocent.

"I have lectured extensively around the country to both lay and professional groups about the polygraph. I have done research with the polygraph, specifically in the field of hypnosis with Mr. Lynn Marcy in 1961 in Redondo Beach, California, at a school operated by Dr. William Bryant, an expert in hypnosis, for the initial purpose of determining whether or not a qualified hypnotist could so condition a man as to enable him to fool a polygraph examiner. The results of that research were that although an amateur might be fooled by some of the things a hypnotist could indeed do with physiological responses evinced on a polygram, one of Mr. Marcy's qualifications would have no difficulty in separating out deception from truth.

"One of the ways in which this was tested was to have Dr. Bryant confess to me as an attorney something that he had done in his past which was factual and was also unlawful, or would put his license in jeopardy. Whereafter I handed Mr. Marcy a list of ten possible crimes and asked him to determine which one the Doctor would be concerned about as a matter of his own history, which Mr. Marcy very quickly did.

"There were other tests run but at least on the point we were satisfied the one possible test of jeopardy, the polygraph was not one to be concerned about, provided the examiner knew what he was doing.

"In my military service as a military and civilian investigator and a criminal lawyer who not only in his own cases but in cases handled by other attorneys who wanted me as a consultant on administration of polygraph in both pretrial and postconviction matters, only once has there been a demonstrable error wherein the examiner gave an incorrect report and his circumstances involved an accusation that an older man and a young boy engaged in a homosexual act. The examiner asked the older man if he did a homosexual act. The man said *no* and he did not respond. He failed to ask the boy if the boy performed a homosexual act on the older man and when the testimony overwhelmingly showed he was guilty he explained in his mind that there was a vast difference between being a passive or active member and that was the explanation given why he did not respond.

"However, I found beyond question that this scientific device can provide a more reliable direction in the search for truth than many of the techniques that we use in the courtroom such as direct and cross-examination of witnesses, contradictory testimony, reliance on the demeanor and articulation, education and intelligence of the witness, vis-a-vis the lawyer who happens to cross-examine him who may or may not be skillful, may or may not be prepared and I am also able, through considerable experience with these techniques, to compare it favorably to the paraffin tests which are admissible in most courts and are used to attempt to solve the question of whether or not the accused recently fired a weapon using a projectile propelled by nitrates.

"It is at least as reliable and probably more so than comparison handwriting. It is at least as reliable in terms of demonstrable errors that are historically compiled by the profession itself, and by the adjunctive professions such as the law and the courts and police profession, at least as reliable as the comparison of fingerprints, and it is at least as reliable as the comparison of firearms identification work of projectiles with gun barrels and castings with firing pins, the kind of things which are routinely used in the prosecution or defense of a criminal case.

"The likelihood of an instrument malfunctioning and contributing to an incorrect result, in my opinion, is extremely remote and I have never heard a case of that happening.

"The instrument itself is very simple and its components, each of them is known to medical science where they are used for other purposes. As an example, I think all of the components of a polygraph are contained in the instrument that is used by doctors for examination and analysis.

"In addition to that and from consultation with many experts in the medical field, and many trial lawyers, my opinion is it is at least as reliable as the opinions which result from electrocardiograms and electroencephalograms where I have observed experts differ in their inspection of the charts.

"I have never in my entire career known two polygraph examiners, both of whom had qualifications of the kind that have been exhibited by the witnesses in this matter and include Sgt. North, who have come to contrary conclusions when both were testing the same subject matter, both had the same subject and both had the same information to work with in structuring the tests.

"As a trial lawyer I have no doubt that the ordinary safeguards of judicial control over who is and who is not an expert in an adversary proceeding wherein qualifications can be examined or challenged and the attorneys control through the process of cross-examination the caliber of the evidence that is handed to the jury, no doubt that the law in its present configuration is as capable of efficiently and safely handling this kind of evidence and preventing it from achieving unwarranted weight as it is in handling the other kind of scientific evidence I have just alluded to.

"In all of the cases that I know where the polygraph has been introduced, including the one in Massachusetts, the one in New Jersey, as substantive evidence against the defendant, the defendant has been acquitted. Those cases that are reported in the case books, particularly the recent ones, around 1962 in Arizona, where they were admitted by stipulation and the defendant failed, I have had no contact with but I read about them.

"I have testified as an expert in polygraph four or five times in court including as a witness for the prosecution in an attempt of a New York prosecutor in Watertown, New York, to lay a foundation for the receipt of evidence of a deceptive chart wherein a criminal defendant was invited to and did take a test.

"Insofar as the overall effect on criminal justice, of the utilization of this test, if ordinary criteria are applied as they have been applied to other kinds of scientific evidence, which over the years have become admissible, in my view the test could consistently, always with the consent of the accused, provide an invaluable contribution to that area of the law where I think our system is weak and that is on accuracy.

"In cases where there are contradictions between articulate witnesses or honest mistakes such as eyewitness identification cases where mistakes have been recorded as legion, I believe that it could prevent miscarriages of justice. I believe that the more extensive use of the polygraph in the pretrial stages, the invitation to take one together with some kind of reward if one takes and passes one, would streamline our court system and clean up the docket to a degree. I believe there would be fewer trials, more pleas and fewer innocent people put to the embarrassment and agony of trial, if this safeguard were used in the early stages, not in the postconviction stages where one is attempting to repair a mistake, but in the early stages as it is now and where every person has a right to submit, if he chose to do so, and the prosecutor did not have the option to decide that a polygraph would not come into the case as the practice now has it.

"I have no reason in the world to think that juries or judges—I have brought this evidence in, in substantive form, before many judges who are more prone to receive it if they are sitting without jury—no reason to think that undue weight is cast upon this kind of expert opinion which is all that it is, any more than it might be cast upon a fingerprint tieing an accused at the scene of a crime. It would be very heavy evidence. Or, a firearm expert who says that this bullet came from a gun which came from the accused, which would be very heavy evidence. There is no question that the polygraph expert opinion would probably sway the jury to go one way or another as to believing a certain witness. And there are times where if a mistake was made and the other evidence was of guilt, that the polygraph examiner's testimony would not have any effect on the jury or affect the jury verdict and that is not an opinion but experience I have had in courts, both civil and military.

"My own experience has been whereas ten years ago there were people around whose qualifications were doubted by some of the other polygraph examiners, this condition has diminished very sharply and it is very rare now for one who is in any way active in the profession of polygraph testing to be a person of less than sound qualifications.

"Very typical is an active examiner like the next to the last witness, Sgt. North, a policeman or private examiner who has run hundreds of tests and whose evaluations, understanding of theory and practice is consistent with that of people who have been in the profession for a much longer time.

"I think that completes it."

MR. GOUSSY: I would like to ask a couple questions, counsel. Do you have any official connection with any of these organizations, the American Polygraph Association, or any other polygraph associations?

MR. BAILEY: I was at one time an associate member of the nonexaminers of the Academy for Scientific Examination which is one of several units that combined to form the American Polygraph Association. I have not been an associate member for six or seven years. I have received as a staff lecturer for the Keeler Polygraph Institution and for the National Training Center of Lie Detection, but I have no monetary interest of any kind in the development of machines or development of examiners. My sole business connection with them is to pay examiner fees to run tests or appear and testify.

MR. GOUSSY: You don't represent them as general counsel as such?

MR. BAILEY: No. They have general counsel but I am not and never have been that person.

MR. GOUSSY: The other thought I have in accepting your opinion from your experience that you feel that at the present stage of the art or science, however we refer to it professionally, that the courts as they are now structured could, through the diligent and judicial exercise, weed out the bogus operators et cetera, the charlatans. Don't you see a substantial danger wherein a state like Michigan that have—I forget how many judicial districts we have in the state, but numerous—we have 83 counties, courts sitting in every one of them—we have all phases of judges and prosecutors and defense lawyers where the standards set in one particular case can be far from the standards set in another case? The demand for people in these areas that the polygraph become admissible I frankly think could become substantial because the State of Michigan having district police posts throughout the state, we would have our examiners, the prosecutor will have his examiners, the defense lawyers will need theirs, and can't you see in the absence of licensing or some type of control imposed independent of a judicial ruling in each case as to the expertise of the operator, that the very concern about the spread of people who freely do just that, buy a book and buy a machine or get together in a co-op and have a machine, is just almost inevitable?

Mr. Bailey: No, I think that danger is of no serious concern both in theory for certain reasons and in practice. In the total range of my experience it has never been a matter of my concern for the following reasons:

There are several ways for the charlatan to reach the courtroom or try the judicial process. He has to be introduced by counsel and the matter of experience, counsel are ordinarily reluctant to produce experts of doubtful quality. If he is produced and put on the witness stand to qualify before the court, there are indicia of expertise which any judge, even though he knows very little about the polygraph itself, can quickly pick up, and it is in this precise manner that those unlicensed experts that we use on a day-to-day basis, such as in handwriting, such as police experts in fingerprints and firearms identification, who must rely on their education, training and experience and either have the indicia of expertise or do not.

An additional safeguard is the amount of polygraph examiners in the community, and I have seen this done in my very first case, where they in droves called me to give me information about the charlatan on the witness stand to impeach him. The polygraph community could come forward very rapidly. If it became known to them that a person in the profession thought to be not qualified was testifying, I think they would appear and say so without hesitation and tell the jury this man has not the experience that you should rely on.

In addition to that, and I think somewhat like the other comparable professions we talked about, I find in the polygraph examiners, both from personal knowledge and indirect contact, they have a very high level of professional integrity and a great jealousy about that integrity. These men are painfully aware of the damage that a corrupt examiner could do. They are less frightened of that now that standards across the industry enable one examiner to read a chart of another. Ten years ago another examiner would never testify on another examiner's chart; today they will. Today it is nearly impossible to structure your test for money to give the accused the benefit of a false opinion to show that he is truthful. It would be fairly easy on cross-examination to check on that expert and so because of that, contradiction is not likely. The attempt by people not really experts is no greater danger than it is in the handwriter or firearm identification or fingerprints, which are not licensed professions anywhere in this country and are subject to judicial control.

I have never seen this present a problem. I think such possibility has been cured by developments within the profession and, again, I think the speculative fears that these are the kind of things that would happen—especially the comparison to psychiatry which comes back to no fixed base line, no photograph, no chart, no graph that another expert can look at and add his opinion to—I think all of that, while it is reasonable under the circumstances for an unfamiliar science, both historically and theoretically, is unlikely not a cause for exclusion.

To say it should wait until licensing comes in is sound in the broad policy sense but terribly unfair to any individual whose trial happens to precede the action of the Legislature in getting moving as in ten states it has already occurred.

MR. GOUSSY: My question would be to you then: Where I can accept your thought and I would never suggest a licensing of fingerprint people, firearms experts, handwriting experts, it has been my experience over the past ten years, having been involved in a considerable number of prosecutions, that they are not routinely used in the prosecution of criminal cases. They are unique in the type of crime that is involved. Where I would anticipate that the polygraph examination did become admissible that there possibly are very few, if any, criminal lawsuits that might not be able to avail itself of this type of evidence. So where the question of firearms and fingerprints and other types of scientific evidence that are used now are the exception rather than the rule—and in a criminal case it would strike me that—

THE COURT: Is this a question?

MR. GOUSSY: Yes.

It would strike me that the admissibility of polygraphs would probably make the use of polygraphs during any given criminal case the rule rather than the exception and, therefore, I am wondering if you could assume this to be the case if you really don't have to have some type of licensing, some type of external control before you find yourself in this situation?

MR. BAILEY: In my opinion it makes very good sense but the conditions of polygraphy in the State of Michigan right now indicate that is far from essential because, by reputation nationwide, a very fine group of examiners reside in this state. Their qualifications meet a certain level as is known within the profession and although the polygraph is not yet used in the open court it is a terribly influential device in the pretrial stages, when a decision to indict or prosecute has to be made. There has arisen no problem in the case of an examiner misleading or misdirecting the issuing of an indictment. There is no empirical danger in saying licensing is something we have to wait for before we can proceed.

The second half of the question: in those jurisdictions where the polygraph controls the prosecution, for instance the military, because in the military in only one case in my experience—and I am still active in the military—was an innocent man or one who passed the polygraph brought to trial and that is because he was accused before they thought to ask him and thereafter refused. But I had Mr. Howard go down and testify. The court didn't hear it, but he was acquited anyway on four counts of molesting a child. It would have destroyed him. In the military and in the State of Maine, for instance, a person is never tried if the polygraph examiner clears him, and if it is to have this kind—

THE COURT: By law?

MR. BAILEY: By policy. There is no rule of law, but the same Parker Hennessey, described yesterday as a polygraph examiner and Keeler graduate—he got a confession out of a thirty-four-year termer who always denied it.

In my view a citizen is better protected against the State of Maine, against the damaging experience of indictment and trial regardless of result. It is damaging and distresses me, and this is the best safeguard. The citizen of Maine has no extra chance to

get away with criminal products because of the great practical
effect of the polygraph, and the military, which has had this
policy in an informal sense for longer than I have been connected
with it—which begins in 1952—which trained many of the examiners that are now senior, which never brings a man to trial if
the G-2 Section gives him a clearing result, has a much higher
conviction rate than the civil courts do and yet consistently is
more accurate in its results. And by that I don't mean a defendant is given all of his rights which may be irrelevant to his guilt,
but that the guilty men are found guilty and the innocent men
are either not tried or are acquitted.

This is the general syndrome in the military courts. Therefore, experience indicates there is no jeopardy to our present system which has its very obvious limitations, but a great improvement.

The phenomenon you expected of contradictory polygraph
examiners won't happen. They don't disagree. Like in handwriting, we don't have battles of experts or true disagreement. Many
cases that are tried would not be tried and this is why the polygraph wouldn't find its way into the courtroom consistently. We
would get more accurate results where the defendant would be innocent and we want his defense on the merits and not because
the burden of proof is on the state; but because he is innocent we
would frequently wind up without a jury and the defendant
would be acquitted by the judge.

I don't think polygraphy would ever fall into the unhappy
category that we experience with psychiatrists, where exuded is a
lot of expertise and jargon the court doesn't understand, let alone
the psychiatrists who testify.

MR. GOUSSY: I don't want to appear to be testifying against
you when I ask this question, but you furnished a copy of the
examination conducted by Mr. Zimmerman to the Michigan
State Police—

MR. BAILEY: I think the questions were furnished. I doubt
that the charts were . . .

THE COURT: Let me ask you this as an expert, and I accept
that you are an expert in the administration of criminal justice.
Are you suggesting the defendant charged with crime be permit-

ted to show the results of the polygraph in his trial? Are you also suggesting that the other witnesses' testimony either be corroborated or impeached with the use of polygraphy?

MR BAILEY: In certain circumstances. In a circumstantial case where an ordinary identification—the only meaningful test is the defendant because either nobody saw him do anything or the person who thinks he saw him may be honestly mistaken—the polygraph can't pick that up, but in a case such as rape or contradiction such as confronts us in this trial, if the defendant requires that he be tested on a polygraph and he is cleared, I think either the witness should be examined and his refusal should be admissible against him.

THE COURT: What if the defendant has not taken the test, the victim comes in and testifies, are you suggesting it would be consistent with the defendant's rights in the administration of justice if the people were able to support that witness' testimony by the polygraph?

MR. BAILEY: Absolutely, and I can think of no limitation against this. This would enhance the likelihood the guilty people would be convicted and the innocent people would be acquitted or not brought to trial.

THE COURT: Wouldn't we get into that in every trial?

MR. BAILEY: Not in every case, no. In some cases the defendant would choose to remain silent and refuse a polygraph test, all within the ambit of his rights and place the burden upon the state and this would be an additional tool.

THE COURT: I am certain there is a right to have a polygraph test as long as you don't have to answer, just listen.

MR. BAILEY: Nobody can be forced to take a test.

THE COURT: You can take his blood.

MR. BAILEY: But that doesn't require articulation.

There has been great talk that people wouldn't take tests if they were admissible. I don't believe that for a minute but I point out the fact the conversation taken during the taking of a polygraph test is admissible if any admission should be made. Second, that the polygraph has always been admissible as an adjunct of a confession to show it was voluntary and not beaten, and there are many cases.

If it were known it were admissible the innocent people would flock to it. The guilty people would refuse it and some people who were guilty would ask for it—and the experts I put on the stand have flunked many of my clients. The man Mr. Harrelson had flunked cold who later for the first time in six years made a forty-two-page confession wanted to be asked, "Did you murder your wife?" He was convicted circumstantially. He denied any knowledge of it and the jury gave him the chair and it was commuted to life without parole. That question was put to him. Mr. Harrelson also said, "Were you present when your wife died?" He was. He did not murder his wife. He hit her and she hit her head against the radiator and on the way to the doctor she died and he buried her.

That case is settled. He would have had a life in Hades for a long time. That is what good it does.

If a rape victim is vindicated where she can be worked over very well by experienced counsel and her credibility hit pretty hard and her standing in the community hurt because she brings a complaint of rape, if her testimany can be supported in that very private kind of offense by a polygraph examiner who says, "I have examined her on these specific questions and she gave no signs of deception," I think justice would be enhanced.

Mr Carlson: May I ask one question of Mr. Bailey?

Sir, how would you prevent only those polygraph tests which had been given to defendants and have cleared them, how would you prevent those tests from the ones that will never be admitted. In other words, if a criminal defendant can neither legally nor practically be compelled to take a test, what is to prevent him from going to a private examiner, take the test, flunking the test, keeping absolutely silent about the results and the results never reach the court; also if he passes the test, then he can come forward and present them? Wouldn't it be one-sided? The reason I ask that is because you said it struck you as unfair that the prosecutor could pick and choose.

Mr. Bailey: That could happen frequently and I would analogize it directly to that common form of evidence which embraces confessions and admissions. No one is compelled to talk to a police officer. Many don't. As a result of those conversations many are convicted on their own statements which are free and voluntary. The state gets convictions with them and gets them without them. Many people who refuse to talk to a police officer tell counsel what happened in order to see whether that would be a good statement to give the state; and if it is not a good statement we conceal it from the state. But the polygraph can be analogized to other kinds of articulated admissions because of the word "yes" as a response, we have the blood pressure going up. I think the manner in which confessions appear or fail to appear in criminal cases right now would closely parallel what you would say happened in polygraphy.

MR. GOUSSY: Could I ask one question just in discussing this generally from the administration of criminal justice, which I am very interested in. Take an office like my own. If what you suggest were to be the law that I be permitted to support each and every one of my witnesses with a polygraph, testimony of a polygraph examination, the office of the Attorney General, because of the number of our prosecutions would probably be totally justified, as would the major prosecuting offices throughout the state, in maintaining polygraph services so that we could create such evidence in all our cases. On the other hand, we have the big problem in this state of indigent defendants and near-indigent defendants. How in the world could those people if we were to go in and come in with a new standard, almost a new standard, ever determine credibility for the jury? It strikes me as a practical matter that polygraph testimony would really substitute its judgment for the jury in the sense that the old indicia of credibility would give way and this new one would come in. How in the world would the system possibly provide these services for the average guy that just can't come in with a well-financed defense or can't come in with any kind of financed defense and has to rely on court-appointed attorneys, et cetera?

MR. BAILEY: Most criminal defendant's wouldn't want anything to do with the polygraph. When going into prison to test a man the administrator says, "Everyone will want one."

THE COURT: Why? Because they are guilty?

MR. BAILEY: Because they are guilty. The vast number of defendants would not require their services. You have provisions to

give experts to indigents where they are required and most innocent people would be afraid to take a test from the state police.

THE COURT: Mr. Bailey, both as an expert somewhat in the
field of the use of polygraphs as distinguished from the operation,
and certainly as an expert in the field of criminal law, do you
know of any way that with the present personnel and present
situation that the use of polygraphs have been used to deceive the
court?

MR. BAILEY: No.

THE COURT: Completely understanding I am not suggesting
you are doing this.

MR. BAILEY: No, no.

The question is, could an unethical lawyer with desire to win
a case for his client manipulate this technique?

THE COURT: That is precisely what I am asking.

MR. BAILEY: No. I think all of the safeguards protect the court
in other instances and certainly it conceivably could be done; a
dishonest examiner with a phoney test and a lawyer willing to
subborn perjury to combine to place the evidence before the
court. And it could be done in many other areas.

THE COURT: The way I interpret it with experts, when I permit an expert to testify it doesn't mean I am satisfied totally with
his expertise but merely there is a sufficient foundation for the
jury to weigh his credibility.

MR. BAILEY: Exactly, or for you to weigh it if you are sitting
jury-waived.

THE COURT: Yes, but lots of times I will permit an expert to
testify when in my judgment he is not a very good expert and I
can't give much weight to his testimony. But, nonetheless, there is
sufficient testimony for the trier of the fact to put it in the scale.
That is pretty much the general practice, isn't it?

MR. BAILEY: You are the filter through whom the evidence
must come and the safeguard against unreliable or let's say evidence so unrealiable that it should not be heard.

THE COURT: Would you concede in the polygraph area at
least perhaps in the beginning a much higher standard should
be applied as to who is an expert, rather severely?

MR BAILEY: If there is any indication to the court the examiner's testimony will be disputed in any sense either by another expert or by the party against whom it militates, that the court should examine very carefully the man's qualifications and his reputation because he can have a pervasive effect on the jury's thinking.

THE COURT: Exercise a rather strict discretion in the area.

MR. BAILEY: Yes, but I point out after the limited exposure your Honor has had in two days of evidence I think your Honor is more than ably equipped to determine whether a man is sufficiently qualified and has that kind of professional standing so he should get through the filter, that is the judge, and reach the jury.

THE COURT: Do you have any further proofs in connection with your special hearing, Mr. Bailey?

MR BAILEY: No, your Honor, I rest so much of the case as requires evidence.

THE COURT: Mr. Goussy, any proofs you wish to offer concerning the use of the polygraph?

MR. GOUSSY: I have none, your Honor.

THE COURT: Any argument, Mr. Bailey?

MR. BAILEY: I would like to present argument. I will try to be reasonably brief.

THE COURT: Very good.

MR. BAILEY: The question which is posed to you which is not a new question in the law and in fact, as one of the witnesses pointed out has been bandied around for almost fifty years now, is whether or not to permit the jury to hear for whatever weight they might choose to give it under the appropriate instructions and under conformity with rules of general testimony, the opinion of a polygraph examiner bearing on the credibility of, in this case obviously, someone testifying for the defense.

Now, in regard to the legal position of this instrument and this technique. In 1923 there was a case called Frye against the United States. Frye was accused of murder and there was at that time in very rough form an instrument which measured blood pressure only and at the case of Frye in an appellate opinion for the United States District Court of Appeals for the District of Columbia, the testimony of this expert was proffered as evidence to indicate that Frye was totally denying his guilt of homicide. It was rejected by the trial judge and Frye was convicted.

The appellate court had this to say and it has been the fulcrum of almost all polygraph jurisprudence since. He said,

> Just when a scientific technique or device emerges from that gray area of uncertainty to the point where the law can utilize it, to be weighed by the factfinder, is an uncertain line, but in examining the criteria that have been applied historically, we rule that before such evidence can be received it must be shown that it has attained some kind of general scientific acceptability.

Subsequent cases, although not entirely consistent, have relied pretty heavily on that language. The polygraph, as the evidence has indicated, has been actively used by law enforcement for over thirty years now and I think the evidence is uncontradicted since no witnesses have been called in opposition nor, in fact, have any of the experts been disputed except for the extent of the cross-examination, that it is pervasively used throughout the United States, and beneficially so.

The law has never said what general scientific acceptability is but a study of the cases, such as have been, I believe, submitted to the court indicates that it is pretty apparent in this case that the level of general scientific acceptability has been set high. Probably because in the view of the judges this kind of expert testimony comes so close to the function of the factfinder that it must be closely guarded and the standard must be high.

Assuming all of that to be the state of the law and I must point out that the court that decided the Frye case was right in prinicple and, of course, the jury was wrong. Mr. Frye was examined seven years later and he was released. We are all happy, of course, he was not given a sentence of death by the jury.

If the court lays down a criterion then, of course, counsel is invited to meet it and no decision has any historical or precedental value of a change of circumstances appears. Uniformly the cases have said it has not been shown to the court by evidence or from other sources that this criterion has been met and, therefore, we must reject. There are exceptions.

In New York in 1938, a test was admitted by a trial judge

who permitted the opinion. That was determined solely on a galvanometer. The judge thought it should be admitted.

By stipulation in many jurisdictions it had been received as other evidence may be received by stipulation that could be objectionable.

Significantly, in 1962 the State against Valdez in Arizona, a defendant was invited to take a polygraph test and to stipulate that the results be admissible. He agreed and so stipulated. He showed response indicating deception. He went to trial. The examiner testified against him. He appealed. The Arizona Supreme Court said this kind of evidence has been rejected and should not have entered in the trial.

The court said, "We think the time has come to take a fresh look, not solely because of the contractual relation between the evidence which might bind him or stop him from complaining, but because of what we perceive from the testimony in the literature to be the evolution and improvement of the polygraph technique, and, therefore, we hold that this evidence is inadmissible and that for future cases it should be admissible under the following conditions:

First, that the parties do agree.

Second, that the test and its surrounding circumstances appear to the court before whom admissibility is sought to have been fair as against the forces which in any way appear deceptive.

Three, the court shall examine the qualifications of the expert through whom the evidence is proffered and if he finds him to be competent shall receive the evidence.

This has exceptional merit because it could have been predicted on solely the offer of the contractual agreement between the parties that something will be received. This court did not place its reliance on that. It placed its reliance in large measure, as I read that opinion, on the scientific reliability of the device and on the general escalation of standards within the profession. This is eight years later.

In the past several years many states have enacted licensing statutes which certainly inhibit charlatans, phony examiners or people who won't take the time to train themselves or to get trained or can't meet the qualifications of intelligence education and other qualifications to become an expert. Licensing inhibits them.

In addition to that the American Polygraph Association, to which each of these witnesses belong, has promoted a uniformity and a regulation of standards wherein they feel fairly confident that one who is not qualified would not do very much business without being known and severely criticized by a body of responsible talent. This safeguard would always be available to a court if it was entertaining testimony from a man of dubious caliber.

General scientific acceptability, as it has related to other kinds of scientific evidence, is a criterion related to other kinds of scientific evidence that surely we have met with the evidence put before you. I call your attention, for instance, to the admissible testimony and I think it is in this jurisdiction wherein paraffin is applied to the hand of a man suspected of having fired a weapon that burns powder, in order to see if nitrates are found.

The Texas court, in saying this kind of evidence should be admissible, said the paraffin test, although disputed, is not so inherently unreliable as to be rejected by the law.

That criterion is enunciated in the decision itself and in a footnote on the very excellent section on the polygraph published by Professor Richardson in 1961, in his book on *Scientific Criminal Evidence* which clearly indicated way back then the polygraph was being held to a completely different standard.

Professor McCormick in his widely respected *Handbook on Evidence* published about 1958, made the same observation. He said an examination of the decisions make it very apparent that the polygraph has already reached that point of reliability which other kind of evidence has been required to meet, but is still rejected, and we must assume that it is because the courts are especially concerned of the impact it could carry.

The evidence before your Honor is the best evidence that could ever be proffered. In theory the technique is sound, but much more impressive, I think, is its empirical history. Each witness was asked about the frequency of erroneous conclusions. Many of the witnesses were asked, "As a matter of policy, or as a matter of experience, how often does a man who is cleared by a responsible examiner wind up either being demonstrated as being guilty or gets prosecuted in the first place?" and it's a rare bird.

So we have this ironic posture; obviously a great deal of money is spent to train people and money is spent on these instruments and I don't know whether the evidence indicated but they are not cheap, and it is public money.

So, society has demonstrated a great concern over the usefulness and has adopted the usefulness of this device. The posture of the criminal law is at this level. We know that from the commission of a crime the isolation of a suspect to the commencement of a judicial proceeding against him, whether it be by information of the prosecutor, complaint of a private citizen or indictment by citizen or grand jury in this state that investigation continually goes on to see whether or not this prosecution should go forward.

For all of the wonderful things we say about our system and it has its admirable aspects, experienced lawyers all know that the fact of indictment and public announcement of indictment is a stain on a human's reputation and his character that is very difficult to get rid of and certainly not eliminated universally or even uniformly by acquittal. Very frequently that is interpreted by the public as simply being the indication of the skill of counsel, but no indication of the innocence of the defendant.

A society which is attempting to improve itself continually, viewing the posture of the utilization of this device without knowing any of the history or controversy or concern that has attended its development, would probably have serious questions about the intelligence of those, who have placed it in a position of overwhelming influence. In that stage of a criminal case where the safeguards are very limited and where the police have almost complete control, the defendant or suspect may have possession of private information but the police have the machinery that they are operating moving toward a point where he may get prosecuted and the defendant is not involved, although he may be greatly effected.

In these stages, if the device is reported so there is a great likelihood, if you believe the testimony, that any divergence in the path of justice may be caught and corrected because of the accuracies of this machine and by the same token where witnesses are verified as telling the truth or a defendant is found to be lying; with greater confidence can the people proceed to indict and try him and spend the money and take the risk of damaging his reputation that is inherently involved.

But if we get into the judicial process this device which loses none of its reliability since the technique has no knowledge of the state of the process it is being called upon, this device is completely excluded and resort to the much more archaic, and in such case plainly barbaric, presumption that by calling witnesses who differ vastly in their ability to articulate and persuade and by relying on the vehicle of cross-examination which varies tremendously, far more than the skill of a polygraph examiner from one attorney to the next, that we are going to empower a group of twelve citizens without further help to pick between witnesses, each of whom claims credibility about necessarily diametrically contrary events.

There is no reason, logically or otherwise, to exclude the value of this ancillary truth-verifying device which can shed remarkable light on which of two articulate witnesses is withholding some relevant information. That is its function.

If there is a way to conceive of holding a scientific technique up to a higher standard that has been developed here in the testimony today, I can not imagine. I do not believe, and I know your Honor is conversant with many of these kinds of testimony, that stronger testimony of reliability, the unlikelihood of contradiction between experts, total experience in the number of errors that are found or the number of disagreements that might have to be litigated is remarkably small. I don't think that kind of testimony could be produced by some of the other devices that are now used every day.

I think that the questions of the court indicate that reliability is not the only problem. The courts have been unfair to this extent, your Honor. They have pegged their refusal on reliability when in fact they were talking about what you were talking about, the practical problem: Who are we going to give it to? Under what circumstances? Is the whole system of justice going to turn on the polygraph? I have seen that long before this case. . . .

If we in the law are really interested in giving the jury all of the best information that can be put before them so they don't make a decision of great importance in partial ignorance of the existence of facts, whether they be logical or scientific, then I don't think we are really doing a very good job.

In some areas of law precedent has rebelled. Stare decises. I suppose one of the things we learn in law school is you really don't have a good piece of information until you have a citation to go with it. Fine. I'm not interested anymore in the decision made by the 1923 court in Frye against United States, because polygraphy as you heard it described, didn't exist—or in the decisions that have intervened.

In the criminal law we are concerned with justice, not whether a will was going to be good in fifty years because the drafter can rely on the fact the law will remain the same; where the area of stability and continuity of the law is of great value, but where the prime consideration is are we using everything now available, whether it be neutron bombardment, particle identification or whether it be the voice print now available to identify telephone conversations and voices, whether it be the blood test in paternity suits which have been deemed so reliable that a jury is not allowed to disagree with it in most cases in court where men were convicted despite blood tests which they offered and had rejected fifty years ago.

I cannot see any reason the state would object to evidence of innocence upon which it continually relies and is guided in making its own judgment, and which it has no reason to believe as a general matter, not in this specific case because we have not heard the examiner, has no reason to believe from its total experience would be unreliable in any given case. Certainly no more impressive witnesses could be called than the adversary and the state police, and certainly the other side of the case, if Mr. Defendant is guilty, they do not want him to escape.

Just as the other experts said, errors just do not occur, or they very rarely occur.

The evidence is available. It would enhance the likelihood of an accurate result. If the other party had submitted and there were contradictory test results for you to have to deal with, that would present a question about which you would inquire of the experts. However, that is not present in this case.

This defendant is supposed to go to jail if a jury finds him guilty. I don't think the jury ought to find him guilty until they have heard this evidence just as you heard it had it been brought into their judgment. Obviously it has too much value.

On these basis and because I think this is that day, perhaps long in coming, that the Court of Appeals in the District of Columbia had in mind in 1923 when they affirmed the conviction of an innocent man, this is the day in this court in Michigan when the polygraph has been demonstrated without one shred of contradictory evidence or one serious contradiction from among the witnesses as being at that stage where it can be helpful to the administration of justice, in the opinion of all of these who are concerned. It is unlikely to ever do it any harm. . . .

Chapter 4

QUALIFYING THE POLYGRAPHIST IN COURT

I~N ALMOST~ every hearing, speech, lecture or simple inquiry relating to polygraphy, likewise similarly inferred in the Alaska
Opinion in the case of Thomas Pulakis, invariably two questions
seem to shoot out: (1) How reliable is the polygraph technique,
and, (2) will an innocent person be shown as guilty?

Stopping to analyze these two questions, we find them to be
serious inquiries concerning judges and the layman. During their
investigations no other profession seems to carry the weight placed
on the shoulders of polygraphy. When a polygraphist renders an
opinion, that opinion frequently overshadows all other forms of
investigation already acceptable by the scientific as well as public
communities. The resulting defensiveness only tends to further
confuse the uninformed and misinformed.

In making a study of the reliability of polygraphy we eventually find ourselves focusing on three basic factors: (1) The polygraph instrument, (2) the physiological responses recorded by the
instrument, and, (3) the interpretation of these responses by the
polygraph examiner.

The acceptance by the layman that the polygraph instrument
is reliable is basic. He understands that it is simply a scientific,
sophisticated, recording instrument. It has been demonstrated by
the scientific world as reliable and valid in its recording of physiological changes.

The layman also accepts the fact that physiological changes do
occur within each and every person. When a person practices
deception the makeup of these physiological changes are remarkably different from those when he is telling the truth.

These facts are well founded in the fight or flight theory, are
easily demonstrated and accepted by the scientific community as
reliable and valid.

Therefore, we are left with the interpretation of polygraph chart tracings by the examiner. The majority of studies thus far done in this regard were conducted without real-life situations and, in numerous cases, in laboratory situations by persons who wouldn't know a polygraph if they stumbled over it. However, even the most ridiculous laboratory experiments have, nevertheless, revealed a very high degree of reliability in determining truth.

In fact, in Lykken's study in 1959, and Davidson's study in 1968, both were able to correctly identify all of the innocent subjects in their studies. Not until Frank Horvath's study in 1969 was it shown that the whole key to accuracy and truth verification strictly depends on the individual polygraphist, his personal knowledge, understanding and interpretative ability. In that study, examiners were not allowed to take into account any detailed background information, to converse with or observe the subject being tested, or to prepare or review the general comprehension of the questions.

Instead, these examiners were only allowed to interpret the subject's polygraph recordings independent of each other. All records used were verified innocent or guilty and all subjects tested went through a regular control question technique.

Horvath showed from his study that the seven examiners with more than one year's experience scored an average of 93.6 percent accuracy in correctly identifying the innocent subjects. He also showed that three examiners still in their training programs (and with less than 6 month's experience) scored an average of 83.3 percent accuracy in identifying the innocent subject. This study by Horvath was the first to uphold the contention that polygraph examiners, themselves, do have a high degree of reliability in determining truth.

In 1971, Fred L. Hunter idealistically explored the question as to whether or not polygraph examiners, working independently of each other, could successfully diagnose the same reactions, within real life situations, at two different points in time. The introduction of a time element would establish that an examiner's chart interpretations would be based on well-grounded and sound physiological principles which would add validity to his work.

As in Horvath's study, the examiners involved were from the staff of John E. Reid & Associates, Chicago. Four examiners, each with more than eighteen months experience, were asked to interpret a number of polygraph records. They were denied the complete diagnostic technique, as in Horvath's study, and were told the following:

The ten sets of polygraph records are those involving a theft case. The standard Reid Control Question Technique was used on each subject. They were told that questions 1,2,4,7 were irrelevant questions; that 6,11 were control questions; and that 3,5,8,9, 10 were relevant questions. All relevant questions were of a pertinent nature with the exception of 9, which was a knowledge question. They were asked to try and make a determination of truth or deception on each and every relevant question. They were also told there was no time limit involved in their interpretation, but were asked to note the time it took to complete all ten sets of records. The examiners were also told not to discuss their interpretations with the other examiners involved in the study.

The polygraph records submitted to the examiners for analysis were obtained from one real-life investigation. The case was typical of the kind presented to private examiners as it represented the theft of some negotiable bonds from a bank. The ten sets of records selected for their analysis included nine innocent subjects and one corroborated guilty subject.

The original polygraph examinations were all conducted using a five-channel Reid polygraph. Each set of polygraph records included five different tests: two straight through the questions tests, a card test, a silent answer test, and a mixed question test.

Before presenting the polygraph records to the examiners, all points of identification concerning the individual tested or the investigation involved were concealed or completely removed. This rendered the examiner unfamiliar with either the case or the individuals they were called upon to analyze. The records were then put in a numbered order from one to ten. After the first analysis by all examiners involved, the numbering of each record was changed and they were placed into another order from one to ten. There were fifty relevant questions contained in the ten sets of polygraph records submitted for interpretation. At the time of the original investigation forty-four of these questions were diagnosed as truthful, two as deceptive and four as inconclusive. Of the four inconclusive questions, three dealt with the guilty subject. Their ambiguity was concluded because of the greater weight to the subject of the deceptive questions. The deceptive questions directly involved the theft of the bonds as where the inconclusive questions dealt with steps taken to hide the theft later. The other inconclusive question involved the knowledge of the theft by a verified innocent subject. For the purpose of this study only the forty-four verified truthful questions were used.

Due to the work loads and schedules of the examiners used in this study, the time element involved between their first and second analysis varied somewhat. However, the second analysis was completed from between thirteen to not more than twenty days after the first.

The amount of time needed by each examiner to complete his analysis of the ten sets of polygraph records varied from twenty-five to eighty-seven minutes. The average length of time needed for analysis, however, decreased from the first to the second. Below are details regarding the individual examiners:

TABLE I

DISTRIBUTION OF TIME FACTORS IN ANALYZING THE POLYGRAPH
RECORDS BY EXAMINERS

Examiners	Time Needed For 1st Analysis	Days Between Analysis	Time Needed For 2nd Analysis
1	87 Min.	13	60 Min.
2	40 Min.	20	35 Min.
3	35 Min.	14	25 Min.
4	55 Min.	15	45 Min.

RESULTS: Overall accuracy in determining the truthful responses.

On the first analysis three of the four examiners were able to correctly identify all nine of the innocent subjects. However, in close analysis we see they averaged a 96 percent accuracy in identifying all truthful relevant questions. On the second analysis three of the four examiners were again able to correctly identify all nine of the innocent subjects. Again in closer analysis we see they averaged 96.1 percent accuracy in identifying all truthful relevant questions. As can be seen from Table II, below, however, there was a significant difference in the truthful questions analyzed as deceptive or inconclusive between the first and second analysis.

In the first analysis, Examiner 1 was able to correctly identify forty-three of the forty-four truthful questions. However, he diagnosed the one other truthful question as being deceptive. In the second analysis he was only able to correctly diagnose thirty-seven of the forty-four truthful questions; however, he diagnosed all seven remaining questions as inconclusive and none as deceptive.

Examiner 2 in the first analysis correctly identified thirty-nine of the forty-four truthful questions; however, he diagnosed the remaining five questions as deceptive. In the second analysis he was able to correctly identify all forty-four of the truthful questions.

TABLE II

DISTRIBUTION OF INNOCENT—GUILTY—INCONCLUSIVE JUDGMENTS OF THE 44 TRUTHFUL QUESTIONS BY EXAMINERS

Examiners	Truthful	1st Analysis Deceptive	Inconclusive	% Correct
1	43	1	0	97.7%
2	39	5	0	88.6%
3	44	0	0	100.0%
4	43	0	1	97.7%

Total average % of accuracy 96.0%

		2nd Analysis		
1	37	0	7	84.5%
2	44	0	0	100.0%
3	44	0	0	100.0%
4	44	0	0	100.0%

Total average % of accuracy 96.1%

It is only fair to point out that in computing each examiner's accuracy score, an error was calculated if an examiner put either an inconclusive or deceptive judgment upon a truthful question. If only the deceptive judgments were counted there would have been an overall 98.3 average percent of accuracy in determining truth for both studies. In other words, there was only a 1.7 percent error made in analyzing a truthful response as a deceptive response when taking both studies together. However, we must note that all errors of this type were reduced upon the second analysis when none of the truthful questions were diagnosed as deceptive by any of the four examiners. But in fact, all errors made in the second analysis were those of a truthful being diagnosed as inconclusive.

The data accumulated from this study clearly supports the claim that polygraph examiners can reliably diagnose truth. This also shows the layman that the polygraph is extremely reliable in eliminating the innocent subjects in a real-life investigation from any undue embarrassment or inconvenience caused by such an investigation.

The fact is clear that without being denied a complete diagnostic technique, the four examiners involved in this study surely would have attained an even higher percentage of accuracy than they did achieve.

The most important point we believe that can be ascertained from this study is the fact that an examiner can and does reliably attain the same interpretation from a set of polygraph records at two different points in time.

The data shows there was virtually little or no difference in the average percent of accuracy from the first analysis to the second analysis. However, one can see the examiners not only becoming more accurate in not making the error of interpreting an innocent response as deceptive but also becoming more conservative in their interpretation.

In conclusion, this study attests to three basic contentions that polygraph examiners have rightfully held to for years:

1. The polygraph technique is reliable in differentiating between truth and deception. It is a technique that can be trusted by the layman.

2. The majority of errors favor the guilty. There is a very small percentage of error made in interpreting truth as deception.

3. Examiners can interpret the same set of polygraph records with reliability at two different points in time. This supports the contention that the interpretation of polygraph records is built on well-founded and sound principles.*

A PROCEDURE FOR EXPERT QUALIFICATION

Throughout the years appellate decisions have either inferred, or occasionally contained the following remarks: "and no proper foundation was laid for admissibility consideration. . . ."

However, particularly in district and superior courts where there has been some acceptance, foundations have been laid to varying degrees. The purpose of this chapter is to fragment a guide for those attorneys who know little or nothing about the subject of polygraphy and who might subsequently have dire need to utilize this science for protection of the innocent in the interest of justice.

In his preparation, counsel should carefully consider each question put to the examiner, attempting at all times to anticipate cross and recross as well as questions which may be interjected by the court, in either voir dire or in open court. A presentation which is factual, informative, and interesting enough to cause a judge to ask his own questions can be a key factor in his ultimate decision to admit or deny.

From court records and from our discussions with judges, doctors and lawyers in four different parts of the country, we have formulated a hypothetical case as follows:

AND, THE COURT RECORD SHALL READ:

Danish, Mistansia, U.S.A.
September 7, 1972.

THE COURT: This is a hearing, in the absence of jury, called at the request of defense counsel. He wishes to make and expand upon certain foundation proofs concerning the use and application of expert testimony with regard to polygraphy. Mr. Defense Counsel?

---

*Hunter, Fred L., John Reid & Associates, Chicago, in a presentation to the American Polygraph Association Seminar, Atlanta, Georgia, 1971.

DEFENSE COUNSEL: If it pleases the court, before I call the first witness, may I outline what my client is attempting to produce here. In other words, we are placing ourselves before the court in an effort to put our submissions in some kind of context or in some kind of context light so the court may ultimately consider or reject our desire to place into evidence polygraph test results on the defendant which indicate innocence.

If it please the court, before calling my first witness, may I outline what we are trying to establish here?

THE COURT: Yes. That would certainly be helpful.

THE DEFENSE: It is the purpose, your Honor, of this hearing to lay a foundation to comport with what the court has almost universally maintained to be criteria for the admissibility of scientific evidence. What we will try to show through expert witness testimony is that the polygraph instrument is indeed capable of recording deception or the absence of deception, which is the sole thing being tested, and the use of the technique.

We propose to show, through empirical experience over a long period of time and through constant use in all areas of polygraphy, that the history based on examiners' judgments and test opinions against intrinsic facts as they later develop, or may already have developed, contains a very, very high degree of reliability.

In order to show that perhaps twenty years ago the polygraph technique was not quite ready for even limited use by the court, at least in the judgment of those courts that passed on it, due to improvements in the technique, standardization in the training, licensing laws in a number of states, but more specifically the upgrading and high qualification requisites for present day examiners, that numerous leading writers who are authorities on the subject have reversed their earlier stands and now take the position that polygraphy can be most useful in the courtroom as well as in many pretrial investigative stages.

In order to commence laying this foundation I should like to call Mr. John Q. Smith as my first witness.

Portions of this chapter are based on Michigan v. Peter N. Lazaros, CR-6237, in the Circuit Court for the County of Oakland, June 23, 1970, F. Lee Bailey, C. Michael Kimber, for the Respondent

THE COURT: Mr. Prosecutor, do you have any statements you wish to make before we proceed?

THE PROSECUTOR: Not at this time, your Honor.

THE COURT: Very good.

JOHN Q. SMITH

being first duly sworn by the clerk to tell the truth, the whole truth and nothing but the truth, was examined and testified as follows:

DIRECT EXAMINATION

BY DEFENSE COUNSEL:

Q. State your name, please for the court.

A. John Q. Smith.

Q. Where do you live?

A. In Danish, Mistansia.

Q. How long have you been a resident of this state?

A. Some twenty-five years.

Q. What is your business or profession?

A. I am a polygraph examiner for X Company.

Q. How long have you been so employed in that capacity?

A. For twelve years.

Q. Would you give the court some of your educational background?

A. I have a baccalaureate degree from Mistansia College in sociology. I have taken additional courses in psychology and criminology at State University. The formal portion of my polygraph training was taken at the Keeler Polygraph Institute in Chicago where I graduated in 1957. Subsequently I have attended and studied at numerous national and state polygraph seminars throughout the past fifteen years.

Q. Do you belong to any professional associations primarily concerned with the ethics and practice of polygraphy?

A. Yes. I am a member of good standing in the American Polygraph Association. I am also a member in good standing of this state's polygraph association.

Q. Are you licensed to practice the art or science of polygraphy in any state?

A. Yes. I am licensed in Florida, Georgia, New Mexico, Illinois and Texas.

Q. To your knowledge, how long has the Keeler Polygraph Institute been in existence for the schooling and training of examiners?

A. I believe since the beginning or early 1940's.

Q. Will you please describe for the court what kind of courses and training you received while attending the Keeler Institute?

A. As I recall, we had intensive studies in the basics of instrumentation, both from a mechanical and functional or operational standpoint. This was followed by many hours of study in question formulation, chart interpretation, applicable psychological and physiological aspects, the physiological correlations between the chart tracings and the polygraph technique again from the interpretative standpoint, the legal aspect applicable thereto, and the various types of approaches available for just about any given situation.

Q. Mr. Smith, would you please explain, for the benefit of the court, the basic components of the standard modern day polygraph instrument?

A. I will refer to one of the newer instruments that I utilized for the test on the defendant in this case. It is a Stoelting double pneumo instrument with an eight-inch chart. It is manufactured by the C. H. Stoelting Company in Chicago. Other polygraph instruments are manufactured by Associated Research, also in Chicago. These two companies probably manufacture and assemble 98 percent of all polygraphs used throughout the world.

The basic components of this four-penned instrument are called the cardiosphygmograph section, the pneumograph section—in this case the pneumograph is comprised of two separate recording units, for both thoracic and abdominal recordings—and a galvanometer. There are other instruments containing as much as twelve recording pens for various types of physiological or physical recordings but the basics still remain the same within the fields of private or criminal polygraphy.

Q. Will you please advise the court, in layman's language, what the cardiosphygmograph section generally as well as specifically records?

A. Yes. This particular section records heart rate, heart beat, systolic and diastolic pressures, relative blood pressure, the dicrotic notch, and any changes therefrom.

Q. From what, or from what area, and by what means is this particular recording obtained?

A. By placement of a standard medical blood pressure cuff, as used by every doctor, over the brachial artery. Similar tracings can also be obtained by using the identical cuff, or a more narrow children's cuff, over the radial and ulnar arteries where they bifurcate just below the elbow. However, it is my opinion that the farther away from the heart, the less sensitivity in mean blood pressure is obtained.

Q. How is the cardiovascular tracing obtained and what comprises the makeup of its recording?

A. The cardiovascular tracing is obtained by placing a standard medical blood pressure cuff over the brachial artery, for example, and then inflating the cuff with air, just as a doctor might do. There is an aneroid sphygmomanometer dial on each Stoelting instrument which is calibrated in millimeters of mercury.

Tubing from the cuff band leads past the pressure indicating dial or gauge to a very sensitive bellows and its connected lever system which powers the pen. This is a pressure differential system. As the pulse wave passes under and beyond the pressurized cuff the differential between the force of the moving arterial blood as against the air in the arm cuff causes the cardio pen to move up and down, with a slight hesitation on the downward stroke.

Q. At what pressure is the cardiovascular system normally operated?

A. At mean blood presure, in a manner of speaking.

Q. I'm sorry. You've lost me. Please describe to the court the meaning of mean blood pressure, as you phrased it. Would you also include in your explanation what is meant by the systolic and diastolic blood pressure recordings?

A. Systolic blood pressure is the greatest pressure exerted outward against the arterial wall as the pulse wave passes a given point. Diastolic pressure is the least pressure exerted outward against the arterial wall during a rest cycle of the heart.

The difference between systolic and diastolic pressures is called relative mean blood pressure.

Q. Is it possible to record a change in systolic pressure without a change in diastolic pressure, and vice versa?

A. Yes.

Q. Would you please explain to the court what the dicrotic notch is?

A. First, I would like to explain that systolic blood pressure is represented by the ascending stroke, or limb, of the cardio tracing. Diastolic pressure is represented by the descending stroke, or limb, of the cardio tracing.

The dicrotic notch is represented by a slight jog, or offset, in the descending stroke. As the blood leaves the left side of the heart headed for systemic circulation, it is going uphill. At this point there is a momentary regurgitation of the blood back against the closed heart valve before vessel constriction forces the blood on forward into systemic circulation. As a result, there is created a secondary pulse wave graphically recorded which is called the dicrotic notch.

Q. About where on the descending limb of the tracing does this dicrotic notch appear?

A. If the blood pressure cuff and the system is activated to approximately that of subject's arithmetic mean blood pressure, the dicrotic notch will normally appear at about the middle of the descending limb of the tracing.

Q. Is there ever occasion in the course of examination when, following a verbal stimulus, or question, that the dicrotic notch might shift its position on the downward stroke of the tracing?

A. Yes. Persons who specialize in cardiovascular tracings generally consider a shift in position of the dicrotic notch as being the most subtle change in relative blood pressure within the body.

Q. Mr. Smith, if the three other sections of your instrument were to malfunction, would it be possible in some cases to detect truth or deception from only this cardio tracing?

A. Let me answer this way. Such is possible. However, I personally would not attempt to base my opinion on the operational function of any one recording unit. As a matter of fact, I would not conduct a test unless all components of my instrument were functioning at full sensitivity.

Q. Why do you make such a dogmatic statement?

A. From my personal viewpoint such would not be fair, impartial, or objective to the subject, interested parties, and particularly to the court if the instance should occur.

Q. Are the recording units, sections, or components of your instrument of independent significance, or only of significance collectively?

A. Individually, in certain cases. Certainly collectively in the majority of cases. Generally, almost broadly to specifically, deception "criteria" can appear in one, two, three, or all four recording areas. It can also specifically appear in only two, three or less areas. It depends on the type of stimulus inserted, what that stimulus means to the person receiving it, and what organs are affected by that particular stimulus.

Q. You have just lost me. Are you a registered physiologist?

A. No.

Q. Are you acquainted with the field of psychology?

A. Yes, as pertains to polygraphy.

Q. In your opinion, have previously published psychological studies of polygraphy, within laboratory confines, contained any real validity. From what I have read they, to quite some extent, have been rather critical.

A. I only have a personal opinion.

Q. Your Honor, will you permit a brief opinion?

THE COURT: Only brief.

Q. Mr. Smith?

A. Well, counselor, I'm not going to criticize the field of psychology. The polygraph profession is almost as old as the field of psychiatry and perhaps a part of it, at least physiologically.

It is my opinion that a psychologist should be concerned with the biological and environmental "whys" in human behavior whereas the polygraphist is primarily concerned with "did you or did you not" in a given situation.

I believe there is a vast difference in theoretical, clinical, and interrogative psychology. To my knowledge very few polygraph laboratory experiments conducted by psychologists have produced realistic validity because they have been so carefully controlled that even the element of surprise loses its validity factor. In polygraphy there is no way individuals can be group classified because no two people will evaluate a stimulus in identically the same manner, nor will two different persons react to a stimulus in the same manner. Likewise, the same person will not normally react to the same stimulus in the same manner, as he initially did, when it is later repeated.

Contrarily, even the most blatant psychological experiments published on polygraphy have turn up so-called accuracy reports of 70 percent or better. Certainly no other method of truth verification comes that close.

THE COURT: I think we've had enough in this particular.

Q. Getting back to the polygraph instrument. Will you please describe for the court the operation of the double pneumograph recording section?

A. Both units of this instrument's pneumograph section consist, independently, of corrugated tubes which are fastened around the chest and stomach regions with a chain. This system, when in operation, functions under closed pressure. As the chest or stomach expands and contracts in the process of breathing, pressure differentials are transmitted from the closed system through rubber tubing to extremely sensitive bellows which, mechanically, causes the pens to move up and down with the inspiration-expiration cycle.

Q. How sensitive and reliable is the pneumograph system?

A. Very highly, perhaps more so than the cardiovascular system.

Q. Basically, what does the pneumograph section record?

A. Every phase of breathing, and every interruption of breathing, momentarily or of some duration, such as breathing or not breathing, a sniff, sigh, cough, clearing the throat, answering yes or no, voluntary or involuntary holding or suppression of the breath, increased respiration, deep or shallow breathing.

Q. How much reliability is placed on the pneumograph recording sections?

A. With the court's permission, may I answer in this manner. Once thought subservient to the cardiovascular system in sensitivity, research and case experience has revealed the body's respiratory system to produce more valid deception criteria than any other bodily function. By the same token, since the cardiovascular and respiratory systems are so closely dependent upon each other and so closely affected by the same type of stimuli, primary chart interpretation is based on the type of tracings each examinee's body produces.

Q. How do you distinguish between truth or deception when you interpret your charts?

A. By the context, or makeup, of the pretest recording norms as compared to the type and makeup of physiological deviations evidenced on the polygram at, during or just following a relevant question which may be of some importance to the examinee.

Q. You previously mentioned a recording component baseline. What does that mean?

A. The recording baseline is established by the examiner as soon as he activates the instrument. It is mechanically set or adjusted in each recording section to permit free flow of the pens so they do not interlock or impose upon each other's tracings. While the chart is underway, readjustments can be made if and when necessary.

Q. Now, the last primary component of your polygraph instrument, I believe, is called a galvanometer or galvanic skin response recording unit?

A. Yes.

Q. Before I ask you to explain the basic causes for its recordings, may I ask you to tell the court, in your own opinion, what it is composed of and its conduciveness to accepted reliability?

A. At one time the galvanometer was used by itself under various commercial names and even in some instances was called a lie detector. Such is considered ridiculous in itself. However, galvanic skin response recordings, containing none of the elements of "work" (a/k/a movement) can become very exacting in the detection of truth or deception. In other words, it strongly supports the pneumograph and cardiovascular recordings, particularly in the recording of physiological deviations caused by pure emotion following the insertion of relevant stimuli.

Q. Have you seriously studied the fields of psychology and physiology?

A. Yes, specifically those areas applicable to polygraphy.

Q. To some extent?

A. Probably just about everything directly or indirectly connected with or correlated with this field of endeavor.

Q. How long?

A. Since 1957.

Q. Do you think formal education at the college level is imperative in this field, particularly if a person is subsequently to be qualified as an expert?

A. Any formal education can be helpful. Certainly college helps to lay a foundation for future efforts if those efforts are properly channelled. But, in the strict sense, college is not mandatory even though the requirement should be in every licensing law.

I believe several criteria should be considered before qualification is excluded. The first big step, of course, is to have attained educational and/or investigative experience, plus the maturity, required to meet entrance requirements of polygraph schools recognized by the American Polygraph Association. The second step would be to have graduated from such a school and attain the requirements to be licensed to practice, where license is called for. The third step would be to have the qualifications for membership in the American Polygraph Association, as an active examiner. I suggest the final step would be considerable testing experience in the private, law enforcement, or government fields where polygraphy is almost hourly utilized, plus a never-ending study and application of not only proven methods of approach but also updated techniques.

Q. Mr. Smith, have you ever been qualified as an expert in court?

A. Yes. I was qualified over objection in a lower court in 1963 and, again over objection, in federal court in 1971.

Q. Approximately how many polygraph examinations have you personally conducted since 1957?

A. At least 25,000 or more.

Q. Could you attempt to break down that number into any kind of classifications?

A. It would only be an attempt. I would estimate that 60 percent would fall into the preemployment category for all kinds of businesses and 40 percent would fall into the specific, problem, and criminal testing categories for private industry, law enforcement agencies, and attorneys.

Q. Now, let's go back to the galvanometer recording section. Mechanically, how does it function?

A. The galvanometer on my instrument generates against a given area of a person's sweat glands, in this instance the last joint on two fingers of the same hand, a current of 50 microamperes at 500 milivolts. The current is connected to the grid of a detector and transmitted through two primary legs of a bridged circuit which contains an established constant. Sensitivity of the galvanometer unit may be adjusted from 1 to 100,000 ohms. The lower the amount of ohms in the system, the higher the power of electricity.

As the body functions it generates its own peculiar form of electrical energy. By using the ohm sensitivity dial, the polygraphist instrumentally matches a machine constant with the body's so-called electrical output. When this is accomplished, pen excursion on the chart should be about one inch for every 10,000 ohms. Of course, this will vary as a result of subject's own resistance factor, physical condition, humidity, and so on.

The GSR components sense small changes in skin resistance, from a subject's general resistance level. A simple Wheatstone bridge circuit utilizes the finger electrodes and compensating resistances in one arm and is so arranged that the subject's general resistance level, across the electrode plate, can be balanced against the other bridge arms. The subject's emotional response to insertion of verbal stimuli by the polygraphist will trigger small changes in his general resistance level, causing a positive or negative imbalance, and fluctuations in the upward or downward motion of the galvanometer recording pen.

Q. For the court's information, will you briefly describe the basic physiological aspects involved in all three recording sections?

A. Since volumes have been written, and are still being written on cardiovascular, respiratory, and galvanic skin response, my answer can only be based on what I have read, studied, and daily experienced in live polygraph testing.

First, and foremost, the physiological activity is meaningless unless the psychological aspects are very carefully controlled by the polygraphist. The subject must have a clear understanding of the nature of the questions to be presented to him. He must have no misunderstanding about the purpose of the test. There should be no element of surprise.

Polygraph chart tracings are based on the function of the brain and its command of the autonomic nervous system which is headquartered in the medulla. The autonomic nervous system, which has been termed the fight or flight mechanism of the body, is divided into two sections, the sympathetic and the parasympathetic. These are antagonistic systems.

Q. What is the role of the autonomic nervous system and its two subdivisions with respect to polygraphy?

A. The internal organs such as the heart, lungs, and viscera, or stomach, intestines, spleen, pancreas, are served by the autonomic nervous system which is by definition a motor system. As I said before, its two subdivisions are functionally antagonistic.

For example, the sympathetic system accelerates the heart action while the parasympathetic slows it down. On the other hand, the parasympathetic accelerates stomach activity, which is checked by the sympathetic.

To proceed a little further, parasympathetic action stimulates nasal and salivary glands, the serous and mucous secretions and smooth muscle of the bronchioles in the lungs, but has no effect on sweat glands and smooth muscle of the skin. Contrarily, sympathetic action has no effect on salivary glands, but inhibits the same organs and stimulates sweating.

In the pons and medulla oblongata are respiratory, vasomotor, and cardiac centers. These centers are functionally restricted in the sense that the respiratory centers do not control the vasomotor centers, although they may affect them. But the hypothalmus, projecting, may control or activate them simultaneously, as when respiration and blood pressure increase during emotional states. These centers also function on a reflex level as in the control of blood pressure. Furthermore, they are frequently integrated with somatic activities. Respiration, for instance, involves the use of skeletal muscles.

The sympathetic system tends to respond, as a whole, particularly during emergencies, and is therefore an important part of the mechanisms by which a person reacts to stress. There are many stressing situations—in this case the emotional factor of fear or lack of fear contained in a truthful or deceptive answer to a relevant question of importance to the person receiving the question—which implicate the sympathetic system.

In addition, in response to stress, there are more slowly developing changes involving both the nervous system and the endocrine system. I am now touching on physiological recordings of the galvanometer section under control of the hypothalmus which is also the temperature regulating center of the body.

Any thought process, specifically an adverse thought process, any emotional stress or increase in excitement level sends nerve impulses racing along the nerve pathways. This is, in itself, energy expended. Whether by physical movement or by emotion, energy expended creates changes in body temperature and affects sweat gland secretions. Hence, any change in body temperature affecting sweat gland activity pits itself against the minute current of an instrument constant and causes the galvanometer pen to fluctuate on the moving chart.

Q. In polygraphy, what stimulates this emergency system into action or operation?

A. The psychological implication contained in a question which causes the individual to perceive some kind of danger. To paraphrase, if I see a truck bearing down upon me at any speed I would ordinarily be motivated to jump out of the way to safety. As the truck narrowly misses me, I would probably find myself breathing heavily, my heart pounding, and my body trembling.

My sympathetic nervous system has then been enervated to meet that momentary emergency. I am lying in bed at night. Suddenly I hear a noise like a door opening. A burglar? A swift, sudden, uncontrollable pang of fear races through me. I perspire. I break out with goosepimples. I have no control over that pang of fear which now has almost complete control of my body. I am weak and literally defenseless.

But, there is no further sound. I lie quietly, and after a while my body starts to return to the norm it was functioning at before the sound occurred. I heave one big sigh of relief. I turn over, and I go to sleep, perhaps at peace with the world. I was not harmed!

Q. And with reference to deception?

A. There is little to no difference. The attempt to deceive is the same kind of emergency occurring at a psychological level, compounding the physiological aspect to varying degrees.

Q. Does a person have any voluntarily control?

A. The "normal" person permitted to walk free and unrestrained in our society does not have conscious control over autonomic function, even though he may temporarily feign it. Consequently, this system will "kick in" depending upon the perception of the individual as to how he personally receives the emergency quality of the total, even partial, perception pattern.

Q. Now you have said that the stimulus which can cause the sympathetic segment of the autonomic nervous system to go into effect might be a perception which I presume may be oral, visual, or auditory?

A. Yes.

Q. Or be perceived by any of the senses?

A. Yes.

Q. Do I correctly understand that when this system is activated under fight or flight conditions the decisional process of the mind—which I believe has been referred to in some psychological studies as well-being, in effect, while the brain contains a more pure physiological connotation—and use of the will are bypassed?

A. Yes.

Q. Then this is an automatically reflex action generated by one or more of the senses?

A. Yes.

Q. Not actually thought out or decided upon?

A. Right.

Q. Insofar as polygraphy is concerned, and specifically as to the pneumograph or respiratory tracings, can you explain to the court why one would not deliberately run a pattern of truth when he knows he is lying, and also knows that his breathing is significant? Why is that not a feasible means of beating the examiner, so to speak?

A. At the time of test commencement the testee's body is functioning at a respiratory pace which we refer to as his physiological norm of the moment. Voluntary attempts at controlled breathing are clearly discernible and are of short duration, even though deliberately repeated. Abstract thinking, holding of the breath, semi-hyperventilation activity, sharp deep breaths, longer periods of "sincere" thinking calls for more oxygen and glucose while creating more carbon dioxide to exhale. Very quickly, the increase in blood pressure and heart rate calls for involuntary and reflex compensation through various sensory centers, the vagus nerve and autonomic action.

Q. Does such voluntary or deliberate respiratory activity pose any chart interpretative problem for the professional examiner as he searches for truth or deception criteria?

A. None whatsoever.

Q. In your opinion, could a person beat the test or foul up a chart's interpretative quality by movement?

A. Only to a very minor degree. With modern instruments having from three to any other number of recording pens, the slightest deliberate movement of just about all portions of the body, externally or internally, will usually cause an instant, clearly discernible break in the tracing. The professionally alert examiner will readily be able to tell the existence of a sup-posedly hidden movement by the content makeup of the trac-ing involved.

Q. Then the primary stimulus which differentiates between truth and deception on a polygram comes from the issue question asked by the examiner which is or is not of relevancy to the person receiving it?

A. Yes.

Q. Are there other kinds of stimuli which might show up in the test or be recorded on the polygram and not contain truth or deception criteria?

A. Yes. These may sometimes be classified as unintentional, un-forseen, extraneous responses caused by unexpected sounds or noises, e.g. the ringing of a telephone, the honking of a horn, or possibly the slamming of a door. However, each examiner is carefully taught to use certain making symbols during his training and practice and to make appropriate notations at the exact place on the chart where the extraneously caused re-sponse occurred.

Q. Do such occurrences have any bearing on chart interpretation or analysis?

A. Not really, no. They are immediately eliminated from chart interpretation. Should an extraneously caused response occur just prior to, during, or just following the insertion of a rele-vant question, that question will later be repeated. Through repeat, follow-up, and rewording in question formulation we have the process of elimination.

Q. Mr. Smith, for years we've listened to stories, perhaps myths—I really don't know if there is any truth in them—that there are certain kinds of people who can lie to the so-called lie detector and not be detected. Do you know in what classifications these persons may fall?

A. From everything I've read and studied, psychologically, the persons you refer to are generally called sociopaths, sometimes psychopaths.

Q. Are they normally capable of beating the test?

A. No. However, sometimes they might present a slightly different pattern than one would ordinarily analyze as produced by the normal or neurotic subject.

This difference does not interfere with chart interpretation. The sympathetic nervous system operates within these people, at their own level or norm, just as it does in anyone else.

Q. Now, with respect to criminal suspects, would you anticipate encountering this type of personality with a fair degree of interpretation if you were doing just criminal polygraphy?

A. Yes.

Q. Do you also find this kind of personality frequently in private industrial polygraphy?

A. Yes, particularly in preemployment and theft cases.

Q. This is the kind of person who often winds up in trouble with the law, or his employer?

A. Yes.

Q. Based on your experience and that of the profession, do psychopaths, sociopaths, neurotics present any special problem insofar as catching them if they are attempting deception?

A. Not for the experienced, professional examiner. The neurotic may present some minor difficulty to the lesser experienced examiner in seeking to distinguish between the whole truth and something less than the whole truth because of erratic charts which contain both anxiety and sympathetic enervation. Actually it just takes more careful and detailed analysis to make these discriminations or distinctions.

Q. What about the mentally retarded?

A. This will depend on the psychologically established degree of retardation, and where these people are—or in what status they are—when tested. The average polygraphist does not come in contact with more than the minutely retarded person. This is easily ascertained, and then all subject matters and explorations are reduced to meet his level of understanding.

Q. Suppose a person evidences suffering from some psychotic episode. Would you test him if you sensed this?

A. No.

Q. Why, please?

A. It would not be fair to him.

Q. Please explain, for the benefit of the court.

A. I have never known a qualified examiner either in criminal or private work who would even think of attempting to test a person known to be suffering from a recent or present psychotic episode. That person might be under some delusional or hallucinatory experience over which there is no immediate psychological control.

Q. I want to rephrase a question. Is there any kind of a situation where the testee might be able to tell a lie and the instrument tracing indicates truthfulness?

A. Under rare circumstance such is possible. If a testee unequivocally believes he is telling the whole truth and nothing but the whole truth, it can happen.

Q. In 25,000 test cases has this happened to you?

A. Yes. One time.

Q. Did he show truth or deception on his charts?

A. I never polygraphed him. I listened to his story and took a signed statement which I almost immediately destroyed because of the psychologically oriented irregularities in its context. He was subsequently proven completely wrong by police investigation.

Q. Mr. Smith, have you ever made a mistake in rendering an opinion?

A. Knowingly, I have made four such mistakes.

Q. In 25,000 tests?

A. Yes.

Q. Briefly explain to the court the nature of those mistakes.

A. During my first and second year of practice I called four guilty men innocent, on separate occasions, while testing them for theft from private industry.

Q. Have you ever knowingly called an innocent man guilty?

A. No.

Q. How do you know that you have not made more than four errors in your interpretations?

A. I can only assume so due to the absence of litigation against myself or my clients, and due to the absence of complaint from the individuals tested, and all those requesting such tests.

Q. Am I correct, then, in assuming that in many of the cases where you have diagnosed truth or deception that either an outright admission, subsequent interrogation or investigation —other circumstances—corroborated the polygraph recordings and your opinions?

A. That is correct.

Q. I take it the test is a useful aid to interrogation in that it assists in obtaining an admission or confession from a guilty but reluctant subject?

A. Yes.

Q. Is it also not most useful in verifying the truth when a person under suspect or accusation is denying guilt?

A. Extremely so. That, in my opinion, is one of polygraph's greatest values.

Q. Would you, as one heavily involved in polygraphy, have any hesitation in relying on the opinion of an experienced and qualified examiner that a certain individual is truthfully denying guilt?

A. I wouldn't hesitate at all.

Q. Now, having in mind the total range of your experience, I ask you to indicate to the court whether or not there has been any serious problems with diagnostic errors; that is, do you frequently bump into a situation where a responsible examiner says a man is innocent and it later turns out he was not?

A. No.

Q. We frequently hear that certain kinds of drugs, if taken prior to a test, can help a person beat the test or can keep the examiner from arriving at a conclusive opinion. Is there any truth to this?

A. Very little. Any doctor will tell you that a person must take a great deal of a certain type of drug before it will affect the function of the autonomic nervous system. In such instances, that person will hardly be able to walk or talk coherently. When there is such a suspicion or verbal and physical manifestations indicating same are observed, a test is not even attempted.

Q. Are there any situations where a person under the influence of drugs or narcotics can be successfully and conclusively tested?

A. Yes. For example, if a heroin addict has just taken his regular shot, his body is functioning at what may be considered his norm. Ordinarily he can be successfully tested. In some cases, the same applies to the chronic alcoholic.

Q. Will marihuana have any adverse affect on chart interpretation?

A. Ordinarily, no. Even if a person is "stoned" on marihuana, as long as he understands the meaning of the question and the purpose of the question; as long as he knows the difference between truth and lie, there will be no problem.

Q. Then physical manifestations are the first clues to the examiner that a person has taken some kind of drugs or barbituates?

A. Yes. Initially we may not know what he has taken until we probe, but any unusual giggling, laughing, yawning, jerking, sleepy appearance, belligerence, the appearance of the pupils, are all red warning lights.

Q. Do some persons take small amounts of tranquilizers or drugs thinking they can beat the test?

A. Yes. However, during the first twenty to thirty seconds of chart recordings the type of pattern produced will alert the experienced examiner. Through direct and controlled question formulation he will probe.

Generally, the only help tranquilizers or small amounts of drugs give to the testee is strictly psychological. He thinks he can beat the test by taking them. When that defense is broken he can even be more easily controlled from a psychological testing standpoint.

Q. Are you familiar with other kinds of scientific evidence used in criminal cases such as the matching of fingerprints, firearms identification, the matching of handwriting, and the parafin test?

A. Yes.

Q. With your total range of experience with these various aids to litigation, which have been ruled admissible by the courts, are you satisfied that polygraphy contains the same plain of reliability.

A. Very definitely.

Q. Do you know of any states in which it has almost become policy not to bring prosecution against someone who has been cleared by a competent polygraphist.

A. Yes. This happens quite frequently in just about every state, and this also includes the military.

Q. I assume you are aware that admissibility of polygraphic evidence has been generally rejected by many courts, and in particular the Appellate Courts?

A. I am.

Q. Are you also aware that polygraphic testimony has been admitted on stipulation and, of recent years, even over objection of opposing counsel in several courts, both criminal and civil?

A. I am.

Q. Do you think the present judicial process would be impaired or jeopardized if, in proper form, polygraphic results were given to criminal and civil juries as a matter of course?

A. In no way, as you said, if properly controlled.

Q. Will you state a brief opinion for the benefit of the court why you feel competent polygraphy should be admitted into record and before the jury?

A. Generally, polygraphic interpretation is little different than the comparison by a firearms identification expert, no different than the comparison of a latent against an existing print by a fingerprint expert; no different than the interpretations of an x-ray, skiagraph, electrocardiogram or electroencephalograph by other experts.

Certainly it is not the instruments utilized in all the foregoing that normally afford the area of mistake. If a mistake is made, it is made by the interpreter. Such would include any doctor, psychiatrist, psychologist, the otherwise specialist in any field, as well as the juror, lawyer or judge who can wrongfully be persuaded by whatever evidence or interpretation of that evidence is presented.

Q. Mr. Smith, there has been some apprehension, certainly in judicial circles as well as the Bar, that juries will be so completely impressed by polygraphic testimony that they may abandon the rest of their function which is examination of the total evidentiary picture. What is your opinion?

A. Jurors will make up their own minds, no matter what, or in what manner, evidence is presented to them.

Q. To your knowledge, have many persons who have been tried before a jury, or a judge, been indicted, found guilty and sentenced, and then freed because polygraphy which verified their innocence was substantiated by corroborative evidence that another person was actually guilty?

A. Yes. There are hundreds, undoubtedly thousands of such cases.

Q. In both criminal and civil fields, where do you think polygraphy might carry its greatest weight?

A. In pretrial by attorneys and law enforcement agencies using it as an investigative tool; for the verification of dual allegations as to a given fact or incident of relevancy; in posttrail where perhaps pertinent facts were not brought out, in presentencing for the element of intent; in postsentencing and confinement cases where there is a question of true guilt or innocence; and in the case of a person who may be taking the rap for someone else because of his past record or other pressing reasons.

Q. Do you think judges or jurors should consider just one examiner's opinion?

A. I see no reason why not, if he be qualified. However, I think that perhaps the same conclusion drawn by three competent examiners, utilizing the appropriate question formulation, as long as they come to the same conclusion of truth or deception, should be given very weighty consideration.

Q. Is each examiner equally qualified?

A. I think not, any more than one can say that each doctor, lawyer, psychologist, psychiatrist, judge, plumber or carpenter is equally qualified. Each individual must stand on his own two feet by his schooling, speciality training, experience, and self-application.

Q. In your own experience, have you ever known qualified examiners to arrive at a different conclusion on a test independently conducted by each, given the same set of real life circumstances?

A. No, not in real life situations of import.

Q. Do you sincerely believe a jury could get closer to the truth—and that is the whole crux of every trial—by being permitted to consider polygraphic evidence or testimony?

A. More so than ever before.

Q. Why?

A. Because there is no other present means of arriving at truth so fairly, impartially and objectively. However, I would entertain any other suggestion, in the same vein.

Q. Mr. Smith, how much credibility do you think a judge or jury should give to polygraph testimony?

A. The same that they would give to all forms of expert testimony already considered by them. The polygraph instrument cannot testify, but its recordings can provide the basis for expert testimony as does any other physiological recording instrument.

   Certainly, the polygraph is far more sophisticated than the other recording instruments, such as the EKG, the EEG, and others. And, it seems almost ridiculous for anyone to even suggest that because a polygraph instrument cannot be cross-examined that the judicial process might be impaired. They don't cross-examine a stethoscope or an x-ray machine.

Q. Do you think a jury would have a better chance of arriving at a just verdict if polygraph testimony were presented for their consideration on the same basis as other evidence?

A. Yes.

Q. I assume you are familiar with the procedure of taking an oath and then testifying?

A. Yes.

Q. Which all witnesses do?

A. Yes.

Q. Drawing upon your vast experience, do you think an oath is as good a guarantor of arriving at truth as would be utilization of the polygraph technique?

A. No, indeed.

Q. Can people more successfully deceive or lie under oath than they could during polygraph examination?

A. They definitely can. Literally thousands of trial records clearly and emphatically attest to this.

THE DEFENSE: No further questions.

THE COURT: The witness may step down.

*   *   *

After the foregoing fragmentation, one can readily visualize how many other subject matters could be brought into laying the proper foundation.

It is also quite clear the extent of the cross-examination which will be forthcoming, and which must be anticipated, and logically countered.

Chapter 5

THAT JUSTICE MIGHT PREVAIL

In the January 9, 1965, issue of *Ave Marie,* two writers, John Coghlan and Bruce Cook, challenged validity of polygraphy as:

> and the source of danger is the law enforcement agency and the private firm that, in the interest of investigative experience, resort to the use of this instrument which is no better than a cousin to an Ouija board. Far more convincing evidence could be obtained through legitimate investigative procedures by trained and experienced men.

Were they right? Or, were they wrong?

Well, while we wonder how a dictionary might describe the word asininity, let's take a brief look at some recent cases where the training, expertise, knowledge and professional application of polygraphy played a leading role.

The medium-size man with the incredibly smooth complexion said he was from the Better Business Bureau and sat down in vice president John Stinson's office at the First Federal Savings and Loan Association in Evansville, Indiana. Quite calmly, he pulled out a revolver.

The two men left the office and walked behind the counter. The gunman then herded eight other employees into the vault. A few minutes later he left, with $22,500.

That was October 8, 1962. For about six months the robbery went unsolved. Then, a medium-time hoodlum named Charles Del Monico was indicted in Los Angeles for extortion. His victim was oilman Ray Ryan, an Evansville native son whose Las Vegas escapades were always front page copy back home—with pictures.

John Stinson recognized the photo of Del Monico as the gunman who had robbed his bank. Other bank employees agreed. Stinson and his secretary were flown to California and taken to the courtroom where Del Monico was being tried on the extortion charge. Again they identified him as the robber.

115

When Del Monico—who got five years on the extortion charge and then was freed on appeal bond—was arraigned in March of 1964 for the Evansville robbery, four other bank employees saw him in court and identified him.

The accumulation of eyewitnesses made for a very strong case against Del Monico. But the thirty-seven-year-old son of gangster Charlie (The Blade) Tourine stubbornly insisted that he had never set foot in the state of Indiana until his arraignment. He also produced two witnesses—reputable ones—that he had been in Miami Beach during the robbery.

Del Monico pursuaded brilliant criminal lawyer Edward Bennet Williams to handle his case and fully convinced his attorney of his innocence by offering to submit to polygraphy.

At first, Williams was skeptical because of the eyewitness identification against his client. Initially he suggested Del Monico take the test so he could get at the truth in order to prepare a proper defense.

Nearly every intelligent criminal lawyer has been doing this for years.

Williams called polygraphist emeritus Robert S. Eichelberger, former police lieutenant with the Washington, D.C. Metropolitan Police Department, then in private practice. Del Monico underwent two days of polygraphy.

At the end of the final testing session, Eichelberger told Williams he was positive Del Monico was innocent. He then prepared a detailed report for his client's use.

Williams went to the Justice Department, advised his findings, and offered to submit his client to another polygraph test by any examiner of the government's choosing. Justice agreed and, on advice of a member of the FBI, named its own expert, Robert Eichelberger, only to learn he was the man whose polygraph findings had already upheld Del Monico's claim of innocence.

Nevertheless, Justice went ahead with the indictment.

Thoroughly aroused, Williams sent his client to nationally known polygrapher, Richard O. Arther, in New York City. Exhaustive testing corroborated Eichelberger's findings.

Williams sensed a landmark case to test admissibility of polygraphic evidence. To make sure, he sent Del Monico to the famous polygraph laboratories of John Reid & Associates, Chicago. Again Del Monico was declared innocent.

Pressing his case, Williams submitted Del Monico to two sessions of narcoanalysis. His client cleared both tests.

By now Justice was confronted with three polygraph tests, one which was morally its own, and two narcoanalysis—all performed by different experts. If not legally and scientifically binding, they still exonerated Del Monico. At last, Justice submitted him to its own narcoanalyst, with the same results: Del Monico was telling the truth.

Having agreed to the tests, the Justice Department suddenly faced an agonizing dilemma: should it rely on the narcoanalysis and polygraph findings, not one of which would be admissible in court—or the ten eyewitnesses? After pondering for weeks, the government decided against the eyewitnesses. On February 1, on the eve of the trial, U.S. Attorney Richard Stein moved in Federal Court in Indianapolis to drop the case.

The eyewitnesses and banker Stinson were furious. "It stinks," Stinson said. "There's something wrong with our judicial system if someone charged with a crime gets off because they gave him a needle. . . .If Del Monico had come before a jury he would have been convicted."

In the face of the citizen's wrath, U.S. Attorney Stein agreed conviction was probable. But the accumulation of nonadmissible evidence, plus lack of corroborative evidence for the eyewitnesses, persuaded him not to prosecute. "I've seen too many cases where a jury convicted the wrong man on eyewitness testimony," Stein said. "'We were afraid of a miscarriage of justice."

By its reliance on the tests, the government set an out-of-court legal landmark—and clearly hastened the time when polygraphy and narcoanalysis may be accepted as responsible courtroom evidence.*

*　　*　　*

In remarks prepared for the general assembly of the American Bar Association in London, England during July of 1971, former

---

*Newsweek, February 1965.

U.S. Attorney General John N. Mitchell said the American judiciary has spent too much time making new law and new public policy, "and too little time determining guilt or innocence."

Taking to task both the bar and the bench, Mitchell said: "We face in the United States a situation where the discovery of guilt or innocence as a function of the courts is in danger of drowning in a sea of legalisms." He added that, in his opinion, judges and lawyers have a responsibility to see that the right of an individual to a fair trial does not outweigh the right of society to speedy justice.

He decried what he termed "the Hydra of excess proceduralisms, arm-chair formalisms, pretrial motions, post-trial motions, appeals, postponments, continuances, collateral attacks, which can have the effect of dragging justice to death and stealing the very life out of the law."

"My plea," he said, "is for the profession to intensify its reforms in these conceptual areas—to revive the court's function as a finder of fact, and to restore finality as one of the attributes of justice."

One of the nation's most respected mediolegal experts once wrote: "Recently while attending a seminar of criminal trial lawyers, I listened to speaker after speaker bragging about the tricks he had utilized to outsmart opposing counsel. During the course of these talks I listened in vain to hear three words which seemed to me to be quite relevant to the discussions in a meeting of this kind. These three words are "truth," "innocence," "guilt." As I left the meeting I had the strong impression that these three subjects were outside the sphere of interest of the speakers.

"The function of a jury is to find and establish fact in an accusation. Once a jury returns to the courtroom with a finding, from that time on its decision becomes a fact—even though that fact may be very wide of the truth. Any time truth and fact do not totally coincide, a miscarriage of justice results."

* * *

For several months, into the spring of 1968, soldiers at Fort Riley, Kansas, complained that they had been mailed money and certain legal documents from home which they never received.

When numerous undelivered envelopes, opened but empty, were recovered from various trash receptacles in the vicinity of the Fort's post office, as well as from inside a particular barracks, a company commander ordered the arrest of one Specialist 4/c Roger Carson, the unit mail clerk.

Since Carson was the only soldier with keys and full access to the mail room, and since he was quartered in the barracks where one stolen envelope was found, he was charged with larceny and tampering with U.S. mails and placed in pretrial confinement. He remained there for some five to six weeks while C.I.D. continued the investigation.

If found guilty, Carson faced five to ten years in the military disciplinary barracks at Fort Leavenworth, Kansas.

While in confinement, Carson's defense counsel encouraged the soldier to attempt verifying his claim of innocence through polygraphy. He knew it was a rarity, at least in recent years, when any accused in the military who had cleared a polygraph test was tried and/or convicted. Carson readily agreed. Up to this point he had a good service record.

Chief Warrant Officer Melvin J. Williams (since retired), Operations Officer and Certified Polygraphist for the Criminal Investigation Division, Fifth Army Area, was assigned the case.

On the day of the test, in the Fort Riley polygraph laboratories, Williams spent considerable pretest interview time establishing rapport and overcoming the accused's fears. Four polygraph charts later, Williams told Carson's defense counsel that he was positive his client was completely innocent. His charts were analyzed and his test opinion confirmed by Robert Brisentine, C.I.D. Agency Lisison Officer, who also had the primary duties of polygraph control officer.

Carson's company commander was incensed. Nevertheless, all charges against the young soldier were dropped.

Some months later, C.I.D. identified the real perpetrator of the mail thefts as a former unit mail clerk, discharged just prior to the investigation pointing to Carson. They also learned that this perpetrator was wanted by U.S. Postal authorities in his home town for breaking and entering numerous mail boxes.

* * *

In September of 1971, attorney for Lt. Col. Anthony Herbert claimed that the army had possession of polygraph test results supporting Herbert's statements that he notified superior officers of Vietnam atrocities and that he requested a probe of them.

Attorney Charles Morgan, of the American Civil Liberties Union, said Herbert submitted to polygraph in compliance with an earlier agreement with the Army—an agrement the Army later canceled. He added that the polygraphist who conducted the test was the same one the Army had earlier agreed to use.

"Regardless of what else may come to light, the expert recognized by the Army agrees that Col. Herbert told the truth," said Morgan. "Since the Army was interested in the polygraph test, I'm glad its results were favorable to Col. Herbert. I don't know where the investigation will finally lead."

Herbert, then stationed at 3rd Army Headquarters in Atlanta, two years previous accused Maj. Gen. John Barnes and Col. J. Ross Franklin of dereliction of duty and covering up incidents of murder and torture of Vietnamese civilians.

When the army had not acted on the accusations by March of 1971, Herbert filed formal charges himself. Charges against Franklin were dropped, but those against Barnes were pursued.

Morgan said the test was conducted September 3 in Atlanta by Benjamin F. Malinowski, former senior instructor (then retired) at the U.S. Army Military Police Polygraph School at Fort Gordon, Georgia. Results were forwarded to Army authorities.

Two questions stemming from Herbert's statements, challenged during the investigation, were submitted during polygraph. They were

1. Did you, on or about February 14, 1969, advise Col. Franklin of the killing of Vietnamese detainees?

2. On or about April 4, 1969, did you personally request Gen. Barnes to conduct an investigation?

Morgan quoted Herbert's responses to the questions as being "yes" and also read the following statement from the examiner's report:

"It is the opinion of this examiner that Lt. Col. Herbert was completely truthful when he answered the relevant questions with a yes."

Morgan said Herbert and the Army agreed on Malinowski as the examiner, that the exam was scheduled for September 7, but that Herbert was notified on September 2 by Capt. Kenneth A. Rosenblum that the Army test had been canceled.

* * *

While it is a rarity that the military will prosecute or has convicted a suspect who cleared pretrial polygraphy, a strange form of irony appears when military legal precedent prohibits admissibility into evidence for the purpose of verifying the accused's innocence or truthfulness.

This is clearly brought out in the case of Captain Ernest Medina, the officer charged with responsibility for at least 100 murders at My Lai, Vietnam, in 1968.

The investigating officer, Col. James Mobley, testified on the third day of the pretrial hearing that a defense polygraphist conducted a test on Medina and stated that test results supported the captain's claim that he gave no order to massacre civilians at My Lai.

The noted defense and criminal lawyer, F. Lee Bailey, asked Mobley if a defense polygraph expert had not testified during the investigation that Medina told the truth when he flatly denied giving any massacre order.

"The witness said his tests indicated Medina was telling the truth when he said that," answered Mobley.

He said the expert also testified that Medina told the truth when he said he fired at a My Lai woman because he feared she was about to hurl a hand grenade at him.

Bailey asked Mobley if he had checked the defense contention that it was the policy of the Army not to try a defendant if polygraph tests indicated his innocence.

"No I did not," answered Mobley.

Bailey then asked if several witnesses repudiated statements attributed to them by C.I.D. agents building a file on this case.

"Several did repudiate—or make statements not consistent with earlier statements," said Mobley.

He added that the inconsistencies, as well as the polygraph report, were reflected in his recommendation that the case go to trial.

Bailey asked if the changes made by the witnesses in their statements were in favor of Medina.

"That was generally the trend—yes, sir," said Mobley.

When the actual court-martial trial got underway, Col. Kenneth Howard, the military judge, ruled that polygraphic evidence was inadmissible, although he did permit lengthy examination of the reliability of polygraph tests.

While contending that the Army regulation prohibiting polygraphic evidence is an "error of constitutional dimensions," Bailey knew the importance of getting polygraph's reliability into the trial record in case Medina was found guilty.

In the absence of the jury, polygraph experts Cleve Backster of New York and John Reid of Chicago testified in no uncertain terms that the technique of this science had more than proven itself reliable for all courts.

Additionally, supporting testimony came from the famous Court of Last Resort member, Dr. LeMoyne Snyder, who said, "The polygraph is infinitely more reliable than personal identification." Snyder also said that any flaws in administering polygraphy are caused by human error.

Shortly thereafter, Bailey wrote President Nixon asking him to change the rules of evidence so that polygraph test results could be admitted into military evidence.

The registered letter also noted that Nixon once spoke out in favor of the use of polygraphy and attested to its reliability in the Alger Hiss case.

It should also be noted that a polygraph test on Captain Medina was conducted by C.I.D's Robert Brisentine with positive results in favor of the accused. Neither was this admitted into trial evidence, but Colonel Howard did permit Brisentine to testify concerning some of the remarks made during his pretest interview with Medina.

During the latter part of September 1971, Captain Ernest Medina was acquitted. The jury of five combat officers deliberated only sixty minutes.

A stifled cheer and some handclapping, quickly suppressed by the military judge, erupted in the small court room when Col. William D. Proctor, president of the court, read the verdict.

Medina saluted the court, strode back to his seat at the defense table, blinked rapidly and drank from a glass of water.

Moments later he went outside and told a crowd of reporters that although he had always maintained "complete faith in military justice," he had not changed his determination to leave the army.

* * *

In October of 1971, Ralph Wilson, Jr., owner of the Buffalo Bills, was absolved of conduct detrimental to professional football in light of his suspension by the New York State Racing Commission.

The announcement was made by National Football League Commissioner Pete Rozelle following an investigation that concluded when Wilson voluntarily submitted to a two-hour polygraph test.

"Our investigation confirmed that Wilson unknowingly violated certain racing rules, relative to transfer of ownership in horses, and was unaware of the background of the individuals with whom he had briefly dealt," said Rozelle. "He was not involved in any way in fraudulent or unethical conduct."

The commissioner added that as part of the polygraph examination, Wilson was asked if he had gambled on professional football games since becoming a team owner in 1960. Polygraphy clearly verified Wilson's claim that he had not.

* * *

In July 1971, caucasian Emily Forrester (with exception of the defense attorney, all names in this case are fictitious), mother of seven children by three different men, including Negro Alvin Forrester, whom she had recently divorced, sat in her Minneapolis home brooding over a glass of whiskey. She was boiling mad at Alvin. He had a hell of a lot of nerve playing around with her nineteen-year-old daughter, Arlene, who claimed she was pregnant but not by Alvin. Arlene's blowing the whistle about Alvin's amorous attentions had resulted in the divorce. Emily gulped a long drink and gagged. She wished she could find some way of stopping Alvin's weekly visitation rights with their own five-year-old daughter, Christine.

At that particular moment her angry wish tragically satisfied itself. Christine came out of the barthroom whimpering, "Mommy, it burns when I go pee-pee. Mommy, it hurts so bad!"

"Come to mommy, baby, and let's see what's bothering you," Emily soothed. She pushed her drink away and pulled Christine's pants down around her ankles. "Bend over, honey, and we'll see what's hurting my precious one."

Emily was shocked at what she saw. She started sobering and immediately rushed Christine to the hospital. That afternoon Emily's fears were medically confirmed.

Five-year-old Christine Forrester had contacted both gonorrhea and syphilis.

Police and welfare departments were notified. Emily blamed her ex-husband in no uncertain terms. The investigation commenced.

Alvin Forrester had worked at General Hospital for eight years. He was chief aide in pediatrics. Prior to that he had operated houses of prostitution, bootlegged liquor, took suckers with various con schemes, and had run afoul of the law many times.

Forrester first became aware of the allegation against him through his job supervisor when he was prohibited from working in pediatrics and demoted to laundry room duties pending outcome of the investigation. His daughter was placed under treatment. Visitation rights were suspended.

When the accused first met Hennepin County Legal Advice Attorney, Michael O'Rourke, his case looked hopeless. Police and welfare personnel take a rather hard attitude toward anyone accused of such a dastardly offense. All of Alvin's vehement denials fell on deaf ears. Prosecution appeared eminent.

O'Rourke, known as the "battling lawyer," thought he would take what he considered a chance maneuver. He advised the two investigating agencies that he would submit his client to polygraphy. "Now," he said, "if Alvin clears this test, will you drop the investigation against him?"

"We'll think about it," answered the welfare supervisor.

O'Rourke made an appointment for Forrester with Robert J.

Ferguson, Jr., then in practice in Minneapolis. He knew Ferguson was a 1958 Keeler Institute graduate, author of two authoritative books on the subject, and had a rarely equaled case load experience behind him.

Forrester underwent two and one-half hours of polygraphy. When Ferguson concluded, he called both O'Rourke and Forrester into a conference room. "Counselor," he said, "Alvin Forrester is innocent."

"How am I going to get the police and welfare to accept your findings?"

"Perhaps the easiest way is for Forrester to take the test which will medically verify whether or not he ever had syphilis."

A week later the result was in. It was negative.

Forrester was reassigned to pediatrics. Visitation rights were resumed. Police and welfare departments channeled their investigation elsewhere.

O'Rourke wondered if they would pursue it with as much determination.

* * *

The liquor store manager peered at the four men facing him in a lineup at the St. Paul, Minnesota, city jail. One of the four was a suspect in the June 5, 1971, robbery of the store.

After a time he told police he couldn't identify any of the four.

Another store employee said he thought "number three" looked most like the robber, except for the color of his hair.

"Number three" was Jack O'Brien, a wiry, thirty-one-year-old ex-convict who lived in St. Paul, 120 miles from the robbery site in Redwood Falls, Minnesota.

O'Brien had already spent two days in jail on the robbery charge. He was to spend thirty-two more days in jail in Redwood Falls, unable to make bail, until he was released for lack of evidence.

In the meantime he lost his part-time job plus the job he was scheduled to start the Monday after he was arrested. Plus a good bit of his faith in the criminal system of justice.

The Municipal Liquor Store was robbed of $800 and a bottle

of Schenley's by a man who pointed a gun at the manager, Ronald Woese, and asked, "Do you want to die?"

The description Woese and employee Reider Bjornstad gave police was a man six feet tall, 175 pounds, about forty-five to fifty years old, with dark grey hair.

In the days following the robbery, they poured over hundreds of pictures with Police Chief Mike Young. In desperation, Young hired an artist from nearby Marshall to draw a sketch based on the description, but before the artist could produce a recognizable portrait, Young had more mug shots to show the witnesses.

One was of O'Brien, because he was "known to be operating in the out-state area," although he had never been arrested for robbery nor convicted outside the Twin Cities area. His specialty was burglary, and he had spent most of the past two years doing time in Montana.

The witnesses described someone in the light heavyweight class but O'Brien, a former boxer, was closer to a featherweight. He stood five feet six inches and weighed 132 pounds, with brown hair.

Besides, five witnesses—including a foster couple for the Ramsey County Welfare Department—said he had been with them all evening in St. Paul on the night of the robbery.

Apparently Woese and Bjornstad were sure enough from the evidence of the mug shot to persuade Chief Young that O'Brien should be arrested.

And, at a preliminary hearing two weeks after the lineup, both of them, plus a customer who had left the store minutes before the holdup, pointed at O'Brien and positively identified him.

O'Brien's attorney, public defender Earl Tighe, was unimpressed. "An in-court identification isn't worth a damn," he said. "Everyone knows who they're supposed to point at—the guy sitting behind the defense attorney at the counsel table."

He said the third witness was a farmhand with a first-grade education who was very suggestible and had been told by police which photo the others had identified before he made his own selection.

But the in-court identifications were enough to have Municipal Judge Donald Crooks bind O'Brien over to stand trial for armed robbery.

In district court, Tighe tried a new tack, bringing a habeas corpus petition to dismiss the charges on the grounds that O'Brien's arrest was illegal.

When Judge Walter Mann denied the request, Tighe threw some papers across the counsel table to prosecutor Wayne Farnberg and said, "Here, sleep with this."

The papers were the results of a polygraph test given to O'Brien on July 7 by Robert J. Ferguson, Jr. Polygraphy unequivocally supported O'Brien's claim of innocence.

If O'Brien agreed to take another test, administered by a state crime bureau examiner, and if he passed it, the prosecutor said he would ask to have the charge dismissed. The second test produced the same result, and O'Brien was released on July 30.*

*   *   *

With a twist of fate, in Dallas, Texas, early in 1971, a county jail inmate who claimed a jury convicted the wrong man for a suburban armed robbery ran into his waterloo when he repeated his confession that he was the holdup man.

Police investigators reported Jimmie Lee Barnett could not clear polygraphy when he said he, rather than Carl Bentley, had held up the Ranier Pharmacy the previous August 19th.

Bentley was found guilty of the robbery in January in Criminal District Judge Charlie T. Davis' court and received an automatic life sentence as an habitual criminal.

Investigation of the crime was reopened in July when Barnett, convicted of murder in May, announced he had pulled the holdup instead of Bentley. Both men were in the county jail awaiting appeal of these cases.

After Barnett's failure to clear polygraphy, District Attorney Henry Wade said further investigation proved it would have been impossible for Barnett to have been at the Ranier Pharmacy at the time it was being robbed.

---

*State of Minn. v. Jack O'Brien, 5th District Court, File No. 1768; Lundegard, Bob, Minneapolis Tribune, Aug. 22, 1971, *Polygraph frees suspect with alibi, different description.*

"On the day of the robbery," Wade said, "Barnett was employed by the Frymire Engineering Company installing equipment at a Fox and Jacobs project in Richardson. "It was subsequently discovered that he had worked a nine-hour day and did not get off work until 5:30 PM, almost an hour after the holdup.

*   *   *

On May 2, 1968, Edward Tisdale, Jr., twenty-five, walked out of Manhattan's Criminal Court Building into a cold spring rain, free after spending a year in prison for a murder he did not commit.

During April of 1967, he was arrested and charged with the murder of twenty-seven-year-old Albert Jackson and the shooting of one John Robinson just after midnight the previous March 31st. Robinson recovered and positively identified Tisdale as the gunman.*

An unidentified witness also told police that the night before the shooting incident Jackson had robbed Tisdale.

The case was turned over to the District Attorney's office. Tisdale was indicted and incarcerated. He could not meet bail.

While biding his time in jail he ran into an acquaintance, a Harlem "policy" man who asked, "Man, what y'all doin' in here?"

When Tisdale explained, the policy man shook his head. "They's crazy. I was there when it happened. I seen clear as hell who gunned Jackson, and that other jasper, too. I'm going out today and I'll tell 'em for sure."

While he kept his word, he spent three days in the D.A's offices before one of the assistant district attorneys asked if he would be willing to verify his assertions by polygraphy. He readily agreed. The test indicated truthfulness when he said he was at the scene and saw one Phillip Del Rio* shoot Jackson and Robinson.

A new investigation was commenced by Detective Paul Tarentola of the 28th Squad, assisted by Detective Theodore Oates of the District Attorney's office. They turned up several witnesses

---

*State of New York v. Edward Tisdale, Jr., Indictment No. 2096 (1967), Murder, Robinson, NYPD B No. 400513.

*State of New York v. Phililp Del Rio, Indictment No. 3120 (1968).

who reluctantly admitted that it was possible someone else besides Tisdale could have done the shooting.

Del Rio was picked up. He agreed to polygraphy. That was his first and last mistake. Charts conducted by polygraphist Natale Laurendi clearly indicated guilt. Del Rio then admitted the shootings.

Assistant District Attorney Melvin B. Ruskin appeared before State Supreme Court Justice Joseph A. Martinis and explained the facts. Justice Martinis congratulated the District Attorney's office for its willingness to pursue the investigation.

Then he dismissed the indictment. Tisdale was freed.

* * *

Herbert Smith was only nineteen years old when arrested on March 11, 1970, and charged with the shooting and armed robbery of a seventy-seven-year old New York West Side man, Morris Levey. He could not meet the $5000 bail.*

While in the hospital, Levey identified Smith from photographs. Later he picked Smith out of a lineup with two other persons, one of them a policeman known to Levey.

Assistant District Attorney Bennett L. Gersham was assigned the case. An indictment followed. However, Gersham was most concerned about discrepancies in the physical description initially given by Levey who said his assailant was 5 feet 4 inches in height. Smith was almost ten inches taller.

At the request of Smith's attorney, Joel K. Bohmart, Gersham stipulated to polygraphy. Again, Nat Laurendi conducted the test. This was on May 19, 1971.

He faced two attorneys with an emphatice: "The polygrams indicate complete innocence in this particular."

Next, Gersham confronted Levey with another series of mug shots, including one of Smith. This time Levey picked out a different photo as the man who shot and robbed him.

As a result, Gersham appeared before Justice Harold Baer on May 26, 1971, and asked for a dismissal of the indictment. It was

---

*State of New York v. Robert Smith, attempted murder, Indictment No. 2299 (1970).

granted. "Had it come to trial earlier," Gersham said, "there is a good possibility he would have been convicted."

*   *   *

On March 30, after spending two years in a crowded cellblock of New York City's Tombs awaiting trial on charges of robbing and murdering Harlem bartender James Shaw, two men were paroled after the Manhattan District Attorney's office said someone else had committed the crime.

One of them, John Garrett, twenty-six, was released immediately by State Supreme Court Justice Mitchell D. Schweitzer. His half-brother, Bernard Gaines, twenty-eight, was held for transfer to federal authorities to serve a six-month sentence on a narcotics charge to which he had already pled guilty.

It was not quite clear why it had taken more than two years for the truth to "come out."

The killing for which two innocent men were arrested took place at 2:30 AM on January 6, 1968, in the Morrison Lounge on Broadway near W. 148th St. During the robbery James Shaw was shot in the chest.

The step-brothers were picked up by police in a nearby pawnshop when they tried to pawn a ring a few hours after the Shaw killing. The ring, it turned out, was one of the items stolen from Shaw.

Garrett claimed innocence, telling police he had bought the ring from a man named Alvin. Nevertheless, he and his brother were taken to the station house, booked and sent to the Tombs. Garrett was subsequently indicted. When still not indicted by April, Gaines was released.

Then, in June, a grand jury returned an indictment and Gaines was again arrested. According to defense counsel, Philip Edelbaum and Alfred Rosner, the grand jury's action was based on testimony of narcotics addict Alvin Entzminger, a former police cadet trainee, who testified Gaines had confessed the Shaw murder to him while the two had previously been confined together in the Tombs.

When a witness to the crime reported he was unsure of the perpetrators' identification, Assistant District Attorney Louis

Aidala was assigned to the case. He was aided by detectives Thomas Ranich and Natale Laurendi.

They began a methodical investigation which quickly turned up Alvin Entzminger, who was identified by witnesses in the bar as one of the actual killers. At that time he was still a police cadet trainee.

Entzminger had no objection to polygraphy. While the test indicated he was not answering the relevant questions truthfully, he steadfastly denied complicity and made absolutely no admissions. Temporarily, the investigation was stymied.

On the eve of the trial of Garrett and Gaines, Nat Laurendi again confronted the prosecution's witness and asked if he would undergo another polygraph test. Entzminger cockily agreed and literally "challenged" Laurendi to ask him specific questions concerning the Shaw murder and also as to whether or not he personally received a ring taken from the victim.

The experienced polygraph specialist calmly accepted the challenge. After the securing of instrument attachments to Entzminger's body, the question formulation began.

Chart tracings containing deception in the areas of complicity were so dramatically evident that Laurendi deactivated the instrument and quietly said, "Look at this for yourself. You are guilty. Now talk!"

Entzminger's facade crumpled.* During his confession he also directly implicated one Glen Fuller as his accomplice.†

Garrett and Gaines were exonerated.

Much investigation credit in helping to solve this case must also go to attorneys Alfred Rosen and his son-associate, Martin. The two turned up invaluable evidence. Police had disputed the assertion by Garrett and Gaines that they were in another bar at the time Shaw was killed, in turn claiming that particular bar had been closed for the entire day and night. However, Rosen and his son obtained an affidavit from the bartender that the bar, in fact, was open.

* * *

*State of New York v. Alvin Entzminger, Indictment No. 1515, June 3, 1971.

†State of New York v. Glen Fuller, Indictment No. 1516, June 4, 1971. Both pled guilty of first degree manslaughter.

The horror story of a twenty-three-year-old Fort Sam Houston soldier accused and arrested for the June 1971 armed robbery of an ice house in San Antonio, Texas, was ended through polygraphy.

Sgt. Gene Danish, chief polygraphist for the San Antonio Police Department, credited his bureau and two robbery detectives with exposing the near miss in the wheel of justice.

The young supply sergeant, with only a few minor traffic infractions on his record, was arrested and jailed after the victim pointed him out to police as the bandit.

The story began when the young man entered the ice house to purchase a quart of milk. An attendant, the victim of a heist several days previous, "positively" recognized him as the hijacker and he and fellow employees followed the soldier to his nearby apartment.

Placing a call to police, the house was then watched until officers arrived and made the arrest.

After two days in jail, robbery detectives A. E. Zapata and Bill Tefteller asked the suspect if he would volunteer for polygraphy.

"I'll even take truth serum," the shaken young man cried.

Danish scheduled the test which more than proved to himself and other officers that the soldier was, in fact, completely innocent.

Danish later reported that the real perpetrator of the holdup was apprehended and charged.

*　　*　　*

Another incident in which the veteran polygraphist, Robert Eichelberger's polygraph proficiency protected the falsely accused was called, "The Case of the Purple Pants."

At 11:30 PM, October 11, 1968, Washington, D.C., Lillian Jones slipped her cinnamon red car into her garage behind the 4200 block of 13th Street, N.E. Suddenly a man pressed a black pistol to her head. After ordering her to "give me the pocketbook," he grabbed her purse and ran off with a total of 10 one-dollar bills.

At 12:50 AM, October 12, 1968, Patrolman Russell Drummond stopped a youth walking at Michigan Avenue and 12th

Street, N.E. The youth wore purple trousers and a tan trench coat. He matched the description of the robber.

The suspect, Ronald F. Faucette, nineteen, a senior at McKinley High, was hauled off to appear in a station house lineup with a policeman in civilian clothes. Mrs. Jones pointed her finger at Faucette.

Thirty-four days later, Judge Andrew J. Howard, Jr., of the Court of General Sessions, found Faucette guilty of petty larceny, making threats and possession of a prohibited weapon.

Free, pending probation report, Faucette denied any part in the crime which was so contradictory to his background and personality that his probation officer, Jeanne J. Wahl, could not let the case rest.

At Miss Wahl's request for help, Judge Charles W. Halleck contacted Eichelberger. As a police detective back in 1957, he had freed a youth who had been in prison two months as a result of "eyewitness identification."

This time Eichelberger donated his time and resources. He began an investigation seeking information on which to base polygraphy, and he methodically poked holes in the case of *United States v. Ronald Faucette.*

1. Faucette had left work in Hyattsville fifteen minutes before the purse snatching and he had walked a girl home. It was too far from the girl's house to the scene of the robbery for the youth to have walked there in time to have stolen Mrs. Jones' purse.

2. When arrested, Faucette did not have the 10 one-dollar bills, nor did he have a gun in his possession.

3. Faucette had no criminal record and he lived next door to a policeman who vouched for his character.

4. Mrs. Jones had told police that the clothes of the youth who robbed her were what she remembered best. Although Faucette's clothes matched those of the described holdup, those of the policeman in the lineup did not.

Following his investigation, Eichelberger conducted a polygraph examination in Judge Halleck's chambers. Faucete conclusively cleared it.

Presented with the new overall evidence, Judge Halleck set aside the conviction. He explained that none of this evidence came out at the original trial. And, Mrs. Jones *had* positively identified the youth in the purple pants and the tan trench coat.

Assistant U.S. Attorney John Ellsworth Stein dropped the charges. Faucette was freed.

*   *   *

During the late evening hours on August 2, 1970, in Gainesville, Texas, Marsha Kelly (name fictitious) was attacked. The investigation, plus the victim's identification of a mug shot, brought about the filing of a complaint.

On October 16, 1970, the Sixteenth Judicial Grand Jury issued the following indictment (in part) per Pat Ware, Foreman:

> IN THE NAME OF . . . the Grand Jurors, duly selected, organized, sworn and impaneled as such for the County of Cooke . . . and before the presentment of this indictment, in the County and State of Texas, aforesaid, John Henry Johnson in and upon Marsha Kelly, a woman, did make an assault; and did then and there by force and threats, and without consent of the said Marsha Kelly, ravish and have carnal knowledge of the said Marsha Kelly, against the peace and dignity of the State. . . .

On January 21, 1971, Judge W. C. Boyd ordered the rape charge dismissed in a hearing in 16th District Court on a motion by County Attorney Bill Sullivant.

Sullivant's dismissal motion disclosed "new developments" which proved Johnson was innocent. His prepared statement read:

> Because of the grave concern we all have had about the recent attacks on women in Gainesville, I want to make public new evidence which has come to light in the *State of Texas v. John Henry Johnson* (No. 70-075) .
>
> There have been new developments which prove he is innocent of the rape with which he has been charged. Johnson consented to take a polygraph examination administered by a Department of Public Safety polygraphist. This man has administered thousands of such tests and is recognized throughout Texas for his expertise in this field.

After having conducted the test on the defendant, W. W. Baker, the polygraphist, stated unequivocally that Johnson was innocent of the crime. He said there was not a single instance in the results of the test that would even make him suspicious that Johnson was guilty of this or any other rape.

The results of this test, coupled with the fact that a hair of Negro origin, discovered by investigators at the scene of the rape, could not be matched by the FBI laboratory with hair taken from the defendant, and the fact that several other people say Johnson was at another location at the time of the rape, convinced me a mistake had been made. Therefore, I have today presented the evidence to the court and moved to dismiss the indictment against Johnson.

I also want to take this opportunity to commend our law enforcement personnel for their dedication to Justice. This case again demonstrates that they work as hard to protect the innocent as they do to convict the guilty. This part of police work is often overlooked by the public but it, of course, is highly important.

*   *   *

Six girls had been killed within a twenty-mile radius of Ann Arbor, Michigan, since August 1967. All except one were University of Michigan students.

Ernest Paul Sims, twenty-six, was released from the Milan Correctional Institute in Michigan on March 25, 1969. He remained in Ann Arbor until about May 8 when he went to Nashville, Tennessee. There he misused some credit cards, then headed for Tupelo, Mississippi. After a short while he moved on into Illinois. In the meantime, a Nashville citizen signed a breach of trust complaint against Sims and a warrant was issued.

On May 29, 1969, Homicide officer Tom Cathey returned Sims to Nashville from Salem, Illinois, where he was put in jail. From his cell, some three weeks later, he wrote a letter to a girl friend in Ypsilanti, Michigan, inferring therein that the co-ed slayings in Ann Arbor could not be solved without his help. Jail censors picked this up. A police "plant" was put in his cell.

When first questioned, Sims simply said to Sgt. Doug Dennis, "I just want to tell the truth."

Then came sixteen hours of weird admission and statements surrounding drugs, a mysterious friend named Don, who reportedly bragged about killing several other people and the murder of two girls and a cab driver.

Sims told police he had killed one girl about the first of April, and then one in the middle of April. He said he did not know details of the first killing because he was so high on marihuana. However, he said the name of his second victim was Dawn. (Dawn Bascom, 13, was found strangled in Ypsilanti April 16.)

Next, he admitted the murder of Marilyn Skelton, sixteen, whose mutilated body was found near the University of Michigan campus March 25. Authorities said she had been sexually molested, beaten and strangled four days earlier.

Lastly, he admitted stabbing a cab driver to death in Oklahoma.

When all the statements were properly made up and signed, Lt. Kenneth Reasonover and his staff began contacting authorities concerned in the various states. They discovered that Sims' story hit the nail right on the head in certain respects while other portions were way off base compared with reported facts.

When Sims' mother first heard of her son's predicament she said, "He'll be dead when he tells the truth. He has never told the truth in his life."

Lt. Reasonover asked Sims if he would verify his statements by polygraphy. The suspect pleaded for the opportunity.

Family members came to visit Sims. They told him of the embarrassment he had brought upon their heads.

The following day, polygraphist Lt. Noble Brymer went through a long interview with the amiable Sims, put attachments on his body, activated the instrument, and then began the question formulation. In part it went thus (condensed) :

Q. Did you lie to detectives about killing the girls in Michigan?

A. No.

Deception criteria appeared.

Q. Did you confess to these killings to get attention?

A. No.

Deception criteria appeared.

Q. Did you kill the girl in Michigan named Dawn?

A. Yes.

Deception criteria appeared.

Q. Do you know who killed the girls in Michigan?

A. Yes.

Deception criteria appeared.

Q. Did you personally kill the cab driver in Oklahoma?

A. Yes.

Deception criteria appeared.

Q. Did you know the letter you wrote your girl friend would be censored by jail officials?

A. No.

Deception criteria appeared.

Brymer deactivated the instrument and began a soft, careful interrogation. It wasn't long before Sims confessed he had lied about killing the Oklahoma cab driver. But he stuck to his story about being responsible for the girls' deaths.

Lt. Reasonover suggested Sims have another visit with his family.

Thirty minutes later detective Tom Cathey resumed the interrogation. "Look, Sims," he patiently said, "we know your entire story is a complete hoax. Marilyn Skelton was dead four days before she was found March 25, which was the same day you were released from the correctional institution at Milan. You couldn't possibly have killed her."

There was a long silence. Furrows of consternation creased Sims' forehead. Detective Cathey pressed a little more. "You further stated you murdered Dawn with your hands, or her blouse, and left her body in a wooded area near some railroad tracks, fully clothed. When she was found, she was clad only in a blouse and from a half mile in one direction up to fifteen miles in another from any railroad tracks. Now, let's cut out the nonsense."

His head dropped. He sighed. "I need help. I don't want to hurt my family any more. My girl friend jilted me. I thought my story would get me extradited back to Michigan. It's just a whole pack of lies."

In spite of himself, polygraphy had cut another notch in the handle for protection of an innocent Ernest Paul Sims.

* * *

During December of 1959, spinster Ethel Little was murdered in Miami, Florida. The case went unsolved for three years.

Then, the Miami Police Department received word from Monroe Spencer, an inmate of the State Penitentiary, that he knew something about the murder, and who did it.

He named Mary Katherin Hampton, his "child-woman," who accompanied him on a transcontinental crime spree in the late 1950's.

So clever was Spencer's story that Mary Kay, who had even born Spencer's son out of wedlock, confessed and was sentenced to double life in St. Gabriel Prison.

On a humid September afternoon, 1962, Warren Holmes, the near legendary polygraphist-criminologist of the South, emerged from a consultation room at the prison. He had just completed a two-hour interrogation of the young woman, concluding with polygraphy.

He had a disturbing announcement for two Louisiana lawmen waiting in an adjoining office. Holmes told them:

"You have an innocent girl in prison."

The two officials nodded sadly. Although they were inclined to agree with Holmes, there was nothing they could do about it.

But Holmes felt a lot could be done about the plight of Mary Kay. He had already devoted much of his time and money to prove what he was certain was the truth at the conclusion of that interview in St. Gabriel Prison.

In his possession was documented evidence, in the form of a traffic ticket and record of cash bond posted in lieu of bail—both still on file in Florida—which showed that both Spencer and Mary Kay were 400 miles from the New Orleans area when the murder in question took place.

These he put in the capable hands of F. Lee Bailey of Boston and his colleague attorney James Russ of Orlando.

Without fee, Bailey went to work for Mary Kay. He was not alone. Among those working closely with him, in addition to Holmes and Russ, were Salvador Anzelmo of New Orleans, and many others in the fields of law and related activities.

Subsequently, the prosecuting attorney presented Bailey with a compromise in the form of a simple four-worded question: "Will you accept commutation?"

Bailey, realizing that refusal of the offer undoubtedly would drag the matter on and on through still more court actions, accepted. At least it meant immediate freedom for the frightened young woman.

Mary Kay agreed. Arrangements went forward for her release. Several days later, thin and drawn, wearing a twenty-dollar mail order suit, Mary Kay's ordeal ended. She bade farewell to Warden Clyde Griffin, who believed in her innocence, then returned to her home in Sandy Hook, Kentucky. Christmas was just around the corner.

* * *

Texas Rangers walked into the offices of polygraphist emeritus, Dee E. Wheeler (now chief examiner with the Fort Worth Crime Lab.) one day with a pretty red-haired teen-aged girl who bragged about writing a string of hot checks.

"She's confessed to thirty-seven forgeries," one of the Rangers said. "We'd like for you to put her on the 'box' and see if we can clear up some others."

Twenty minutes later Wheeler emerged from his examining room.

"Did you get any more?" the Ranger asked.

"No," Wheeler said. "She didn't even forge the ones she's confessed to."

"Hell," the Ranger laughed, "we didn't bring her up here for you to ruin our case."

The girl's father was a constable—a strict disciplinarian. She wanted to strike back at his authority, she said. The teen-ager confessed to a crime because she wanted to shame his name. She was freed against her will.

Another redhead, identified by a handwriting expert, later confessed.*

*   *   *

That any responsible person could seriously question polygraph's reliability or efficacy when such testing is done by a competent examiner is beyond normal comprehension.

Every week in our country there are hundreds of cases in which the polygraphist helps to exonerate innocent person after innocent person, *prior* to the real perpetrator of the crime being found and confessing.

What better way is there to prove that the polygraph technique "works" on both the innocent and the guilty?†

Can psychologists or psychiatrists bring forth proof that even one of their many procedures, techniques or tests is as valid as polygraphy in determining the truth?

While we could indefinitely go on illustrating cases of similarity with the foregoing, starting with the Frye case back in 1923, we wonder if those real life individuals involved also think polygraphy is a "cousin to an Ouija board!"

---

*Ferguson, Robert J. Jr.: *The Scientific Informer.* Thomas, Springfield, 1971, pp. 61-69, 79, 80.

†Arther, Richard O., Polygraph's enemies, *The Journal of Polygraph Studies,* Vol. 1, No. 3, Nov.-Dec. 1966.

PART II

Chapter 6

FUNDAMENTAL CONCEPTS BEHIND EMOTION

Trial transcripts and investigative records officially reveal that nearly all confessions taken from the pathologically innocent have been, for the most part, obtained through (1) lengthy interrogative sessions which have completely confused and exhausted a subject both mentally and physically, (2) interrogative "prayer sessions" involving some type of brutality, for example placing a subject in fear of his life, (3) incomplete or ineffective investigations compounding the foregoing, and (4) subject suffering from undetected guilt complex or mental abnormalities not even connected to the issue in question.

The record speaks for itself when one researches the endless court cases where a pleading of insanity has been made by the defense. For every psychiatrist the state brings in to testify one way, the defendant, if he is wealthy enough, can bring in two other psychiatrists—just as well qualified and outstanding as the state's—to claim the opposite.

Even when fees and/or prestige are not involved, great differences of opinion are evidenced. This has caused considerable concern, as well as investigation, not only in America but also in European countries.

One study of this subject matter showed that in seventy court psychiatric reexaminations there was a difference of "expert" opinion in 54 percent of the cases. Two-thirds of these differences had to do with basic diagnosis and the other one-third had to do with whether or not the accused party was legally responsible for his acts.*

Psychological testing with its subjective evaluations certainly has its place, but at the same time one must carefully consider the

---

*From a talk presented by Dr. Udo Undeutsch, Director of Psychological Institute No. 1, University of Koeln, West Germany, 1965.

limitations. An I.Q. of 100 must not be thought of as "exactly 100," but rather probably between 95 and 105, very probably between 90 and 110, almost certainly between 85 and 115.†

I.Q. tests, even with their limitations, generally are considered to be the best of the paper-and-pencil tests. The important thing about I.Q. tests is that they cannot be "beaten" in the usual sense, since they are measuring intelligence.

However, psychological tests used to determine motivation, job interest, latent tendencies, can so easily be circumvented because applicants, since kindergarten, have become "test-wise" and can generally figure out the correct answers. For example, one of the odd-ball questions included in many governmental, private industrial and police applicant psychological tests (to determine an applicant's manliness) reads: "What would you rather do, go to a football game or read poetry?"

Can any psychological test detect physiological or pathological abnormalities?

Just how long does the average doctor spend examining an applicant for employment? Probably not as long as he would like to. No doubt he would acknowledge that certain medical techniques and procedures, such as an examination by a heart specialist, followed by the EKG, should be utilized but are not.

Modern polygraph instruments would not be used as important psychological and physiological investigators in certain areas of our space-health programs, research clinics, hospitals, law enforcement agencies and private industry if their sensitive recordings were not dependable.

Observation of peculiar patterns of behavior would be of no value to psychologists unless such observation had proven itself valuable in some respects.

Psychiatrists, who are more and more utilizing various types of cardiovascular, respiratory and galvanic skin response instruments, which save time due to their emotional recording capabilities, would not entertain such instrumentation if these instruments were of no value.

---

†Thorndyke, R.L. and Hagen, E.: *Measurement and Evaluation in Psychology and Education.* John Wiley & Sons, New York, 1955, pp. 227-28.

Physiologists and doctors would never have researched with certain types of respiratory recording drums, kymographs, electrocardiographs, kymographic temperature recording instruments, mercury manometers, electrical galvanometer and chemical agents with relation to GSR and nerve conduction, along with cathode, anode, battery in polarization and depolarization, and blood pressure recording devices unless these instruments were sensitive enough to record responsible results.

The same principle is involved in the construction and sensitivity of the polygraph instrument used in preemployment and criminal testing in that some or most of the same types of recordings are obtained.

It seems only common sense that polygraphy cannot be fairly appraised in laboratory experiments unless the laboratory is set up for "live" testing wherein an issue question has some specific "meaning" to the person being tested. If the test means nothing, the necessary emotional factor will not be present.

Every person has an emotional balance and counterbalance of some intensity. We may play games, using word associations, numbers or names all day. Let us have the subject pick a number between one and ten. With number eight as our hypothetical selection we will find that a person will respond very clearly on a chart for perhaps three sessions. From that point on he will react less and less until there will be no response at all. Why? Because, whether or not the examiner detects the correct number on the chart means absolutely nothing.

Obviously, 10,000 controlled tests, where generation of a meaningful emotional aspect is lacking, would produce no conclusiveness of anything.

But now, let the polygraphist and the subject wager $1000 on each game. Instead of permitting the subject to retain his selected number in memory only, he must write it on a piece of paper and put it out of his reach. Suddenly the whole perspective changes. Whether he wins or loses commences to mean something.

A person's body functions at one physiological pace during chart time (2 to a maximum of 4 minutes per chart) whether fast, slow, calm, "nervous," or excited. This pace will henceforth be referred to as "norm." The instrument merely records this norm and any deviations therefrom. The instrument plays no other role and, as long as it is functioning properly, accounts for perhaps only 10 percent of the entire examination. Not withstanding, this 10 percent is vitally important because it facilitates chart interpretation.

A deviation from norm, commonly called a response or reaction, is the result of a verbal stimulus (a question). The question is picked up by the ear and transmitted to certain brain centers for evaluation.

As long as the subject can hear the question and understand its meaning, the question will be involuntarily transmitted to a brain center and evaluated, no matter what thoughts or daydreams the subject tries to conjure up to get away from its meaning.

If a certain brain center interprets the question to mean harm to a person's well-being, providing the question is answered truthfully, a series of nerve impulses is generated. Specifically, the brain has delegated responsibility for protection of the body to the autonomic nervous system and its emergency subdivisions, the sympathetic and parasympathetic. As this emergency system goes into action, a minor to major change from norm is recorded on a moving chart.

When a deviation from norm appears, the polygraphist does not "accuse a person of lying." This would be pure folly. Instead, he probes what thoughts subject associated with the particular question at, during or immediately following the chart response. Generally, the subject knows well what reflections or associations he entertained. If not important or relevant to the issue, there is no valid reason why he should not tell the examiner. If the subject thinks he has a valid reason for not answering the question truthfully or explaining the cause of the response, he also knows this and must make his own decision as to whether or not he will confide in the examiner.

Some reasons why a person's body may produce chart tracing changes immediately following a relevant test question, which have no direct relation to the question, itself, may be listed as follows:

1. Anticipation.

2. Sensitivity to a word in the question, or the inference contained therein.

3. Does not hear the question.

4. Question does not reach subject's level of understanding; confusion as to meaning.

5. Improper question formulation.

6. Improper voice control and enunciation by examiner.

7. Extraneous noise or stimulus.

8. Arm discomfort resulting from lengthy cardio cuff band pressure.

9. Subject movement.

10. Subject suffering from abnormal mental or painful physical conditions.

Strict cognizance and explicit examiner consideration of the primary factors which bear heavily on the successful test conclusion must be maintained thus:

1. Adequate examination facilities.

2. Privacy must be assured.
   a. Proper lighting; dimness frightens and oppresses.
   b. Walls must be of a color not psychologically disturbing, and free of eyesight distractions.

3. Instrument must be in proper working order according to manufacturer's specifications; attachments spotlessly clean.

4. Establishment of proper rapport between examiner and subject.

5. Reaching subject's level of understanding.
   a. Terminology important.
   b. Communion is the primary ingredient.

6. Understanding purpose of the test by both subject and examiner.

7. Permitting subject to tell his side of the story.

8. Proper explanation of the instrument's role.

9. Question formulation.
   a. All relevant questions must be short, to the point, and readily understood.
   b. Irrelevant questions should not be capable of response producing potentials due to individual interpretation.

10. Subject's past associations, economic and educational status,

employment background; his sensitivity toward right and wrong.
    11. Subject's physical and mental capabilities.
    12. Subject's personality projection.
        a. Security manifestations.
        b. Insecurity manifestations.
        c. Observation of physical manifestations.
    13. Chart interpretation.
        a. Differentiating between responses which do or do not contain deception criteria.
        b. Explanation and discussion with subject of responses which his body has produced.
    14. Guilt complex potentials; collusion potentials.
    15. Subsequent consequences facing the guilty subject.
    16. Examiner techniques and approaches.
    17. Physical condition and mental attitude of examiner.

Through an understanding and pretest evaluation of the ingredients contained in the emotions called fear, rage, repugnancy, anger, jealousy and sympathy, the examiner must psychologically "control" the subject in order that the testee becomes suitable to be fairly, impartially and objectively polygraphed.

One cannot hold an emotion while he examines it. He can sometimes retrospect and describe what it was like, but even then his description is a poor representation of the "real thing." Kindness attracts. Rudeness and indifference rejects; compassion and understanding are the first keys to success.

In order to open the psychological doors to ultimate communion, the following emotional aspects must be a part of examiner-awareness:
    1. Attention.
    2. Organic sensation.
    3. Perception.
    4. Memory.
    5. Forgetting.
    6. Emotion, itself.

ATTENTION

When a subject enters the examining room he does so with an exterior presentation of his "norm" of the moment.

If we examine our consciousness at any moment we find that a part of its content stands out in bold relief from the rest—that we are mentally occupied with some one presentation of the senses, or engaged in the elaboration of some thought or idea, at the expense of other possible presentations or ideas. In other words, we find that some part of the content is clearer and more definitely in consciousness than the rest of it. We further observe that there is a constant shifting of the elements of the total content. Now one, and now the other part of the content becomes clear and definite and then fades to give place to its successor. We also find that at any one time, although there are a number of different objects collected by the senses or different ideas that might be entertained in the mind, it is always one of them, or a single group of them, that occupies the center of the stage. Another fact we notice is that the changes in the content take place in a definite order, either in accord with some inner plan of action, or thinking, or in conformity to the order of presentation of outer objects.

We also notice that these changes in the nature of consciousness are accompanied by nerve impulses to movements in the various parts of the organism, especially in the muscles of accommodation of the sense-organs. The eyes are adjusted in seeing; they may be narrowed or wide open; pupils may be contracted or dilated. The head is positioned for hearing, to one side, lowered, held back, turned away. Observation of the thoracic and abdominal respiration may evidence a fast or slow rhythm in either one or both areas. These movements serve to make the stimulus in each case more affective. Facial expressions and bodily attitudes conform to changes of thought. The wrinkled brow and constrained attitude are usually present in deep thought, apprehension, skepticism or consternation. The smile and the frown correspond to definite qualities of consciousness. Changes in heart action and respiration parallel the changes in mental activity.

Attention is not a power—it is an act, a process or function. It is an aspect of perception. From this angle it may be defined as an anticipatory perceptual adjustment or as a readiness to perceive. It is a common and constant function of all efficient consciousness, fully and effectively active.

ORGANIC SENSATIONS

Occasionally, during a polygraph examination interview, a subject will complain of thirst, hunger, nausea, fullness, tension, abdominal and urinal pressures, stuffiness and even suffocation.

When these expressions are made, or when there is activity on the part of the subject, such as constantly licking his lips, cracking his knuckles, gasping for breath, crossing and uncrossing his legs, wringing his hands, repeated swallowing or belching, we are presented with vital clues suggesting that one or more organic sensations are taking place within the subject's body.

The organic sensations include a mass of undifferentiated and vague sensory experiences that are located in and about the vital organs. From the visceral or abdominal region come dull internal pains of varying intensities. From the upper part of the alimentary canal we get more definite experiences. Hunger is located in the stomach as a dull, gnawing pain or ache. Thirst is felt quite definitely in the back part of the mouth, accompanied by a dryness of the lips. Nausea is felt in the esophagus and stomach and is difficult to analyze into its constituent elements of sensation. In the thoracic region we sometimes experience a sense of want of air due to the physiological conditions of the lungs when shut off from an adequate air supply. The sensations coming from the acts of respiration arise from the intercostal muscles and diaphragm and should be classed among the kinesthetic sensations.

While ordinarily we do not sense the condition of the heart, in fright, anger and other emotions, sensations arise in the cardiac region. In fright there is a sinking sensation, caused suddenly by a change in the heart's action. In anger there appears a vague rhythmic tension about the heart. The heart "jumping up" in the mouth probably comes from the sensations of muscular contraction in the pharynx.

The muscles, tendons and articular surfaces are supplied with sensory nerve endings which give, when stimulated, sensations of movement. The stimuli which excite these nerve endings are the contractions and relaxation of the muscles, the pull and tension of the tendons, and the gliding of the tendons over the joints. Herein we are not specifically speaking of the exterior but, rather, emotional nerve impulses which bring about the inner physiological aspect and develop that into observable outward manifestations.

A set of rather obscure and unobstrusive sensations arises in the vestibule and semicircular canals of the ear. With slight stimulation of these organs, it requires very careful introspection to detect their presence. They appear as swimming sensations in the head, dizziness, sensations coming from the position and sudden change of movement of the head or the body as a whole. Naturally, the examiner cannot see these, but often times he will "sense" their presence. Quite frequently the subject will verbally confirm their existence.

Another organic sensation projection the examiner is constantly alerted to is the possibility that subject might be experiencing a feeling of undue warmth or cold. While pathological disturbances may be the cause, a similar feeling of the same type of organic sensation may be the result of aroused emotional disturbances, such as fear, shame, anger, guilt.

PERCEPTION

While sensation is the consciousness of the qualities of objects, perception, on the other hand, is the consciousness of objects, the result of the presentation of a group of physical qualities to the senses. For instance, we do not say that we have the sensation of a murder weapon, but rather that we perceive it. We may consider sensation as the awareness of the qualities of an object, while perception is the consciousness of the qualities of an object synthesized into an object. In sensation what we experience is determined by the stimulus. On the other hand, in perception we supplement and interpret the presented stimuli by past experience, e.g. prior to association, or handling of a murder weapon. However, if an object which is entirely unlike anything we have known is presented to us, it will be experienced as a mass of sensation, having no significance for us—a bare sensory consciousness. Such a state of consciousness rarely occurs, however, for it is difficult to find an object wholly unique and not in some way related to past experience. The sensory material which enters into perception is, we say, assimulated by past experiences.

We find in perception the beginning of imagination, judgment (recognition in a primitive form of judgment), and the concept (presence of meaning).

In normal perception, the "revived sensations" are in keeping with the actual sensations received and true to the sensible qualities of the object. "Recognition" is a primitive form of judgment. In its developed form the consciousness of relationship is explicityly experienced. In perception, recognition is implicit. When a familiar object is brought to our notice, or attention, we experience the relationship of the object "now" sensibly present to the same object or similar objects as experienced in the past. A pure sensation has no meaning and suggests nothing beyond itself. Perception arouses further knowledge.

Every object is presented to us with a background attaching to it. The background is the object's history, its associates, its functions. The object when presented points out, signifies, suggests this background to us—in short, has meaning to us. An object was a thing to be reacted to in a certain way—a bottle meant to put-in-mouth, ball meant to roll, knife meant to cut or stab.

The sensible presentation of the object, if it awakens a maximum of meaning, may function as a "concept." If the emphasis in consciousness is placed on the meaning rather than on the sensible qualities of an object, the perception is conceptual in its nature.

We may note in passing that perception of objects is most complete in just those features which call out our practical reactions. The objects that we have handled, touched and worked with produce in us the clearest perceptions. In turn, they create mental associations which develop the stimulus which frequently results in projections of discernible or visible manifestations.

MEMORY

The physiological basis of mental images rests (1) in the retention of the modifications made upon the brain by previous experience, and (2) in the recurrence of the same or similar nerve processes in the brain centers. The activity of the sense organs, however, is not present. We may suppose that the neural process of perception produces some modification of the nervous substance in the brain, and that the retention of this modification is the condition for the representation of previous experience.

Perceptions are externally aroused. Images are aroused by inner brain processes. Though this is reasonably true, such is not a difference in the nature of the experiences themselves. However, image does differ from perception psychologically. Careful observation reveals that images are less vivid, less distinct, less stable, and less coercive. They are less detailed and more fragmentary than perceptions. Nor do they hold or command attention or move to action as perceptions do.

Memory is the retention, recall and recognition of past experiences. It is reproductive imagination plus recognition. Before we can have knowledge of an event or fact, it must be retained and recalled. We must think of retention in terms of brain modifications. It is not the mind but the nervous system that retains our experiences. The normal brain has thousands of modifications wrought upon its tissue, and these modifications determine the nature of its activity. They represent the past experiences of the individual.

The passage of a particular sensory impulse through a brain center leaves the center capable of and liable to react in the same way again, even when the external stimulus is not present. When this inner neural activity takes place again we have the phenomenon of "recall." Whenever a particular event or object is recalled, observation will show that we are reminded of the event or object by some thought or presentation already in consciousness. We recall past events by means of their associates. Any thought, percept or image already in the mind tends to arouse the experiences which have been associated with it, because our experiences are chained together by association. Given any single link in the chain, we are able, in reproductive consciousness, to repass to the other links by virtue of these associative connections.

We may suppose that if the neural activity in a given brain center is followed or accompanied by the stimulation of another center, the pathway between the centers is opened and there is a passage of nervous energy over this pathway. Then, according to the law of neural habit (that nervous impulses tend to follow the pathways that they have made on former occasions), we are able to get a general idea of what happens in the brain when, for example, a murder weapon revives an image of the murder scene, the act of violence and the deceased.

In psychological terms we may say that the process of recall follows the law of habit—that in any series of revived experiences each is followed by one of its former associates, and any part of a system of thought tends to reinstate other parts of it. But since a single mental experience may have had a number of different associates, what determines which one will be recalled? Evidently, a given mental state will recall the associate that is most closely connected with it or, to return to neural terms, recall will follow the most permeable pathways.

The permeability of neural pathways, or the closeness of association between mental states, is determined by any one or several of the following factors: (1) recency, (2) frequency, (3) vividness of associated experiences, (4) dominant system of thought or the conscious context at the time of recall, and (5) the plan or purpose present in the mind. Varied or painful experiences can continually appear and reappear for days. However, some cases of recall seem to depend upon the strength and vividness of the original impression, rather than upon associative connections.

The final stage of memory is "recognition." The chief subjective mark of recognition is the feeling of familiarity. Whenever we remember an event or object there comes with the sensory content of the event or object the added feeling—content of familiarity. The feeling of familiarity is a subjective sign of the degree of certainty of recognition. The feeling of familiarity is not, however, absolutely truthworthy. It may accompany a false memory act. It often happens that a witness or suspect gives in perfectly good faith erroneous descriptions of events, perhaps through guilt complex, which have in some way acquired a feeling of familiarity, in turn making the event real for him.

Recognition may be immediate or mediate. Immediate recognition takes place without further recall. The experience recalled is recognized on its own account. On the other hand, mediate recognition does not take place until the associates of the recalled experience are also recalled and made to serve as a guarantee for it.

FORGETTING

Attention is never evenly divided over the field of our experience. It is concerned with certain portions, while it neglects or slights others. The portions which lie outside the focus of attention impress us less deeply and are therefore more easily lost. Consequently, forgetting is as normal a function of consciousness as remembering. The factors which lead to such lapses of memory are very numerous and refuse to be placed under any one principle. It is generally and popularly believed that disagreeable and painful experiences are not forgotten. This, however, is not entirely true. There is a marked tendency to strive to forget the disagreeable. Special cases of forgetting, sometimes amounting to complete loss of memory, accompany certain changes and abnormal conditions of the organism.

An interesting lapse of memory takes place after an accident in which we lose consciousness. On recovery we find that we are unable to recall the events which led up to the accident. A blow on the head may, in extreme cases, cause us to forget all our past experiences, creating a form of partial amnesia.

The polygraph technique presents itself as an excellent detector of faked amnesia.

In psychologically evaluating any subject during an interview we must also consider the possibility of paramnesia, a defect in recognition. In some cases a purely imaginative scene or event may be accompanied by a false recognition, making it appear to the subject as a real occurrence. In more normal individuals a pure fabrication may, after being repeated many times, acquire a false recognition, so that such individuals come in time to believe their own ideas. Illusions of memory may also be brought about by suggestions.

If there is the presence of undue fatigue, or if the subject has been overstimulated by intense or lengthy interrogation, the normal associative connections are weakened by the intensity of the inquisition. Under such conditions a highly nervous, mentally unstable subject becomes prey to suggestion and may be made really to feel that he saw or took part in events entirely foreign to him. He may in this way be induced to give false testimony. If questions have suggestions in them, the force of the suggestions may modify the actual connections made in the subject's mind so that he is unable to give a correct report of what happened. In certain cases, questions which presuppose a certain answer—leading questions—or questions which demand the answer which they suggest will actually set up associative connections in the mind causing a subject to give false testimony.

Specific investigative approaches must be initiated to evaluate the differences in thought content and thought processes as conditioned by sex, age, background; to ascertain the possibility of motive; to determine the effect of fatigue, drugs on subject's associative recall; to diagnose abnormal mental disturbances and to detect hidden mental tendencies and wishes or intentionally withheld information pertaining to the issue.

In polygraph interviewing and during actual chart time, the examiner will not only study the character of the association but will also consider the time required to recall an association word or situation. When a stimulus word is pronounced, it requires a certain length of time before the subject can think of an association. If we measure the time between the giving of the stimulus and the response, we shall find that the association time varies. Under certain conditions there is a marked lengthening of time. If the stimulus word or object arouses an emotional complex, or if the subject does not give the first association for fear of "giving himself away" and hunts for another association, the association time is lengthened.

EMOTION

Cannot we say with a reasonable amount of accuracy that emotion is the originator of motivation? In the same breath, we must caution the fallacy of attempting to read more into the emotion than is actually there. Emotion has several ingredient factors developing in early childhood, such as anger, smiling and laughter, happiness, affection, jealousy, sympathy, facial expression, postural reactions, vocal expressions, which create the foundation for emotional countenance in the adult. We must also caution that bodily organic sensations might well form an important or necessary part in emotion and yet not be the emotion.

The widely accepted belief is that the primary central excitation reaching the brain from external objects or events is the basis of emotion. But we must go further to say that the perception of an emotional object or event and the ideational processes which are awakened by the perception as well as the mass of organic sensations aroused by the bodily reflexes enter into the emotional complex. In addition, the various affective accompaniments of cognitive factors also help to determine the character of the emotion. All these components form a synthetic unity, which we call emotion.

If we consider a list of the most important instincts we shall find that they all manifest an emotional aspect. For instance, fear is both an instinct and an emotion—an instinct in so far as it is a tendency leading to native forms of motor reactions, such as flight, crouching or hiding—an emotion in so far as it is a feeling. Pugnacity and anger, curiosity and wonder, parental instinct and tender emotion are other pairs of terms. The instincts which are strongly marked by an emotional counterpart, like those of anger and fear, manifest in addition to their outward acts motor reactions which affect the inner organic processes. If we ask why certain instinctive impulses are thrown back into organic channels instead of into the more evident environmental adjusting mechanism of the body, we may find an answer in certain biological theories.

Why, for instance, does the mouth become dry and the skin moist with perspiration in fear. Why do we tremble when confronted with a fearful object? Accordingly, all emotional reactions which are not now plainly useful are looked upon as organic survivals of acts that were once useful and adaptive reactions in racial development. Fear, when strong, expresses itself in cries, efforts to escape, in palpitations, in tremblings; and these are just the manifestations that go along with an actual suffering of the evil feared. The destructive passion is shown in a general tension of the muscular system, in gnashing of teeth, dilated eyes, a flare at the nostrils and in throaty mutterings.

The essential condition for emotion, however, is that conflicting motor tendencies are aroused and that these tendencies are initiated by the appearance of conscious states which suddenly block conscious activity and interrupt the continuity of our plans and purposes.

Emotions may be classified upon the basis of their predominant and primary effective states as pleasant and unpleasant; or according to the intensity of these affective states as weak or strong; or according to the character of their bodily reactions as sthenic or asthenic; or according to the forms of their occurrence as slowly rising or suddenly arising; or according to the external situations which occasion them as food emotions, sex emotions; as egoistic or nonegoistic; as sensuous or intellectual; as subjective or objective, and many more.

The methods by which individuals cope with emotional conflict at the psychological level are usually referred to as mechanisms of defense. The general purpose of defense is to ameliorate an unsatisfactory psychological condition. In any attempt to understand an individual's behavior we must be aware of these mechanisms of defense since all behavior represents an attempted integration or resultant of many drives operating at the same time. The ego tries to produce integrated and satisfying behavior by synthesizing, compromising, delaying, displacing, or repressing these tendencies. The learned mechanisms of defense come into operation in this process. Behavior is always the resultant of two or more competing drives, and some amount of psychic energy is expended in the struggle between competing motives and in their resolution (to confess or not to confess). The individual develops anxiety because of internal or external factors which interfere with the expression of the drives, or, in other words, because there is a conflict. Anxiety then is the signal of the conflict, and the emotional drive seeking expression can only find discharge by way of some defense. Unless the defense is entirely successful, however, there is an insufficient discharge, and a repetitive cycle begins to be established until the conflict is entirely resolved or until some symptom stabilizes, for a time, the tension state.

In an interview the examiner must approach the major defenses set up by the subject somewhat separately, but it must be remembered that the individual usually uses two or more defenses in combination. These defenses may be condensed into singles of repression, denial, isolation, undoing, introjection, reaction formation, projection, regression and sublimation.

Emotion may further be described as a mental state or strong feeling affect usually accompanied by physical changes in the body such as alteration in heart rate and respiratory activity, vasomotor reactions, and changes in muscle tone, e.g. a mental state or feeling. These constitute the "drive" which brings about the motor adjustment necessary to satisfy instinctive needs. Frustration is normally associated with displeasure and intensifying of need; the process of gratification is accompanied by a pleasurable feeling tone which persists for a variable period in less intense form. Somatic (e.g. postural) changes precede and immediately follow the emotion; at least the two are inseparable and the recognition of "affect" (apart from one's subjection sense) is dependent upon the presence of its appropriate physical correlates.

SOME NORMAL AND ABNORMAL EVALUATIONS

Whether the test is of a criminal, problem, or preemployment nature, the polygraphist must give serious evaluation to personality projections of the person who has volunteered for truth verification. In most instances the subject can readily be classified into normal or near-normal groups.

If the case is of a criminal nature, initial groundwork for the examiner's evaluation and assistance will be presented in the form of findings by field investigators.

When the case is preemployment only, the examiner is presented with an identifying employment application (at least sometimes), which if not completely falsified offers some guide-lines.

Otherwise, he has very little to go on. In view of this, the poly-graphist in preemployment testing utilizes a "data sheet" ques-tionaire to get a deeper insight into the mental, physical and job qualification potentials of the applicant. He then uses the poly-graph instrument for confirmation or verification of answers given by the subject to data sheet questions during the interview.

In criminal testing the examiner's major concern is not actual-ly an evaluation per se of subject's guilt or innocence, for the sub-ject will reveal this in spite of himself. The primary concern is the proper type of approach which bares subject's defenses and results in his confession of the truth.

In preemployment testing the examiner's main concern is not necessarily discovering the falsity in an application's contents but, rather, in factually establishing the degree of falsity, if it exists, and determining whether or not it is relevant to employment.

Both applications of polygraphy require careful consideration and psychological evaluation of the type of subject being tested. The main questions are, therefore, (1) is he in the normal or near-normal group; (2) is he in the psychoneurotic or psychotic groups; (3) what are his emotional behavior projections?

If one is normal, one's life functions and experiences are sub-ject to some of the faults, failings and abnormalities that charac-terize the existence of specific human beings at a particular time in world history, in a definite culture to which the individuals belong in accordance with age, sex, social status, attainments and so forth. Thus, there is no single psychology which holds for all mankind. What is normal oftentimes depends upon the observer who evaluates it.

The normal individual functions chiefly on a rational emo-tional basis. That is why emotional factors and disturbances are significant. The emotional influences in infancy and childhood are especially important. These influences help, hinder, or warp the development of emotional patterns of behavior which persist in later life. The individual tries to harmonize the conflicting im-pulses within himself to the demands of the environment; this is adjustment. In general, the more mature the individual is, the more flexibly he adjusts. Maladjustment causes a return to previous childhood forms of satisfaction, feeling, thinking and behavior. These reactions constitute and produce symptoms which can be grouped or classified as neurotic, psychosomatic, antisocial, criminal. The ego reacts secondarily to those symptoms and tensions, denying or utilizing them to the individual's purposes.

Characteristics manifested by the "normal" person, generally may be listed thus:

1. He reveals relative freedom of symptoms of immature and neurotic attitudes. He discloses no serious preoccupations, hypochondriasis, or undue fantasy or indecision.

2. He expresses adequate personality functions, physically, mentally, emotionally and morally. He is useful to himself and society, and capable of learning to be more useful. He shows proper rapport and good interpersonal relationships. He has healthy desires, abilities and attitudes, including sexual adequacy. He is neither frigid nor fearful of emotions. He is able to find happiness in living and working. He is capable of withstanding difficulties; he has a considerable tolerance or capacity for enduring frustration, tension or anxiety.

3. He fits satisfactorily into personal and social situations; he does so in accordance with his intelligence, abilities and resources, training, special skills and opportunities. He enjoys work, has no undue fatigue, and he maintains efficiency.

4. He accepts and reciprocates affection without guilt feelings, hostility or loss of self-esteem.

5. There is adequate personal and group emancipation; he can emancipate himself from his parent, as a manifestation of maturity. He can exhibit desires conflicting with group demands, but he can make up his own mind, show a tolerance for cultural differences, and he does not need an excess of reassurance or flattery.

6. Life goals are well directed; they are realistic, achievable and pro-social rather than egocentric.

In every normal or near-normal group we find other characteristics revealed in part or in whole. We shall divide these into categories of "insecurity" and "security." Further, it should be noted that each category overlaps the other, and that every item is a cause and effect of every other single item. In a word, this is a syndrome.

Insecurity Manifestations

1. Feeling of rejection, of being unloved, of being treated coldly and without affection, of being hated or despised.

2. Feelings of isolation, ostracism, aloneness or being left out of it; feelings of being "unique."

3. Perception of the world and life as dangerous, threatening, dark, hostile or challenging; as a jungle in which every man's hand is against every other's, in which one eats or is eaten.

4. Perception of other human beings as essentially bad, evil or selfish, as dangerous, threatening, hostile or challenging.

5. Constant feelings of threat, danger, and anxiety.

6. Feelings of suspicion and mistrust, of envy or jealousy toward others; much hostility, prejudices.

7. Tendency to expect the worst, general pessimism.

8. Tendency to be unhappy or discontented.

9. Feelings of tension and strain and conflict; together with various consequences of tension, e.g. nervousness, fatigue, irritability, nervous stomach and other psychosomatic disturbances, nightmares, emotional instability, vacillation, uncertainty and inconsistency.

10. Tendency to compulsive introspectiveness, morbid self-examination, suicidal tendencies, discouragement.

11. Guilt and shame feelings, sin feelings, feelings of self-condemnation, discouragement.

12. Disturbances of various aspects of self-esteem complex, e.g. craving for power and for status, compulsive ambition; over-aggression, hunger for money, prestige, glory, possessiveness, jealousy of jurisdiction and prerogative, overcompetitiveness and/or the opposite; masochistic tendencies, overdependence, compulsive submissiveness, ingratiation, inferiority feelings, feelings of weakness and helplessness.

13. Continual striving for, and hunger for, safety and security, various neurotic trends, inhibitions, defensiveness, escape trends,

ameliorative trends, false goals, fixations on partial goals. Psychotic tendencies, delusions, hallucinations.

14. Selfish, egocentric, individualistic trends.

Security Manifestations

1. Feeling of being liked or loved, of acceptance, of being looked upon with warmth.

2. Feelings of belonging, of being at home in the world, of having a place in the group.

3. Perception of the world and life as friendly, warm, pleasant, benevolent, in which all men tend to be brothers.

4. Perception of other human beings as essentially good, pleasant, warm, friendly or benevolent.

5. Feeling of safety, rare feelings of threat and danger, unanxious.

6. Feelings of friendliness and trust in others, little hostility, tolerance of others, easy affection for others.

7. Tendency to expect good to happen; general optimism.

8. Tendency to be happy or contented.

9. Feelings of calm, ease, and relaxation. Unconflicted. Emotional stability.

10. Tendency to be outgoing.

11. Self-acceptance, tolerance of self. Acceptance of the impulses.

12. Desire for strength, or adequacy with respect to problems rather than for power over people. Firm, positive, well-based self-esteem. Feeling of strength, courage.

13. Relative lack of neurotic or psychotic tendencies.

14. "Social interest," cooperativeness, kindliness, interest in others, sympathy.

While any classification is arbitrary, if the polygraphist has a good understanding of the fundamentals outlined herein he will find it easier to sense, then handle, certain singular or multiple symptoms as they arise during the pretest interview.

Briefly, let us interject a connecting factor called "motivation," which is very complicated, and touch upon one or two of its basic aspects.

Motivation is divided into two basic areas, biological and social. The greatest of all drives is breathing. Everything else is secondary. Next comes water, sleep, food, shelter, and so on. These are the biological drives which must be satisfied or the organism soon dies. For example, the biological drive for food can and has made a person steal.

Second in importance are the social drives, such as wanting to be liked or loved, to be wanted. These drives can become so strong at times, such as a motive which encompasses religion, that they will prevent a subject from stealing food, though he may starve. Very few crimes are committed just to meet biological drives. In contrast, social motives are never satisfied.

Everything that is learned is because there is a motive and a reward. When a person is engaged in a crime, there is a motive. He commits the crime as a means of receiving a reward. Therefore, the motive or reason usually makes sense to him. If we know why a person does something, whether or not it makes any sense to us, then we have better control in handling that person and "reaching" him.

Gough* studied some common misconceptions regarding neuroticism. He isolated seven clusters of belief popularly thought to be characteristic of neurotic individuals: (1) numerous physical complaints, (2) feelings of victimization and misunderstanding, (3) exaggerated irritability, tenseness, fear, and anxiety, (4) lack of independence and self-sufficiency, (5) dissatisfaction with family background and childhood, (6) sexual conflicts and preoccupations, and (7) bizarre, eccentric ideas.

Thus far we have carefully avoided the implication that each emotion has a set, stereotyped behavior pattern. The reason is that variations in emotion, even within a particular culture, are often more obvious than uniform expressions. Even under the same external circumstances, emotional behavior differs considerably from one person to another, depending on how one perceives or interprets the situation.

For example, it is much easier to differentiate expressions of

---

*Gough, H.G.: Some common misconceptions about neuroticism. *J. Consult. Psychol., 18:*287-292, 1954.

pleasant and unpleasant emotions than it is to differentiate expressions of specific emotions, say, joy vs. love, or sorrow vs. fear. It is obvious, however, that when people almost universally judge an expression to be a certain emotion, they are differentiating that expression from expressions of other emotions. If they can do this, moreover, the different emotions must have distinctive expressions.

The chief difficulty with attempts to discern the inborn, universal expressions of emotion is that of disentangling these from acquired expressions. One drawback in all research in this field is that only a few emotions can be aroused under laboratory conditions where techniques for analyzing them are alone available. These are emotions like fear, anger, disgust, and humor. Even the fact that these are aroused in the laboratory rather than under more natural conditions (refers back to the fact that polygraph research must be made on "live" subjects to be conclusive) perhaps makes their expressions less spontaneous than one would desire.* The general conclusion is that neither a given situation nor a given emotional experience brings out a uniform pattern of expression.

Certain emotions tend to arouse different general postures, although there are great differences in reaction of one individual to another. Fear often involves either flight or "being rooted to the spot." Violent anger often involves not flight but aggressive movements, either abusive or involving actual attack. Love usually involves movement in the direction of the loved one and, where tactual stimulation is involved, movements conducive to continuation of the stimulus. Sorrow is often associated with a general slumping posture. Movements of the hands, as in clenching the fists and gesticulating are often quite expressive emotionally.

PSYCHOPHYSIOLOGICAL RESEARCH CONCOMITANTS

Much of psychological research on emotion has been focused upon such physiological concomitants as respiration, blood pressure, pulse rate, limb volume, sweat gland activity, gastrointestinal

---

*Munn, Norman L.: *Psychology*, 2nd ed. Houghton Mifflin, Boston, 1951, pp. 342-43.

functions, metabolic rate, and chemical changes in the blood. This prior direction of research may be said to have two aims: (1) to discover how various physiological processes change during emotion, and (2) to discover whether there are different patterns of physiological change underlying specified emotions.

Most studies of the physiological concomitants of emotion record several physiological changes simultaneously (as does the present day polygraph instrument). Activity of the heart in emotion is often studied by examining the shape of the curve obtained with an electrocardiograph. This instrument makes records of the electrical activity of all aspects of the heart beat. In the research on emotion, the analysis of electrocardiograms indicates changes in heart action and duration of such changes. Harvard University, Department of Social Relations, has made lengthy and extensive studies of physiological responses due to emotional stimulus with polygraph instruments. These particular instruments usually record through their electroencephalogram, pneumography, psychogalvanometer, sphygmomanometer, and plethysmograph components.

Modern polygraph instruments are equipped with the same recording components for general criminal and private industrial examination, excepting the electroencephalograph unit attached to the scalp.

Galvanic skin response has been studied by some psychologists who used a psychogalvanometer. This instrument (the galvanometer is an integral part of the polygraph) measures or records changes in electrical resistance in the skin electrodermal areas. The polygraph examiner commonly refers to these changes as activity of the sweat glands. At one time psychologists thought galvanic skin response, GSR, was specific to emotion, that is, present only when emotion was aroused.

It has been clearly established, however, that the response also occurs in manual and mental work. However, GSR is also present in emotional upset, and may even provide a rough measure of the degree of upset.*

*Lund, F.H.: *Emotions.* Ronald, New York, 1939, pp. 195-198; Woodworth, R.S.: *Experimental Psychol.,* Holt, New York, 1938, pp. 291-292; Munn, N.L.: Psychology, 2nd ed. Houghton Mifflin, Boston, 1951, p. 348.

In the past, galvanometers involved the principle of the wheatstone bridge. They still do with certain modifications. The subject is placed in one circuit, the potential of which may be balanced with that of a fixed circuit. The two circuits are connected through a galvanometer. When they balance, the galvanometer reading is zero. If the subject's skin resistance changes, however, the potentials are thrown out of balance and a deflection of the galvanometer results. Changes in the galvanometer following emotional stimulation are due to a lowering of electrical resistance between the two electrodes which are attached to the skin. This lowering of electrical resistance is itself due to the fact that beads of sweat oozing out of the skin facilitate conduction of the minute current. GSR may be studied in terms of its latency (how long a period elapses before the change occurs), its amplitude (degree of change from zero), its duration (the time which elapses between onset of the response and the return to normal), or some derivative of such indices.

Psychologists, following laboratory experiments, have asked themselves: Is is possible by studying such changes to tell whether or not the individual has been emotionally aroused, and can we tell anything about the intensity of emotional arousal?

It is necessary to add a note of caution. In studies of physiological expressions, the investigator knows that an emotion-provoking stimulus has been presented, hence he can correlate physiological changes with such stimulation, and with emotion as reported by the subject. Under such circumstances someone else who knows that the subject has been emotionally aroused may, from the physiological record alone, be able to tell at what point the subject became emotionally aroused. However, physical and mental work often produce physiological changes like those associated with emotion. Thus, if one saw a record of respiratory, circulatory and electrodermal changes without knowing whether work or emotion was involved, the chances are that he would be unable to deduce which had produced the changes— work or emotion. For example, those stimuli which the individual rates as pleasant or unpleasant tend to arouse a more marked galvanic reaction than those rated as neutral in affective value. A high intensity of emotion (as reported by subject) is also usually associated with a more marked galvanometer deflection than is a weak intensity of emotion*

*Munn, N. L.: *Psychology,* 2nd ed. Houghton Mifflin, Boston, 1951, pp. 349-50.

Dr. Munn suggests two problems in this respect, the first of which is to discover whether the direction and degree of change in a particular physiological process or aspect of a physiological process is different for different emotions. In other words, does respiration differ in, let us say, fear and anxiety? The second question poses a more difficult problem, that of discovering whether the great variety of physiological changes associated with a particular emotion fall into a given pattern which may be differentiated from the pattern of some other emotion.

Dr. Munn answers:

> The answer to the first question is that little success has been achieved in differentiating emotions in terms of changes in a particular physiological variable. Most of the results are negative. The answer to the second question is that a large amount of research on this problem has disclosed no distinct pattern of physiological changes which would enable us to differentiate one emotion from another.

We wholeheartedly agree with this brilliant scholar, as far as he goes. It is true that, from a psychological laboratory experiment viewpoint, emotional reactions cannot be specifically differentiated by use of any physiological recording instrument, particularly a galvanometer. Unfortunately this belief is still part of many psychological approaches to the accuracy of the so-called lie detector although, admittedly, these investigators acknowledge that the instrument does not detect a lie, per se.

Let us pull out the fallacies with respect to polygraph examination on "live subjects."

First and foremost, it must be emphatically stated that the polygraph examiner is not concerned with attempting to differentiate one emotion from another. He is only concerned that a verbal stimulus did provoke an emotion which produced sufficient nerve impulse intensity to create a deviation from norm on the chart. Then he searches for what caused the deviation.

Polygraph galvanometer recordings are generally considered the most inconclusive because deflection may be caused by subject's mental and manual work, aside from emotion. Manual work is referred to as subject movement, voluntary or involuntary.

There are times, however, when galvanometer recordings provide the only key to deception.

In a subsequent chapter we shall detail how "work" is readily discernible by the type of tracing produced. General irrelevant mental activity is countered through the process of elimination via question formulation.

Psychology, then, may briefly be described as the study of human behavior. By behavior we mean what a person says and does.

In polygraph examination one must be extremely conscious of the wording of a question as it is asked, that is, the use of words and what they may mean to a subject, in order that the particular question does not condition the answer.

Compounded, double meaning and interpretative questions are what we are speaking of. The stimulus which provokes the emotional reaction is the question itself and what said question means to the person who hears or receives it.

Chapter 7

PHYSIOLOGICAL CORRELATES
OF AUTONOMIC ACTION

P OLYGRAPHY IS NOT CONCERNED with stereotyping emotions into specific categories. No polygraph test will ever say that a graphically recorded response belongs only to the emotion called anger, rage, embarrassment, or otherwise.

While psychological researchers have made tremendous strides forward in the past fifty years in their exploration of emotion-producing causes, acknowledging the neural mechanisms in emotion, much of their research has centered around bodily movements of a more muscular or reflex nature, following a stimulus. As a result, only the skin senses and the peripheral nervous system, along with hardly more than a diagrammed reference to the autonomic nervous system, have received primary attention.

In their attempts to ascertain whether or not there are different patterns of physiological change underlying specified emotions they have apparently overlooked one important factor—what the stimulus, under the circumstances at hand, means to the subject receiving it.

Quite simply, if we provoke a normal person sufficiently he will become angry. If we frighten him enough he may become fearful. If we humiliate or embarrass him to the extreme he will generate some degree of hate toward his antagonist. If we physically hurt him enough he may feel intense pain and even cry, and if we tickle him he may laugh.

However, if the person being subjected to the foregoing is bombarded by all four stimulants within one experimental session he can be intimidated to produce an emotional manifestation of anger from being tickled. In such instances the value of the experiment is voided. If we have a controlled experiment to generate fear, the fact that the recipient knows it is controlled will frequently result in a "self-conditioning" of sorts to counteract the unexpected when it does come. Even the element of surprise is somewhat curtailed.

It would seem, therefore, that controlled experiments seeking to differentiate emotions should be placed in the unconditioned group category or conducted on "live" subjects where the stimulus used to provoke an emotional reaction really means something. In other words, it must not be anticipated. Only in this manner can reasonably accurate statistical percentages be compiled.

During polygraphy, the primary emotion-provoking factor which perhaps 95 percent of all subjects experience, and verbally confirm, is "fear," three-dimensional. The degree of fear may vary according to the brain centers digesting the stimulus.

There is fear that falsification of something material on one's employment application may be discovered during the test. Another is fear that the test may reveal a previous phony back injury claim (suit), and perhaps a sizeable out-of-court settlement. More common is the attempt to cover up existing physical disabilities because the subject "really needs the job."

In problem testing we see the fear of being caught with its potential consequences predominating. The most misconceived fear is that of invasion of personal or intimate privacy.

Secondly, we see fear, through mental association, pulling similarities from the past into the present. In both pretest and posttest discussions a subject will often say, "Do you know that before I came in here my mind relived nearly every wrong I've committed in my whole life, including things I haven't thought of in years."

Third, we see the fear of sensitivity, uncertainty, and even guilt complex which unfolds as a test progresses: "No, I didn't steal the $500 in question, but two months ago I stole a five dollar bill and that's my real problem in this test."

Collateral hereto, we see fear occasionally turned into resentment coming from persons who turned one or two past wrongs into a straightforward productive life.

What causes or develops the various degrees of fear within a person's thoughts as he approaches polygraphy?

Particularly during the pretest period we could describe the

fear-emotion as evolving from (1) misconception, misinformation, misapprehension, fear of the unknown, and (2) fear of
anything foreign which projects any type of potential harm to
one's well being, direct or implied.

With these pretest factors a relatively known quantity, a proper explanation of the purposes of the test to a subject lessens ten-
sional fear and gradually guides the subject through a psychological conditioning phase to a point where he can be fairly, impartially and objectively tested without associational complications.

We have established that the instrument records certain physiological phenomena through its primary components. Therefore,
though somewhat fragmentary herein, the bodily systems of acute
importance to the polygraphist are

1. Circulatory System.
2. Respiratory System.
3. Integument Sensitivity.

THE CIRCULATORY SYSTEM

It is the function of the circulatory system to ensure that
blood reaches all parts of the body in order that every cell may receive nourishment; so efficiently is this duty discharged that even
the most trivial cut on any part of the surface of the body is in-
evitably accompanied by bleeding and, because tissue fluid derived from the blood bathes every cell, the circulatory system has
been likened to an irrigation system. But blood is not uniformly
distributed. Tissues in which cells predominate require and receive a proportion of blood greater than do those in which inter-
cellular substances predominate.

Blood reaches the capillaries because the circulatory system is
provided with a pump; this is the heart. From the heart an ever-
branching system of arteries and arterioles conducts the blood to
the capillaries. Venules and veins corresponding to the arterioles
and arteries conduct the blood back to the heart.

Arterioles possess a structure similar to that of arteries but the
emphasis is on muscle tissue in the media rather than on elastic
tissue. When it is further observed that it is to the arterioles especially that nerves are distributed, it is apparent that the phenom-

ena of vasoconstriction and vasodilatation are special functions of the arterioles. It is by this change in calibre of the arterioles that the quantity of blood delivered to a capillary field can be increased or diminished according to functional activity, e.g. the blush of maiden modesty, the blanching of fear, and the cold hands of apprehension.

Veins are thin-walled because the pressure in them is very low compared with that in the arteries. Because the flow in veins is much more sluggish than it is in arteries, the veins are larger calibred so that they may return to the heart in given intervals of time a volume of blood equal to that leaving it. Veins that have to return blood against the influence of gravity are equipped with valves. These, by breaking up the column of blood, relieve the more dependent parts of excessive pressure and encourage the flow of venous blood toward the heart. For example, the venous congestion that the hot and tired feet feel at the end of a busy day is relieved by reclining with the feet higher than the pelvis.*

The flow of blood through capillaries differs from flow in arteries. The heart pumps blood into the aorta "only during systole." During the whole period from the end of one systole to the beginning of the next, while the semilunar valves are closed, most of the blood in the first few centimeters of the aorta is stationary. The onward flow here is intermittent, occurring mainly during contraction of the heart. Even in arteries a little farther removed from the heart there is a degree of intermittency of flow. As the capillary bed is approached, the intermittency becomes less and less marked, and in the capillaries themselves the flow is usually constant.

As the heart ejects blood into the aorta, the spurt of blood distends the elastic aortic wall. During cardiac diastole the stretched aortic wall clamps down again, squeezing the blood forward, backflow being prevented by closure of the semilunar valves. This, in turn, distends the next segment of the aorta or artery, which presently recoils elastically. This gives rise to the "travelling pulse wave" which can be felt in any artery.

As each pulse wave passes through the brachial artery, where

*Cates, H.A., Basmajian, J.V.: *Primary Anatomy,* 3rd ed. Williams & Wilkins, Baltimore, 1955, pp. 234-35.

the polygraph cardio cuff band is attached, we see the ascending stroke of the cardio tracing graphically recorded.

The result is that even during diastole of the heart, the blood is kept moving forward. As we progress farther from the heart the difference between rates of flow in systole and disastole becomes less and less until no spurting at all is normally apparent in the capillary region.

This may also be expressed in terms of energy transformations. *Motions of all kinds, including blood flow, demand the expenditure of energy.* In systole of the heart energy is liberated, most of which is converted into energy of motion, and blood is pumped out. Some of the energy, however, is expended to distend the elastic aortic and arterial walls; that is, some of the energy liberated by the heart muscle is stored as potential energy of the stretched vessel walls. Then, when energy liberation by the heart temporarily ceases in diastole, the potential energy of the distended vessel walls is converted into kinetic energy. The vessel walls recoil elastically and push blood along.*

As the pulse wave passes beyond the cuff band covering the brachial artery, we see graphically recorded the descending limb of the cardio tracing.

The Heart

The most vital organ in our body has two duties to perform: (1) It must pump venous blood to the lungs, so that the red blood cells may exchange their cargoes of carbon dioxide for new cargoes of oxygen; (2) it must pump this oxygenated blood, received from the lungs, to all parts of the body.

The right side receives the venous blood and pumps it to the lungs; the left side receives the arterial blood from the lungs and pumps it to the body at large. Circulation to and from the lungs is called the lesser or pulmonary circulation"; the circulation to

---

*Portions of the foregoing physiological material may be found on pages 44, 45, 47, 48, 170-1, *Machinery of the Body*, 4th ed., by Anton J. Carlson and Victor Johnson. Reprinted by permission of the University of Chicago Press. (Copyright 1937, 1941, 1948, 1953, by the University of Chicago. All rights reserved. Published 1937. Fourth ed. 1953. Third Impression 1956. Composed and printed by the University of Chicago Press.)

and from the body at large is called the greater or "systemic circulation."

Each side of the heart consists of a receiving chamber, the atrium, which pumps its blood through an orifice guarded by a valve into a discharging chamber, the ventricle, which pumps its blood through an orifice also guarded by a valve into an artery. The artery leading out of the right ventricle is called the pulmonary artery, that out of the left ventricle, the aorta.

Control of contraction of cardiac muscle is exercised by the vagus nerve (which retards) and the sympathetic nervous system (which accelerates). These act on a curious lump of special tissue in the wall of the right atrium—sinu-atrial or S.A. node—to regulate the strength and rate of heartbeats. The S.A. node is known as the pacemaker of the heart. From it, at the rate of about seventy per minute, an impulse (whose nature is not known) spreads over the heart, resulting in a contraction. The spreading impulse is picked up and quickly relayed by another node—atrioventricular or A.V. node—through a prolongation (A.V. bundle) down to the ventricles. The atria contract just before the ventricles and they both relax completely just before the next impulse arrives. The cardiac cycle is thus:

1. Auricles beginning to fill. Auriculoventricular valves closed. Ventricles relaxing.

2. Auricles still filling. Ventricular valves open. Ventricles begin to fill. Semilunar valves closed.

3. Auricles begin to contract. A-V valves floating toward closing position. Ventricles tense through filling; pressure still great in arteries.

4. Auricles resting. A-V valve closed. Ventricles begin to contract; still not as great as arteries. Semilunar valve closed.

5. Auricles beginning to fill. A-V valves closed. Ventricles contracting. Pressure is now greater than in arteries. Semilunar valves open. (Cycle repeats 72 times per minute.)

We see the blood squeezed into the aorta, regurgitate momentarily and then, through smooth muscle contraction, be forced into systemic circulation. Beyond the aortic valve the first two inches of the aorta run upwards and to the right within the pericardial sack and are known as the ascending aorta. From the summit of the arch of the aorta arises the innominate artery which ends behind the right sternoclavicular joint by dividing into the right common carotid and the right subclavian artery.

The subclavian artery is the vessel of the upper limb or, rather, this is the name given to the first part of the continuous arterial channel which reaches the elbow before bifurcating into terminal branches. This main channel changes its name when it enters the axilla (axillary artery) and when it enters the arm proper it becomes known as the brachial artery.

Nervous Factors

The nervous control of the blood vessels involves efferents which are designated as vasconstrictor or vasodilator nerves, depending upon whether they cause contraction or relaxation of the arteriolar muscles.

Vasoconstrictor nerves are usually in a state of continuous or tonic activity. The partial sustained contractions of the arteriolar muscles are dependent upon constant stimulation of those muscles by impulses in the vasoconstrictor nerves. Therefore, cutting the vasoconstrictor nerves should abolish this tone and lead to dilatation. When a vasodilator nerve of a group of arterioles is stimulated, the circular muscle fibers of the vessels relax. They relax to an even greater degree than the relaxation which attends cutting off of the tonic vasoconstrictor nerve impulses. For example, if we cut off the vasoconstrictor nerves of the salivary gland, a slight increase in blood flow through the gland occurs, reflecting the loss of vasoconstrictor tone. If now the vasodilator nerves of the gland are stimulated, the blood flow is still further increased. The dilatation greatly exceeds that of mere loss of constrictor tone.*

While skeletal nerves are absolutely dependent upon an intact innervation for their function—physiologically they can be stimulated only via their nerves—this is not the case with the

---

*Portions of the foregoing material may be found on pages 180, 181, *Machinery of the Body,* 4th ed., by Anton J. Carlson and Victor Johnson. Reprinted by permission of the University of Chicago Press. (Copyright 1937, 1951, 1948, 1953, by the University of Chicago. All rights reserved. Published 1937. Fourth ed. 1953. Third Impression 1956. Composed and printed by the University of Chicago Press.)

heart muscle. The heart continues to beat in the absence of its extrinsic nerves; to a limited degree it may even adjust its rate and strength to the bodily needs by means of thermal and chemical mechanisms. But in the normal intact animal the adjustments are effected mainly by cardiac nerves. Though not indispensable for the actual beat, they nevertheless modify the rate of the heart. The efferent nerves are of two kinds, a pair of accelerators and a pair of inhibitors.

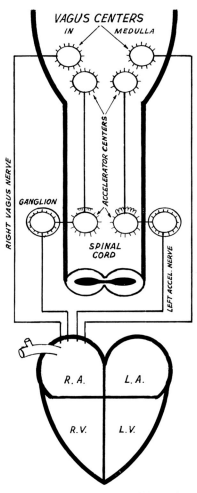

Figure 1. Efferent nerves of the heart. (Modified after Carlson & Johnson, *Machinery of the Body*, Fig. 43, p. 157.)

The accelerator nerves arise in the spinal cord in the chest region and reach the heart by a somewhat devious pathway. The inhibitory nerves arise in the medulla of the brain. The fibers course downward in two rather large bundles called the vagus nerves. The vagus is a vagabond type nerve in the sense that it wanders through the body to many of the internal organs. Artificial irritation of these nerves diminishes the strength and rate of the heartbeat or may even stop the beat for a brief period. The nerve impulses do not act upon the cardiac muscle, causing it to contract, but upon the pacemaker, stimulating it to act at an accelerated tempo. The beat is accelerated because successive activations of the cardiac muscle by the pacemaker now occur at shorter intervals. The vagus fibers also terminate in the sinus node and exert their inhibitory effect on the heart rate by slowing the rate at which the sinus node activates the heart. The depression of the contraction strength is probably due to a direct action of these nerves on the heart muscle.*

Cardio-inhibitors exert a constant controlling action on the heart rate. Nerve impulses are continually passing down to the heart. The brakes are dragging a little at all times. When vagus nerves are severed the heart rate accelerates. In such an instance, nerve impulses continually arising in the medulla cannot reach the heart, and it is said to have been released from its continued inhibition. Vagus nerves are tonically active, tonically inhibiting the heart. Increases in heart rate can be affected simply by a diminution of vagus tone, entirely independent of any effects of accelerator nerves.

At this point we should already begin to see that the cardio-vascular section of the polygraph instrument is recording something very positive—a norm and deviations therefrom.

The nerve impulse travels because each active region of the nerve becomes itself the stimulus to the next adjacent region. When the termination fiber is reached, the impulse passes on to the muscle fiber. There is a continuous transmission of activation,

*Portions of the foregoing may be found on pages 156 through 164, *Machinery of the Body*, 4th ed., by Anton J. Carlson and Victor Johnson. Reprinted by permission of the University of Chicago Press. (Copyright 1937, 1941, 1948, 1953, by the University of Chicago. All rights reserved. Published 1937, 4th ed. 1953. Third Impression 1956. Composed and printed by the University of Chicago Press.)

which in the nerve is a nerve impulse, and which in the smooth muscle fiber is a contraction.

The cause of the diametrically opposite effects these nerve impulses produce upon the heart seems to be dependent upon the chemical and physical organization of the fiber terminations in the heart and upon their relationship to the sinus node fibers. A nerve impulse reaching a vagus fiber termination induces certain localized changes which are not nerve impulses and which inhibit the sinus nodal tissue. Impulses arriving at accelerator terminations induce opposite local changes at the sinus node and stimulate it.

Nerves are activated at one end only, and the impulse travels the full length of the fiber in only one direction. Nerves like the vagi or the accelerators, which are efferent nerves, transmitting impulses away from their origin in the brain or cord, are always activated, then, in the central nervous system.

Cardio-inhibitory fibers originate in the "vagus center," in the medulla. Here also originate the cardio-accelerator fibers. Thus, any nerve impulse in the efferent vagus fibers must come from the vagus center.

These cardioaccelerator and cardioinhibitory centers, which are of vital concern to the polygraphist, may be influenced by nerve impulses reaching them from other parts of the central nervous system through connecting fiber pathways. Certain activities of the brain or spinal cord consequently modify the heart rate.

Emotional states are predominantly affective. Excitement leads to a rapid heart rate, and extreme fear may cause cadiac slowing by affecting the cardio-accelerator or cardio-inhibitory centers respectively. It is probably that emotional states also affect the heart rate and produce other circulatory changes by nonnervous mechanisms, such as causing increased epinephrine secretion.

Of equal importance are the reflex effects upon the cardio-regulatory centers. Stimulation of the sensory nerves of many body regions affects heart rate. Sensory nerves, or afferent nerves, transmit impulses from the periphery toward and into the central nervous system. Such impulses travel in afferent fibers to the brain or spinal cord, whence they are relayed through appropriate interconnecting nerve-fiber pathways to the cardio-regulatory centers. These nerve centers are essentially reflex centers or way stations in which afferent nerve impulses are shunted into efferent pathways, completing a reflex act.

It is found that stimulation of almost any afferent nerve of the body can effect heart rate.

There is a pair of nerves called the depressor nerves, whose fibers terminate in the arch of the aorta and in the ventricular muscle at the root of the aorta. They are afferent nerves and transmit impulses from the aorta into the medulla of the brain, whence they are relayed to the vagus center and the vagus fibers to the heart are involved in the reflex.

When the aorta is stretched the depressor nerve is stimulated, and the heart rate is reflexly slowed. The stretching of the aorta is caused by an elevation of blood pressure within the aorta. The following drawing more clearly illustrates.

Color Plate I. Mechanisms of blood-pressure regulation. It has been known for many years that an animal can be deprived of its sympathetic nervous outflow and still live and maintain sufficient blood pressure for moderate normal activity (Cannon). However, in stituations demanding unusual effort or sustained activity above the normal, such operated animals cannot function adequately, because, among other things, the animals have lost the ability to increase cardiac activity and partially divert the flow of blood from the viscera to the muscles and nervous tissues. Therefore, it is to the advantage of the organism that it possess means for regulating blood flow and blood pressure in accordance with current body needs. Even in the absence of sympathetic outflow, some mechanisms for this regulation exist: (1) the *adrenal medulla* still secretes epinephrine, though its production is poorly regulated; (2) the contractions and relaxations of somatic muscles (in movement) help in forcing blood through the *peripheral vessels;* (3) under the influence of adrenal cortical hormones, sodium and water may possibly accumulate in the walls of blood vessels, thus reducing their caliber and increasing general pressure. However, nervous control is more efficient, since it provides both the rapid and the fine adjustments necessary for maintaining adequate general blood supply at all times and for protecting the heart from undue strain. Such regulation consists essentially in the capacity of the blood vascular compartment to change the caliber of its vessels and to alter the stroke volume and rate of the heart. Both the variable arterial caliber and the heart's output modify blood pressure and, according to regional changes in the vessels, may affect the blood supply to various systems or regions of the body.

Local changes in blood flow may be due to local or segmental reflexes.

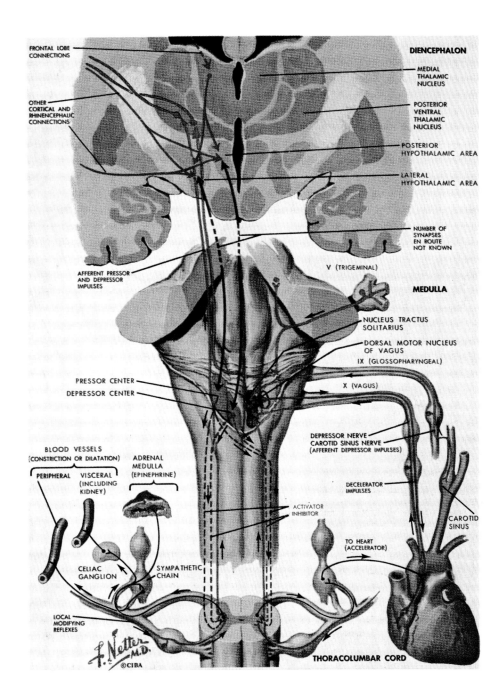

FRONTAL LOBE
CONNECTIONS

DIENCEPHALON

MEDIAL
THALAMIC
NUCLEUS

POSTERIOR
VENTRAL
THALAMIC
NUCLEUS

OTHER
CORTICAL AND
RHINENCEPHALIC
CONNECTIONS

POSTERIOR
HYPOTHALAMIC AREA

LATERAL
HYPOTHALAMIC AREA

NUMBER OF
SYNAPSES
EN ROUTE
NOT KNOWN

AFFERENT PRESSOR
AND DEPRESSOR
IMPULSES

V (TRIGEMINAL)

MEDULLA

NUCLEUS TRACTUS
SOLITARIUS

DORSAL MOTOR NUCLEUS
OF VAGUS

IX (GLOSSOPHARYNGEAL)

PRESSOR CENTER

DEPRESSOR CENTER

X (VAGUS)

DEPRESSOR NERVE
CAROTID SINUS NERVE
(AFFERENT DEPRESSOR IMPULSES)

BLOOD VESSELS
(CONSTRICTION OR DILATATION)

PERIPHERAL   VISCERAL
(INCLUDING
KIDNEY)

ADRENAL
MEDULLA
(EPINEPHRINE)

DECELERATOR
IMPULSES

ACTIVATOR
INHIBITOR

CAROTID
SINUS

TO HEART
(ACCELERATOR)

CELIAC
GANGLION

SYMPATHETIC
CHAIN

LOCAL
MODIFYING
REFLEXES

F. Netter
M.D.
©CIBA

THORACOLUMBAR CORD

Certain types of stimuli might effect spatially restricted *vasoconstriction* or *vasodilatation*. The latter might result in part from axon reflexes or antidromic impulses. More generalized changes may occur in repnose to peripheral and visceral stimuli, principally noxious or libidinous, which activate ascending pathways and thus modify cardiovascular activity by their influence on regulatory mechanisms in the brain. Such afferent impulses may directly affect mechanisms in the *medulla oblongata,* or, more likely, *thalamic relays* which act through the hypothalamus and down again to the *bulbar and spinal outflow.* Also, through *cortical connections of the thalamus,* psychic elements may be brought in to modulate the responses. This type of effect is principally pressor, with increased cardiac activity and visceral and peripheral arteriolar constriction. The efferent limb of this long reflex arc travels mainly in *descending hypothalamic pathways,* and perhaps also pontile relays, to the vasomotor mechanisms (often and for historical reasons called "centers") in the bulb and spinal cord, which, in turn, affect the blood vessels and the heart. The number of relays or synapses in this descending path is not known, and it is very likely that complex reverberating circuits are involved in this as in most neural activities.

The effects of situational circumstances on psychic activity and hence on vasomotor and cardiac regulation, according to the constitutional make-up of the individual, must be mentioned, because they are very important indirect modulators of autonomic activity in modern man.

Depressor effects are also part of the modulation system, e.g., the moderator mechanisms which are set up through the *carotid sinus* and *aortic reflexes.* Situational modification of psychic activity may also act through hypothalamic and/or lower brain stem circuits to lower the blood pressure and depress the heart. It is thus evident that *connections of the hypothalamus with both pressor and depressor systems* do exist. Their true course cannot be properly allocated and can be indicated only symbolically by arrows. The definite pressor and depressor regions in the hypothalamus are not clearly known, because in animal experiments a change in stimulus parameters, without altering the locus of stimulation, may reverse the response from elevation to depression of blood pressure.

It should be remembered that not all blood vessels of the body respond to a pressor situation by constriction. It is quite likely that, during neuroregulatory visceral and peripheral vasconstriction, the vessels of the muscles, and perhaps of the heart, dilate. This is logical enough, since the most active tissues require the most blood, which is provided through dilated channels if the pressure elsewhere is high enough.

All this serves to illustrate the inadequacy of the term "center," as it has been used in the past and is still found from time to time in modern literature. The cardiovascular regulatory system extends from receptors to telencephalon and back to effectors, through various complicated circuits.

We can visualize the impact of an emotional stimulus increasing the heart rate. More blood is rapidly pumped into the aorta. When it distends, afferent fibers of the depressor nerve are stimulated, and the heart is reflexly slowed. Its beat would tend in this way to be restored to the rate obtaining before the original emotional stimulus.

RESPIRATORY CORRELATES

Once thought secondary in importance from the standpoint of polygraph chart interpretation, the pneumograph (respiratory) tracing (s) has now risen to vital status.

While sensitivity and "nervous fluctuation" of the cardio tracing can be somewhat affected by certain drugs, barbituates, narcotics, alcohol, this is not normally so prevalent with respect to respiration.

A hardened nonemotional subject may not react blood-pressure-wise to a verbal stimulus, but if a nerve impulse is generated beyond threshold intensity his body will, in spite of itself show some deviation from norm in both respiratory and GSR tracings.

Just as in the case of blood vessels, the walls of the respiratory passages become thinner and thinner as we progress to tubes of smaller and smaller caliber.

The chest is a closed cavity with only one opening from the outside, the trachea. It follows, therefore, that the increase in size will aspirate a quantity of air into the lungs by way of the trachea. In this manner the "inspiratory phase" of respiration is effected.

Expulsion of air, the "expiratory phase," is done entirely by the elastic contraction of the lungs. In either case there is no actual compression of the lungs. The chest walls do not squeeze the lungs and forcibly expel air. In expiration the diminishing size of the thorax simply makes possible the elastic contraction of the lungs themselves. The active agent in drawing air into the lungs is contraction of the muscles of inspiration. The active agent in expelling air from the lungs is elastic recoil of the lungs. Air passages themselves are entirely passive in these processes, except in the larynx where vocal cords are widely separated in each inspiration.

Respiratory movements are important in the flow of venous blood to the heart. This organ lies within the intrathoracic space and is subjected to the intrathoracic pressure changes. The maintained lower-than-atmospheric pressure in the thorax also causes the venous pressure near the heart and the intra-atrial pressure in diastole to be less than atmospheric.

The volume of air taken in and discharged in each breathing movement is called "tidal volume." Remaining in the lungs after a normal expiration is air known as "supplemental" air, which can be forcibly expelled, and the "risidual volume" which cannot be expelled. "Minimal" air remaining in the lungs gives the tissues a specific gravity less than water. The volume of air which can be inspired in addition to the normal tidal air is called "complemental" air. The tidal volume, plus the inspiratory and expiratory reserve volumes, constitute the "vital capacity."

Respiratory Nerve Control

While rhythmic contractions of the muscles of breathing might be compared with the automaticity of the heart, the respiratory muscles themselves possess no intrinsic rhythmicity. There are several efferent, motor nerves, primarily the phrenic nerves, which innervate the diaphragm, and those nerves (the intercostal nerves) which innervate the (intercostal) muscles whose contractions elevate the ribs.

Nerve control of breathing is located in the medulla oblongata and passes downward in the spinal cord.

Thus, we form the picture of a paired cluster of nerves in the medulla oblongata which discharge volleys of nerve impulses rhythmically down nerve pathways of the spinal cord, which in turn connect functionally with the various efferent nerves of breathing. Unlike the situation in the case of the vasomotor or cardio-regulatory centers, physiologists find here no accessory centers in the spinal cord. The paired cluster of nerve cells in the medulla is the chief and only governor of external respiration.

A number of reflexes must be considered—numerous afferent nerve systems play upon the respiratory center. For example, certain afferent nerves which furnish the sensory innervation of the lining of the larynx—the superior laryngeal nerve, a branch of the vagus—and of the pharynx (a branch of the glossopharyngeal, the ninth cranial nerve) have a protective function. Stimulation at the central end of either of these nerves produces a brief inhibition of respiration.

Solid particles in the larynx mechanically stimulate the sensory nerves, perhaps evoking a forcible, sudden, reflex expiration—a cough. If we pay attention to our own eating activities, we will notice that when we swallow we also stop breathing momentarily. This indicates that as food goes from mouth to gullet it crosses the pathway for air—nose to pharynx to larynx. Air can get into the gullet rather safely but for a particle of food to enter the larynx is serious or even fatal. Therefore, it is virtually impossible to take a breath and swallow at the same time. (We shall see the effects of this in pneumograph tracings in a subsequent chapter.)

The action of the vagus nerve is primarily responsible in causing the cells of the respiratory center to discharge nerve impulses in their characteristic rhythmic, intermittent fashion. If the central end of these vagus fibers is stimulated, the respiratory center is immediately inhibited and breathing movements temporarily cease. However, while normally the vagi are responsible for the cessation of each inspiratory movement, there is also another factor which functions in the absence of the vagi. In fact, even in the absence of all afferent influences, the center still discharges intermittently and the characteristic rhythm of the breathing movements is still maintained.

Certain sensory nerves in various parts of the body affecting respiration are stimulated by chemical changes in the blood. If the oxygen content of the blood is diminished or its carbon dioxide content increased, nerve endings near the carotid sinus and in the aorta are chemically stimulated, effecting a reflex acceleration of respiration. The carotid sinus and aortic arch areas contain two types of receptors: those responding to stretch, lying in the walls of the carotid sinus and aortic arch, and those responding to chemical changes (oxygen lack or carbon dioxide excess), lying in the adjacent carotid body and aortic body, which are involved in the reflex respiratory acceleration described.

There seems to be little question but that the chief effect of changes in the chemical composition of the blood is produced directly upon the cells of the respiratory center itself. However, while oxygen does play a minor role, the prepotent stimulus to the respiratory center is carbon dioxide which is more effective than any nervous inhibition. When carbon dioxide reaches a great enough concentration, the most determined effort of the "will" cannot nullify its effect on the center. One could not commit suicide by voluntarily holding the breath.

Coughing and sneezing, which clearly affect all three polygraph tracings, result from irritation of the linings of the respiratory passages. Essentially these are modified respiratory acts, in which at first a strong forced expiratory movement is started with the vocal cords tightly apposed (with the glottis closed). This greatly elevates the pressure within the lungs so that when suddenly the glottis is opened, a blast of air is abruptly forced from the lungs through the mouth in a cough, or through the nose in a sneeze, tending to expel the irritating objection from the breathing passage.*

To summarize, control of respiration is provided by the autonomic nervous system from automatic centers in the medulla, centers in the spinal cord, the phrenic nerve, peripheral nerves along with occasionally afferent regulators occurring in response to some visual or auditory stimuli.

The phrenic nerve originates in the cervical plexus, entering the thorax and passing to the diaphragm. It is also a motor nerve to the diaphragm with sensory fibers to the pericardium of the heart. When stimulated sufficiently its action causes an involuntary contraction of the diaphragm (associated with apnea). The sympathetic division of the autonomic nervous system services the general segments of respiration, except as noted below.

As we have previously indicated, in the coronary arteries, con-

---

*Portions of the foregoing material may be found on pages 234-237, 241, 248, *Machinery of the Body*, 4th ed., by Anton J. Carlson and Victor Johnson. Reprinted by permission of the University of Chicago Press. (Copyright 1937, 1941, 1948, 1953 by the University of Chicago. All rights reserved. Published 1937. Fourth ed. 1953. Third Impression 1956. Composed and printed by the University of Chicago Press.)

nected to the aorta, are the carotid bodies. They contain epithe-lioid cells which serve as chemoreceptors, responding to changes in carbon dioxide and oxygen content of the blood and to changes in pH. A dilated area at the bifurcation of this common carotid artery is the carotid sinus and is richly supplied with sensory nerve endings of the sinus branch of the vagus nerve. These, when stimulated by distention of the vessel wall brought about by a rise in blood pressure, bring about a reflex vasodilation and a slowing of the heart rate. Parasympathetic control is sometimes shown in this action.

INTEGUMENT CORRELATES

In polygraph examination, as referred to herein, we have chosen the skin and its relationship to sweat gland activity, the general senses afferently, thence efferently, in order to lay an appropriate foundation for tracings which the polygraph instru-ment's galvanometer section records on a moving chart. We be-lieve that nearly any activity of all the major bodily systems, synchronously or individually, have some direct bearing on the amount of sweat gland secretion.

As an excretory organ, skin possesses sweat glands capable of eliminating a considerable part of excess quantities of water and salts (the conducting ingredients to the electrical constant of the polygraph instrument). It is, therefore, an important aid to the lungs and kidneys. Between and within its surface cells naked nerve fibers serve as temperature and pain end-organs.

As a heat-regulating organ, skin possesses a rich blood supply, and its arterioles by constriction can conserve heat and by dilata-tion can dissipate it.

Contrary to popular belief, hairs are actually modified skin, not hollow but solid. The bulb of the hair at the bottom of the follicle receives the ends of sensory nerve fibers. Smooth muscle fibers pass downwards from the epidermis to the deep part of a hair follicle. Their contraction, resulting from cold or fright, produces "goose flesh" and causes the hairs to "stand on end."

Sweat glands lie in the subjacent superficial fascia. From them two networks of arterioles are formed; one is in the deepest part of the dermis; the other is just beneath the papillae and from it the papillae receive capillary networks.*

During polygraphy the examiner takes acute cognizance of any or all of the following factors which have bearing on changes in sweat gland activity:

1. Increases in air temperature.
2. Increase in relative humidity.
3. Increase in circulation to sweat glands.
4. Certain types of muscular exercise.
5. Nausea.
6. Pain.
7. Mental excitement or nervousness.
8. Dyspnea—shortness of breath.
9. Changes in body temperature.
10. Certain drugs.

Sweat gland activity generally decreases as a result of the following:

1. Cold environment.
2. Avoiding large quantities of urine.
3. Dehydration.
4. Certain drugs.
5. Certain diseases.

The first adjustments made by the body are on the side of heat loss. When a room becomes cool the first thought is to seek warmth. In this regard the "wisdom of the body" is equal to that of the intelligent householder.

In mammals heat loss is modified in several ways. In the cold the skin blood vessels constrict so that less of the warm blood from the internal organs circulates through the surface skin vessels. Less heat is therefore lost by radiation; heat is conserved.

A vasodilatation of skin vessels, on the other hand, bringing more warm blood to the surface of the body and facilitating heat loss, normally occurs in a warm environment. This is the express reason why every polygraph examining room should have a constant temperature regulation of about 70 degrees, along with an effective humidity control unit.

*Cates, H.A., Basmajian, J.V.: *Primary Anatomy,* 3rd ed. Williams & Wilkins, Baltimore, 1955, pp. 325-26.

So far we have only fragmented effector structures. That heat directly stimulates the sweat glands, the skeletal muscles or lowers the temperature is a common misconception. If the efferent nerves of these structures are cut, the reaction to temperature changes fail to occur. Sweat fails to be secreted, vasomotor responses do not take place, changes in muscle tension are absent, blood vessels and skeletal and hair muscles are denervated, no matter what the temperature of the environment.

Thus, to a large extent, the responses are "reflex" in nature, resulting from specialized nerve endings in the skin: the "cold" receptors which are stimulated by a temperature fall, and the "heat" receptors, which are stimulated by a rise, as noted in the table below:

TABLE III
REFLEX ADJUSTMENTS TO EXTERNAL HEAT OR COLD

Skin Receptors Stimulated	Reflex Changes Produced	Effects of Reflexes
Sensory Nerve Endings for Colds	1. Vasoconstriction of skin vessels	Decreased heat loss
	2. Erection of hairs	
	4. Fluffing of feathers	
	Increased muscle tension	Increased heat production
Sensory Nerve Endings for Heat	1. Vasodilatation of skin vessels	
	2. Increased sweat secretion	Decreased heat production
	3. Increased salivation and panting	
	Muscular relaxation	Increased heat loss

(From *Machinery of the Body*, p. 335)

The primary temperature-regulating center of the body (unlike the respiratory center which is in the medulla) is located in the thalamus above the midbrain and above and to the right of the cerebellum.

Earlier we briefly noted that although respiration is controlled in part reflexly through the respiratory center, conditions in the region of the center itself, namely, the carbon dioxide concentration, also determined activity of the center and therefore of the efferent systems leading from it to the breathing muscles.

Similarly, in the case of the temperature-regulating center, nervous discharges through the appropriate efferent systems can occur reflexly as a result of afferent influences from the skin. But they can also occur as a result of changes locally in the center itself. When the center is warmed, efferent discharges from it to sweat glands and skin vasodilators lead to increased heat loss; when the center is cooled, the heat-conserving mechanisms are activated, and muscle tension is increased by nervous discharges through the efferent nerves of the muscles.*

Nerve impulses coming from the skin enter the spinal cord over afferent neurons and, at the same level, make synaptic connections with association and efferent neurons. When this circuit (reflex arc) is completed, the muscles respond. Thus, a prick causes the hand to be withdrawn. However, as impulses come in over the afferent neuron, they not only travel around the arc, but also ascend the cord. At the upper end of the cord, in lower brain centers, other circuits may be made, carrying the impulses back to efferent neurons at the level of stimulation.

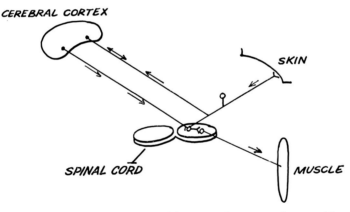

Figure 2. This simplified diagram, with connections on only one side, shows the reflex arc, ascending and descending.

---

*Portions of the foregoing may be found on pages 330, 332, 337, *Machinery of the Body*, 4th ed., by Anton J. Carlson and Victor Johnson. Reprinted by permission of the University of Chicago Press. (Copyright 1937, 1941, 1948, 1953 by the University of Chicago. All rights reserved. Published 1937. Fourth ed. 1953. Third Impression 1956. Composed and printed by the University of Chicago Press.)

Radiating from the central nervous system are the various nerves known as "peripheral nerves." These convey impulses into and out of the spinal cord and lower brain centers. Those connecting with the spinal cord are referred to as "spinal" and those connecting with the brain stem as "cranial nerves." Impulses from the skin enter the spinal cord. The muscles also contain receptors and when these contract or relax, afferent impulses like those from the skin also enter the spinal cord. Each spinal nerve has two attachments to the spinal cord: one (afferent) serving a sensory, and the other (efferent) a motor function.*

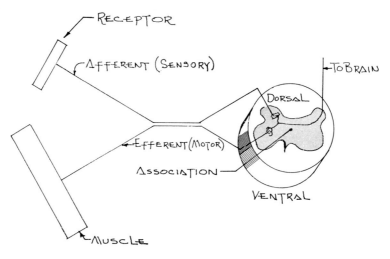

Figure 3. Reflex-arc System. Impulses from receptors travel toward the spinal cord over afferent neurons of the spinal nerve. There they initiate impulses in the association neurons. These impulses in turn arouse efferent neurons along which impulses travel to the muscles. Nerve fibers also carry impulses toward the brain and from the brain down to various levels of the spinal cord. Note that cell bodies of afferent neurons are outside of and cell bodies of association and motor neurons within the spinal cord. Afferent fibers connect with the back of dorsal and efferent fibers with the front or ventral portion of the spinal cord. (Modified after Munn, *Psychology*, Fig. 23, p. 55.)

---

*Munn, N.L.: *Psychology*, 2nd. ed. Houghton Mifflin, Boston, 1951, pp. 48, 54, 55, 64.

Reference to kinesthesis should be made since voluntary movements by the subject (wiggling his toes, pressing on fingers, during polygraphy) generates almost immediately a deflection in the galvanometer recording pen (sometimes an immediate break in the tracing with an abrupt fall of the pen).

Kinesthetic receptors are subjected to pressure or release of pressure as our muscles, tendons and joints are moved. They send impulses to the thalamus and then to the parietal lobe of the cerebrum, thus informing our brain of the position of our limbs.

Incoming impulses are shunted over in the brain stem, or cortex to motor fibers. These carry impulses back to the muscles, tendons and joints, thus stimulating further activity. Any movement of the body stimulates the skin and, in turn, has some bearing on sweat gland activity. In the blocked schematic below we see some of the nerve endings acting as kinesthetic receptors.

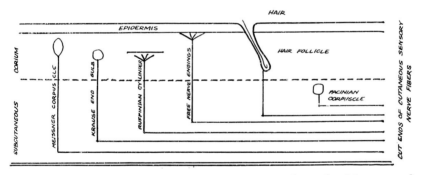

Figure 4. Meissner's corpuscles, some free nerve endings, dendrites around hair follicles, and Pacinian corpuscles all respond to pressure, but the latter only to heavy pressure. Other free nerve endings mediate pain sensitivity. (Modified from Munn, *Psychology*, p. 478.)

AUTONOMIC CORRELATES

As far as we know the seat of consciousness is in the cerebrum and the thought control center in the cerebral cortex. Every other area has apparently been found subordinate. Research has further defined that a strong enough emotion generated at the seat of consciousness can result in a nerve impulse (or series of nerve impulses) being directed to one or several organs of the body which in turn creates some type of proprioceptive, interoceptive or viscereoceptive reaction. In the instance of the fear emotion, with respect to polygraphy, we might picture consciousness of the fact germinating in the associational areas of the cerebral cortex. In these centers are the highest mental faculties, with ideational processes such as memory, imagination, conception, learning, intelligence, reasoning and personality. We further picture development of a conscious thought touching upon the memory process through past learning, evaluated through reasoning (and meaning) generated into a degree of fearful emotion, transmitting a nerve impulse via direct and indirect thalamic relays, through the medulla and to organ destination.

Besides the reflex mechanisms concerned in the regulation of normal blood pressure, psychologic factors also participate, especially in persons who are susceptible to stresses and strains. Circumstances producing emotional reactions, internal conflicts and worry may so upset the normal regulatory machinery that excessive systolic and diastolic blood pressures result. Such effects are brought about through neural channels. The turmoil in the cerebral cortex of a worried individual is brought to focus, in a sense, upon the fundamental cardiovascular regulators at the lower level. The hypothalamic neuron systems, brought to supernormal activity by the bombardment of cortical impulses, discharge down the brain stem and spinal cord by pathways involving unknown numbers of synapses and interrelated circuits. These impulses act upon the bulbar cardiovascular centers, increasing the activity of the heart. Discharges to the spinal level activate the thoracolumbar portion of the autonomic system through which arteriolar constriction is brought about, especially in the great visceral vascular bed. The adrenal medulla is stimulated to produce norepinephrine, which adds its vasopressor effects. All this may lead to hypertension which persists for the duration of the emotional storm. In normal persons an acute elevation in blood pressure is soon over. In emotionally overwrought, tense, compulsive persons, this hypertension may persist for some time.

What are some of the outward physical manifestations projected by a person which permit us to sense the specific types of internal autonomic action related thereto as it takes place from his struggles with his own peculiar degree of fear-emotion?

Blushing

In a pretest preemployment interview we find that Mrs. A is an applicant for a particular job. She is an attractive woman of twenty-three. She enters the examining room projecting nervousness and apprehension and is instructed to be seated. The examiner glances over her employment application, explains the purpose of the test to her, and commences the interview utilizing subject matters on the front of his special data sheet which are, in effect, the beginning of question formulation.

EXAMINER: Mrs. A, have you ever taken this test before?

ANSWER: My goodness no, and I'm scared to death.

Information: Her application shows her maiden name to be M; divorced, three children ages three and four years, and six months respectively.

EXAMINER: What year were you married?

ANSWER: 1962.

EXAMINER: What year were you divorced?

ANSWER: 1964, in Columbus, Georgia.

EXAMINER: You have three children, correct?

ANSWER: Yes. (She blushes deeply.)

EXAMINER: Are you receiving any child support?

ANSWER: None. I haven't seen that ex-husband of mine since 1961. (She catches her breath and again blushes).

EXAMINER: Mrs. A, I assure you there will be no personal or embarrassing questions during this interview or test.

MRS. A.:   (Sighs.) Oh, good. I've heard that all kinds of personal questions are asked in these tests.

EXAMINER: Mrs. A, anything I've asked you thus far is a matter of public record and simply a verification of what you have written on your own employment application.

We may readily presuppose that Mrs. A's fear-emotion partially comes from self-embarrassment of facing a stranger who might think less of her because of a six-month-old child born out of wedlock. We can further presume rather safely that she suspected this unpleasant subject matter might be explored by the examiner.

Blushing is evidence of the emotional aspect, and her own sensitivity to the subject matter. Once assured there would be no probe of the intimate circumstances involved she quit blushing, relaxed and projected her job-seeking personality the best she knew how.

Physiologically, from flight or fight standpoints, what are we sensing?

The body's vasoconstrictor center is located in the medulla and is apparently able to maintain a great deal of its tonic action independent of nervous influences playing upon it. Such influences may reach the center from higher regions of the brain or from afferent systems and may induce either rather generalized or quite localized vasomotor changes. Excitement may stimulate the constrictor center through nervous channels, elevating the blood pressure.

Embarrassment causes the vasodilatation of face blood vessels which results in "blushing." It is another one of the vasomotor phenomenons induced by conscious process, though it is sufficiently localized to prevent any fall in blood pressure. The schematic below presses our point.

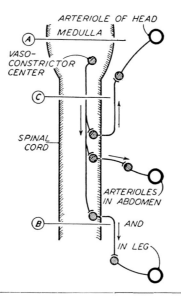

Dry Mouth and Lips

Mr. B has been working in a grocery store for two years. He likes his job and has applied himself diligently. One day he is told he is up for promotion. He knows he faces the "loyalty type check" polygraph examination, which is company policy. He also knows he must satisfactorily clear this test as a condition of promotion.

Suddenly, he remembers every grape, banana, plum, peanut, cupcake, pint of milk, cookie and candy bar he has consumed in the store without paying for same. While he knows he hasn't done anything really serious—or that which other grocery store employees haven't done at one time or another—these minor infractions begin to magnify themselves in his thoughts. In effect, he is thinking, "Will what I have done be considered serious enough to hold up my promotion?"

When Mr. B enters the examining room his mouth turns dry. He is worried. He knows that consuming any merchandise without paying for it is strictly against company policy and even grounds for dismissal.

Mr. B's fear-emotion is generated in the higher centers of the cerebral cortex. The emotional factor creates the nerve impulses which curtail normal salivary secretions in the mouth, and so it feels dry. Nervously he licks his lips. This is almost an unconscious reflex action, an attmept to bring back normal salivary secretion.

Examiner observation: Constant licking of the lips; slight hoarseness of voice; apparent difficulty in swallowing; consternation in the face and eyes; apprehension.

EXAMINER: Mr. B, I imagine this promotion means a lot to you.

MR. B.:   It sure does. I really hope I pass this test.

Observation: Appearance of slight white dry film (alkaline in

---

Figure 5. Nervous connections between the vasoconstrictor center in the medulla and vasoconstrictor nerves of various arteries. A cut across the medulla at A or across the spinal cord at B will not sever the connections between the vasoconstrictor center and the blood vessels. A cut across the spinal cord at C will completely remove the blood vessels from control by the vasoconstrictor center. Arrows indicate the curse of nerve impulses from center to blood vessels. (From Carlson & Johnson, Machinery of the Body. Fig. 61, p. 193.)

color) on lower lip. Shifts position in chair frequently. Voice raspy.

EXAMINER: Mr. B, I don't want to waste any time in this test discussing petty things. By this I mean the normal in-store "grazing" which all employees do on occasion.

Observation: Relief setting in. Relaxation of postural tension and facial muscles. Softening of the eyes. Smile more normal.

MR. B.:   My mouth is so dry. Do you have a drink of water?

Autonomically, what may we sense taking place within this subject's body which can be correlated with his own expressions and physical manifestations?

Simply, we might see this involuntary nerve stimulus from the higher cortical centers shuttled down via thalamic relays into the medulla, through white ramus, preganglionically, into the cervical sympathetic ganglia, to a cholinergic synapse and vasoconstriction of the salivary glands.

Once the subject's fear-emotion has subsided, moisture returns to his mouth via parasympathetic vasodilation, or via parasympathetic preganglionics (glossopharyngeal pathway) to cholinergic synapse, and then parasympathetic postganglionic to salivary glands. Stimulation of autonomic ganglion cells or their axons results in the liberation of chemical substances which play essential roles in the transmission of the nerve impulses from the nerve fibers to the effector tissues. The substance liberated most commonly at the neuroeffector junctions, due to stimulation of sympathetic ganglion cells or sympathetic postganglionic fibers, possesses properties of adrenin. This substance has been called sympathin. The substance liberated at the neuroeffector junctions most commonly, due to stimulation of parasympathetic ganglion cells or postganglionic fibers, possesses properties of acetylcholine. It has been called parasympathin.

Constant Swallowing

Mr. C is applying for a job. One year ago he and two other men were on a drinking spree in a neighboring state. That

Saturday night they stopped an older woman as she walked along a back country road, threw her in their car, drove to an even more secluded spot and took turns raping her. The next day Mr. C fled. Subsequently he learned his two companions had been caught and sentenced to long prison terms. He doesn't think they informed on him but he is not sure. Therefore, he's been job-hopping quite regularly. He is broke and desperately needs this job.

Mr. C's fear-emotion is primarily caused by his mental association of the polygraph preemployment test with the so-called "lie detector" test given in police departments. Specifically, he is afraid the test might reveal his past crime and result in his going to prison. Of secondary importance, he is afraid that if he doesn't answer the questions truthfully he will not get this job and perhaps later be picked up by the police for vagrancy.

As Mr. C approaches the examining room he feels a tightening in the stomach and a sensation that he might soon have to urinate. More so, he is experiencing an unusual amount of saliva secretion in his mouth. In the examining room chair he experiences some difficulty in talking. He has the feeling that every time he tries to say anything saliva wants to run out of the corners of his mouth.

Observation: Constant swallowing. Some difficulty talking; tongue frequently licking at the corners of his mouth.

MR. C.: Just what kind of questions do you ask in this kind of a test?

EXAMINER: (Condensed) Those questions which verify your employment background and contents of your own employment application.

MR. C.: What do you hold against a guy? No one is perfect?

Observation: Constant swallowing continued. Shifts position in chair.

EXAMINER: We don't hold anything against anyone. We are completely neutral, having no axe to grind. The polygraphist's only concern is whether or not you answer the test questions truthfully.

Observation: Relief setting in. He smiles and nods. Postural movements begin to cease. He relaxes with a big sigh. Swallowing becomes less frequent.

Physiologically, what can we sense is taking place? First, we see the fear-emotion has developed an excess of saliva secretion in the mouth. We might say that nerve impulses have travelled from the higher cortical centers down through any number of thalamic synapses into the medulla. From there the impulses travel parasympathetic preganglionically via the glossopharyngeal nerve to a cholinergic synapse, thence postganglionically to the parotid and other salivary glands, creating a vasodilation thereof.

The constant swallowing is more or less a reflex reaction which the brain somewhat unconsciously initiates protectively. The first part of swallowing consists of a series of muscle contractions in the mouth region which pushes the saliva back into the pharnyx. In the act of swallowing we imagine sensory innervation in the lining of the larynx and in the pharnyx, activating the superior laryngeal nerve, a branch of the vagus, and a branch of the ninth cranial nerve, the glossopharyngeal nerve. These afferent nerves are especially significant. These same sensory nerves whose stimulation reflexly causes the swallowing movements can, at the same time, transmit impulses to the respiratory center and inhibit it.

Once the fear-emotion has subsided, the rapidity of swallowing diminishes and sympathetic vasoconstrictive tonicity returns. Subject returns to normal saliva secretion and swallowing activities.

Faintness and Nausea

Mr. D is forty-two years of age, married, has two children, has been active in church work with his wife, has well above average income, and is sales manager of a large furniture store. He projects impeccable integrity. Some six months ago, at an after hours office cocktail party he became infatuated with his new secretary, succumbing to her flattery and witty conversation. She made him feel more alive than he'd felt in years. One thing led to another. Gradually she became a drug upon his senses. When she discouraged any real seriousness he began embezzling company money to buy her expensive gifts. Suddenly the girl disappeared.

Four days after her departure company auditors made a surprise visit. They discovered large shortages. Mr. D denied any complicity, yet was afraid not to submit to polygraphy when the company president suggested it.

On his way to the examining room Mr. D imagined loss of his wife and children, friends, and embarrassment to his own society-minded parents. He further imagined publicity, an appearance in court, and even imprisonment. He began to feel nauseated. His eyes watered and he felt a strong urge to urinate. As he entered the examining room and sat down his vision blurred. He experienced a "knot" in his stomach and he felt "giddy." His shirt collar was too tight; it seemed he couldn't get enough air.

Observation: Downcast eyes, deep gasping breaths, paleness of face and lips, crossing and uncrossing of legs, trembling voice, slumped posture, shakes his head from side to side occasionally, wrinkled brow.

EXAMINER: Mr. D, I assume you know why you're here. Has this really upset you as much as it appears?

MR. D.:   You'll never know how much. Why, this can ruin me. They just can't believe I would do such a thing.

EXAMINER: What could ruin you?

MR. D.:   This whole mess. How can they think I used company money to buy that girl some. . . . Oh, God! I feel sick. Where is the restroom?

EXAMINER: (Mr. D has returned.) The best thing you can do is calm down and get hold of yourself. My only role here is to fairly and impartially verify whether or not you answer the issue questions truthfully. I have certain information given to me by your company's auditors. They make no mention of any woman. Here is what they say: . . . . Now, basically, are these facts reasonably correct?

Observation: Mr. D nods in the affirmative, eyes still downcast, but makes no verbal comment.

EXAMINER: If they are correct, and you actually did embezzle the monies, then there is really no need for a test, is there? Why don't you just get it off your chest

here and now. You'll not only feel better but also be
able to more realistically face the future no matter
what it holds.

Mr. D.:   Do you have some water? I feel faint.

If we take another look at the foregoing illustration, what can
we sense has taken place in Mr. D's brain and body to produce his
verbal remarks and outward physical manifestations?

The fibers of any nerve, even those of the skeletal muscles,
have a corresponding center in the brain or cord. Certain activities
of the brain influence the various nerve channels inside the brain
or spinal cord and consequently modify the heart rate and respiratory activity, primarily through the vagus center. In the protected
civilization in which most of us live, extreme fear is uncommon
in waking hours. When it does happen we see afferent and efferent
nerve reflex action.

When abdominal organs in the viscera are stimulated we sense
afferent nerve impulses passing up to the medulla and vagus
center, thence efferently to cardio and respiratory inhibition or
acceleration. Most internal organs receive a double efferent innervation. In other words, we have parasympathetic augmentation
of the stomach and small intestine, a contraction of both the
rectum and bladder, and an inhibition of the heart via the
medulla. Efferent sympathetic impulse inhibition, relaxation and
acceleration travel down the thoracic and lumbar pathways into
the chain of ganglia, through ganglion centers and thence to
parasympathetic counterparts. From the higher cortical centers
the fear-emotion bombards the fight or flight center where protective nerve impulses are sent out. Sufficient stimulation of the
vagus nerve causes a cardiac inhibition, thus decreasing the heart
rate, and lowered arterial pressure. In turn, there may be an
insufficient blood flow volume to the brain resulting in "giddiness" or "faintness." The emotional effect upon the respiratory
system has, of course, created an imbalance of oxygen and carbon
dioxide in the blood and vasoconstrictor impulses are decreased.
(See Fig. 6.)

When fainting does not actually occur, and only the sensation
of giddiness is expressed by the subject, we sense that reduced

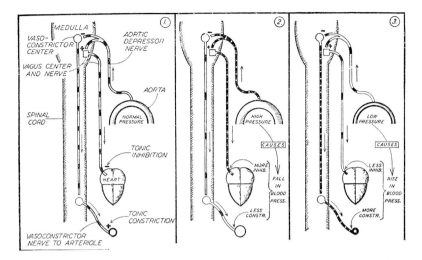

Figure 6. Schema of reflex action of aortic depressor nerve upon blood vessels and heart rate. Nerves are indicated by double lines. Nerve impulses are shown as shaded segments. Arrows indicate direction of nerve impulses. The spacing of the impulses indicates the frequency of impulses in the nerves. Plus signs indicate a stimulation; minus signs, an inhibition. The same reflex effects are produced by changes in pressure within the carotid sinus. Note that in all cases impulses in the depressor nerve inhibit the vasoconstrictor center and stimulate the vagus center. The extent of these two effects depends upon the number of impulses in the depressor nerve which are moderately numerous in part 1, many in part 2, and few in part 3. (From Carlson & Johnson, *Machinery of the Body*, Fig. 64, p. 201.)

arterial pressure has diminished the constant stimulation of the aortic depressor, or carotid sinus nerve, the vagus is less stimulated, and the heart accelerates. Also the vasoconstrictor center is less inhibited and vasoconstriction is increased. The net effect is an increase in blood pressure.

With Mr. D's complete confession, the generated fear-emotion gradually subsides and the physiological functions of his body return reasonably close to his "norm." When such occurs, the polygraphist may then conduct a fair and impartial test designed to verify the truthfulness of subject's answers with respect to amounts, and so on.

Chapter 8

POLYGRAPH'S GRAPHIC CORRELATIONS

W<small>E REPEAT</small> that the principal recording units of the polygraph instrument are its cardiovascular, pneumograph, and galvanograph sections.

The instrument's kymograph motor moves the chart under the pens at a uniform speed of six inches per minute.

The basic purpose of the cardiovascular section is to record, at mean blood pressure, via the brachial or radial artery, the following:

1. Relative blood pressure.
2. Norm pulse pressure, and changes therefrom.
3. Heart rate and beat.
4. Pulse wave amplitude.

The pneumograph section is simply constructed and primarily records.

1. Normal respiratory patterns.
2. Deviations from norm respiratory patterns.

Common theories of what the galvanograph, an electrical system, measures are

1. Increased flow of perspiration.
2. Changes in sweat gland activity.
3. Changes in temperature of the capillaries.
4. Changes in oxygenation of the blood.
5. Polarization of skin tissues.
6. Change in body homeostasis.

Now, brief attention should be given to the significance of each.

RELATIVE BLOOD PRESSURE

As popularly used, this is the pressure existing in the large arteries at the height of the pulse wave; the systolic intra-arterial pressure. More generally, it is referred to as the pressure exerted by the blood on the wall of any vessel. This pressure reaches its highest values in the left ventricle during systole, it is lower successively in the arteries, capillaries and veins, and sinks to subatmospheric values in the large veins during diastole.

The systolic arterial blood pressure itself rises during activity or excitement and falls during sleep, relaxation or from a reduction of tension. In the normal, relaxed, sitting adult, it is likely to be between 110 and 145 mm of mercury.

The following findings are considered abnormal: (1) systolic pressure persistently above 150, (2) diastolic pressure persistently above 100, (3) pulse pressure constantly greater than 50.

Blood pressure varies with age, sex, altitude, muscular development and according to states of worry and fatigue. It is lower in women than in men; low in childhood and high in advancing age as a rule. With new modern instruments for the more accurate evaluation of blood pressure measurements the foregoing is more a guide than a specific. Diastolic blood pressure is the lowest point to which it drops between heart beats. Average in the brachial artery of the adult is 60 to 90 mm.

Normal should show a high systolic pressure of about 145 mm with 1 mm less for women. Normal diastolic pressure, 60 mm to 90 mm; 120 mm average systolic pressure at age of twenty and $\frac{1}{2}$ mm for each year above that age, which would give 135 mm as normal systolic pressure for a man of about fifty.

Basic factors determining blood pressure are (1) minute output—the amount of blood ejected from the heart into systemic circulation, (2) peripheral resistance—general sensations, special senses, voluntary movements, peripheral control by adrenalin, epinepherine and actions of the pituitary, (3) capacity of system, (4) volume—the amount of blood in the system under pressure.

The difference between the highest and lowest forms of blood pressure, systolic and diastolic, is "mean" blood pressure. This mean is the standard cardio conducting pressure during the instrumental phase of polygraphy.

Some polygraph instruments have a "Resonance Control Knob" (although such is really not necessary) situated on their face panels. When this knob is screwed all the way down it removes the cardio tambour assembly from total operation and, with the sphygmomanometer so isolated, the examiner can readily ascertain systolic, diastolic and mean pressures as would a doctor.

An example of obtaining MBP would be the addition of diastolic and systolic pressures, dividing by two.

$$\begin{array}{l} 120 \text{ Systolic} \\ \underline{80} \text{ Diastolic} \\ 200 \text{ divided by } 2 = 100 \text{ MBP} \end{array}$$

NORM PULSE PRESSURE AND CHANGES

Pulse pressure, as commonly accepted, is a rhythmical throbbing caused by the regular contraction and alternate expansion of the brachial artery; the periodic thrust felt over the artery in time with the heartbeat. Normal pulse rate in the adult is about 70 to 75 per minute.

A medical laboratory sphygmograph tracing consists of a series of waves in which the upstroke is called the "anacrotic" limb, and the down stroke (on which is normally seen the dicrotic notch) the "catacrotic." When the dicrotic notch is in the center of the catacrotic downstroke the cardio pressure is generally figured to be at mean pulse pressure.

Correlation with the polygraph tracing is as follows (exaggerated) :

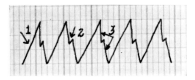

1, Anacrotic limb (ascending—systolic). 2, Dicrotic notch. 3, Catacrotic limb (descending—diastolic).

To compute pulse pressure, the expressive tone of the arterial wall, we shall assume that systolic is 120 and diastolic is 80. By subtracting, the difference of 40 is pulse pressure. Normal pulse pressure suggests that systolic pressure must be about 40 points over diastolic pressure. Generally a pulse pressure over 50 points and under 30 is considered abnormal.

Changes in pulse pressure usually denotes some organic defect, or malfunction, or the presence of nerve impulses which have reached threshold intensity. In polygraph examination recorded changes from normal may be caused by question stimulus, excitement, hypertension, sensitivity, guilt complex, physical discomfort, excepting of course organic defects or artifacts.

HEART RATE

The first sound of the heartbeat (systolic) results from contraction of the ventricle, tension on the auriculoventricular valves, and the impact of the heart against the chest wall, and is synchronous with the apex beat and carotid pulse. This sound is prolonged and dull; after the first sound is a short pause, then the second sound (diastolic) which results from the closure of the aortic and pulmonary valves. This sound is short and high-pitched. The rate of the heart is figured by its minute volume, or its output per minute. In an average size adult with a pulse rate of 70, the amount is approximately 4 liters. Two to 3 oz of blood are driven into the arteries by each heartbeat. The human heart beats about 72 times a minute or 104,000 times per day.

PULSE WAVE AMPLITUDE

The strength of the heartbeat itself, along with the volume ejected into systemic circulation, plus a momentary aortic regurgitation immediately eliminated by nerve-controlled vasoconstriction creates a forceful pulse wave transmission. The force of this pulse wave in the brachial artery increases air pressure within the arm cuff band, thereby forcing air volume from the bladder through the tubing into the instrument's cardio tambour. This movement provides power to move the pen fork, and its recording pen, in an upward direction. Such is called the ascending limb of the cardio tracing.

When the pulse wave passes beyond the cuff, such allows a drop in air pressure (diastole) within the cuff. A partial vacuum is created within the system, thus decreasing the air in the tambour and causing a downward movement of the pen fork.

The force of the wave, itself, and the pulse pressure in the brachial artery determines the amplitude (height) of the tracing.

Amplitude: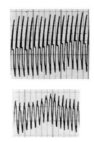

Amplitude:

In helping the examiner to accurately compute heart beat, kymograph chart paper manufacturers have vertically lined the paper in one- and five-second intervals. With the paper moving at six inches per minute, a five-second interval utilizes one-half inch of chart. The examiner counts the heartbeats inside any ten-second interval and then multiplys by six.

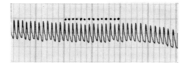

A, 14 beats in 10 seconds. B, Heart beat = 14 × 6 = 84 per minute.

NORMAL RESPIRATORY PATTERN

The instrument's pneumograph recording system is designed on a vacuum (or pneumatic) principle.

Normal adults produce a respiratory pattern of from fifteen to twenty breaths per minute. At the moment of closing the pneumo vent to the system, the air pressure equals outside air pressure and on inhalation creates a slight negative or vacuum to norm, while on exhalation it creates a slight pressure to norm. The system, as such, does not have a vacuum produced by the operator of the instrument; but only through subject's chest expansion is a "slight" vacuum or negative to the normal air pressure thus produced.

A transfer of air volume allows the instrument bellows to move backwards. This causes an upward movement of the pneumo pen and is referred to as the ascending limb of the tracing. As subject exhales, the reverse instrumental process takes place, causing an increase in air volume against the bellows, thus producing the downward or descending limb of the tracing.

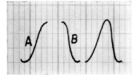

A, Ascending—inhalation. B, Descending—exhalation.

In normal respiration the lungs become involved in two successive phases: (1) breathing, which brings air and blood together in the lungs, and (2) the transportation of oxygen and carbon dioxide between the lungs and the cells.

Control of respiration is provided by autonomic nerves from automatic centers in the medulla oblongata, centers in the spinal cord, the phrenic nerve, peripheral nerves, along with occasional afferent regulators occurring in response to some visual or auditory stimuli.

Normal respiration, vesicular breathing, is heard over the body of the lungs by means of a stethoscope, and is characterized by a soft, breezy inspiration and a short, low-pitched expiration. Generally, expiration is not more than one-half as long as inspiration. Ausculation over trachea or main bronchi in the interscapular space yields bronchial breathing.

DEVIATIONS FROM NORMAL BREATHING

Abnormal breathing patterns are usually pathological in origin. In women and children breathing is largely thoracic or costal; in men and in the elderly of both sexes, it is largely abdominal or diaphragmatic. Restricted abdominal breathing is observed in pregnancy, in abdominal tumors and effusions; in diaphragmatic pleurisy; in paralysis of the phrenic nerve from pressure or bulbar disease and occasionally in hysterical abdomen.

Some pathological abnormalities in breathing are "rales"—abnormal bubbling sounds; "asthmatic"—harsh breathing with a prolonged wheezing expiration; "bronchial" or "tubular"—high-pitched expiration which has sometimes a tubular quality; "cogged wheel or jerky"—respiratory murmur not continuous, but broken into waves; "odorus"—due to drugs, alcohol, tobacco, diabetes, kidney disease.

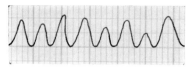

Normal respiratory tracing.

Abnormal respiratory tracing.

In polygraph examination an evaluation is made of subject's respiratory norm and deviations therefrom. If there is a pathological abnormality, and it is consistent, a norm is still established. Therefore, the polygraphist studies the nerve stimulus deviations from whatever norm is present. If we look at the breathing patterns aforegoing and then compare them with the deviations in each as noted below, which are the direct result of nerve stimulus, the correlate picture becomes more clear.

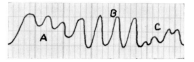

Deviation from respiratory norm. A, Normal. B, Deviation, C, Normal.

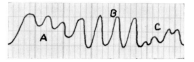

Deviation from pathological respiratory norm. A, Pathological normal. B, Deviation. C, Pathological normal.

On one occasion we asked a newly married female to volunteer for an experiment which turned out to be rather interesting. We attached the pneumograph tube just below her breasts and instructed her to breath normal. At B below, the examiner asked this question: "Since you have recently married, do you mind if I ask you a very personal question?" The legend explains what transpired. (Of course, the personal question was never asked, its purpose being only to induce nerve impulses beyond threshold intensity.)

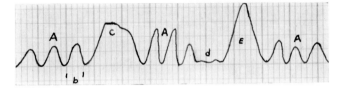

A, Normal tracing. B, Personal question stimulus. C, Top line suppression. When asked what she was thinking about at this point she replied: "I was thinking, what in the world have I got myself into?" D, Bottom line suppression. When again asked what was going through her thoughts she replied: "Well, when is he going to ask his darn question?" E, Deep breath and return to norm. After the instrument was deactivated subject remarked: "I got tired of waiting for that personal question so I guess I just took a deep breath. Anyway, I said to myself, 'the heck with it'."

Respiration is considered accelerated when more than twenty-five per minute, after fifteen years of age. The inspiration-expiration ratio is three to five. To compute the normal rate of breathing per minute the examiner counts the respiratory norm within a thirty-second period and multiplies by two:

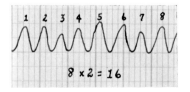

However, when obvious relevant deviations do appear in the respiratory pattern, such as an increase or decrease in the amount of breaths taken within a given period of time, it is wiser to count each individual breath in a whole sixty-second period, specifically noting how much time each deviation consumes.

A common abnormal type tracing which often falls into the norm classification is called "labored breathing" and is usually the result of hypertension, fear of the test, sensitivity to irrelevant past associations or conduct, magnification of petty things in the imagination, producing itself thus:

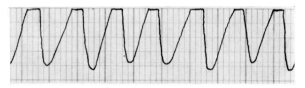

Nerve stimulus following a relevant question of importance to the subject will frequently change a norm respiratory pattern into labored breathing. However, it will usually return to norm.

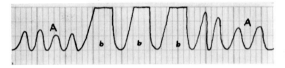

A, Norm pattern. B, Labored deviation from norm.

INCREASED FLOW IN PERSPIRATION

As measured by the galvanograph, at subject's palm or fingertips, there are numerous causes for an increase in perspiration. These come under the headings of changes in temperature and humidity, diluted blood, exercises, pain, nausea, nervousness, mental excitement, dyspnea and diaphoretics.

Perspiration is controlled by the sympathetic nervous system through true secretory fibers supplying the sweat glands. These are invaginated, epithelial, coil glands which penetrate the corium into the subcutaneous fatty tissue and permit sweat secretion.

The perspiration controlling center is in the medullary area. The corium of the skin is formed of connective tissue containing lymphatics, nerve and nerve endings, blood vessels, sebaceous and sweat glands, and elastic fibers. It is divided into two layers, a superficial papillary layer and a deep reticular layer. The papillary layer contains conical protuberances, the papillae, which fit into corresponding depressions in the epidermis. Within each papilla is a capillary loop which furnishes the epidermis with a blood supply.

If an auditory stimulus sets the body's fight or flight mechanism into motion there will be a minute to major change in sweat gland activity. The basic cause of this is a change in the electrical potential of the nerve impulse, efferently, along its pathway towards and at its junction with the sweat glands themselves. There is a lowering of electrical resistance as beads of sweat oozing out of the skin facilitate conduction of the current. Only electrodermal changes in the skin produce the galvo deflections. We repeat, instrument current is constant.

Another cause for changes in sweat gland activity is nerve stimulation resulting in a speedup of the heart action, secretion of adrenalin, increased blood pressure and constriction of small blood vessels in the skin, plus a stimulation of the temperature-regulating center in the thalamus.

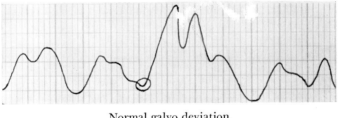

Normal galvo deviation.

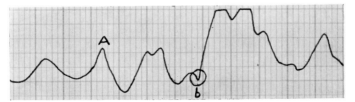

Induced galvo tracing. A, Normal galvo balance and fluctuations. B, Sudden loud noise produced reaction; nerve impulses race afferently to cortical brain centers, down thalamic relays, thence efferently to medulla and to sweat gland destination, off-setting electrical balance between subject and instrument.

CHANGES IN TEMPERATURE OF THE CAPILLARIES

The capillaries are minute blood vessels, 0.008 mm in diameter, which connect the smallest arteries with the smallest veins. They form an anastomosing network which brings the blood into intimate relationship to the tissue cells. Their wall consists of a single layer of squamous cells called endothelium through which blood and oxygen diffuse to the tissue and products of metabolic activity enter the blood stream. Their permeability is influenced by anoxia, adrenal cortical hormone and the concentration of cations in the blood.

As the blood coming from the heart reaches the periphery it goes into the various capillary beds, then into venules, thence into veins and commences its return to the heart. An increase of the muscular tone, a further vasoconstriction of the circular fibers and arteriolar vessels diminishes the caliber of the arterioles and reduces the supply of blood to the capillaries. A reduction of the circular muscular tone, or a vasodilatation of the smooth muscles, present an increase in arteriolar caliber and an increase of blood volume into and through the capillaries. The latter not only permits blood to flow into the capillaries more rapidly but also fills capillaries which prior to dilatation contained no blood.

Vasomotor actions affect changes in the temperature of the capillaries, sympathetic acceleration, parasympathetic inhibition. Vasodilatation brings to the surface areas more warm blood from the interior of the body. Constriction cuts off the warm supply of blood. Simply by touching the ear, whether it is cold or warm (flushed), evidences the presence of vasomotor changes.

It follows than that changes in temperature of the capillaries may be affected by emotional nerve impulses which cause varying changes in sweat gland activity.

CHANGES IN OXYGENATION OF THE BLOOD

Pure air is made up of 21% oxygen, 0.8% argon, and 78% nitrogen. However, the air we actually breath in every day encounters, particularly in metropolitan areas, is somewhat polluted. The proportions, especially of water vapor, are variable.

Therefore, we inspire about 20.96% oxygen, 79.00% nitrogen (including small amounts of argon and other inert gasses) and about 0.04% carbon dioxide. We expire about 16.3% oxygen, 79.7% nitrogen, and 4.0% carbon dioxide.

Oxygen is necessary for a balanced metabolism. It carries off waste products of metabolism in the form of heat, carbon dioxide and aqueous vapor. Oxygen is carried in combination with hemoglobin; oxyhemoglobin gives arterial blood its red color, reduced hemoglobin gives venous blood its blue color. Carbon dioxide is carried in combination with metalic elements in the blood as bicarbonates and also as carbonic acid. In internal respiration oxygen is carried to the cells by the blood, utilized and then the reverse process takes place with carbon dioxide.

Since normal respiration, at rest, is from about sixteen plus times per minute, with each breath consuming about one-half liter of air (inspired and expired) for regulation of normal bodily function, we can easily imagine that a sudden sharp intake of more air—or a sudden holding of the breath—will immediately affect the quantities of oxygen content with relation to other air components. When nerve impulses from the medulla inhibit normal function of respiration we may, for example, catch the breath. When the oxygen content of the blood is diminished, or carbon dioxide is increased, a reflex acceleration of respiration takes place.

In many instances, factors controlling blood flow simultaneously influence breathing. In general, these two physiological processes are attuned to the rate of tissue and organ activity. To elaborate further, stimulation of the phrenic nerve may cause a temporary, involuntary, holding of the breath which upsets the respiratory-cardiac equilibrium. The heart reacts by increasing its output. One ultimate effect is a change in temperature and capillary pressure which affects sweat gland activity. We see this graphically illustrated on page 214.

POLARIZATION OF SKIN TISSUES

A useful index of nerve activity is the play of nerve impulses upon some structure such as a muscle or gland with which the nerve is in physiological association, that is, which is innervated

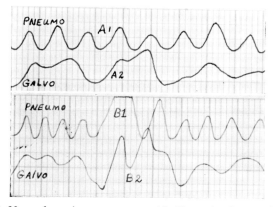

A1, Normal respiratory pattern. A2, Normal galvo tracing.
B1, Excessive intake of air. B2, Double rise and fall of galvo from changes in sweat gland activity.

by the nerve. A muscle with its nerve can even be removed from the body, and upon stimulation of the nerve the muscle will twitch. Here the muscle is not directly activated by the artificial stimulation but is thrown into activity by some influence reaching it via the nerve. This influence is the nerve impulse or a series of impulses. Indirect evidence of the activity can be observed also in the nerve fiber itself. In active nerve the oxygen consumption and the carbon dioxide production increase, indicating that oxidations occur; these presumably liberate the energy concerned with conduction or with the recovery of the nerve after conduction.

Heat is a by-product which has been quantitatively determined. With each nerve impulse there are accompanying electrical changes which are easily detectable with suitable sensitive instruments. These changes spread from the sight of stimulation along the fibers to their termination and serve as a most useful index of impulse conduction in the nerves.*

---

*Portions of the foregoing material may be found on pages 385, 386, *Machinery of the Body*, 4th ed., by Anton J. Carlson and Victor Johnson. Reprinted by permission of the University of Chicago Press. (Copyright 1937, 1941, 1948, 1953, by the University of Chicago. All rights reserved. Published 1937. Fourth ed. 1953. Third Impression 1956. Composed and printed by the University of Chicago Press.)

In the schematic below we see how stimulus applied creates electrical changes in an active nerve.

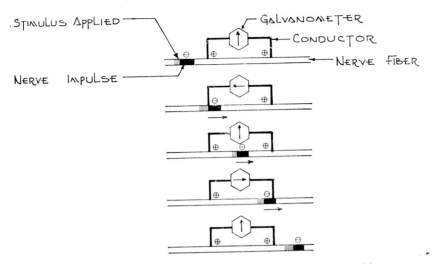

Figure 7. Observed here is a galvanometer making 2 contacts with a nerve fiber. The stimulus sets off a wave of negative electrical potential which passes along the membrane and deflects the galvanometer as illustrated. With suitable instruments such deflections may be recorded on photographic film. (Modified from Munn, *Psychology*, p. 52.)

One of the most generally accepted notions of the nature of the nerve impulse is known as the "membrane theory." As it stands today, the theory is that a nerve fiber is regarded as a long cylinder with a conducting core and a surface membrane of relatively high resistance. In the resting state the membrane is assumed to be more permeable to potassium than to sodium ions. Since potassium ions are more concentrated inside the fiber they tend to set up a potential difference with the inside negative and the outside positive. Propagation is brought about by the flow of current between resting and active nerve.

The schema below shows the flow of current in an unmyelinated axon. Suppose that point A is active and point B is resting. A is sodium permeable so the inside of the fiber is positive. B is potassium permeable so the inside is negative. Electric current therefore flows in a local circuit between resting and active nerve. This current reduces the membrane potential just ahead of the active region by drawing charge out of the membrane's capacity. As a result of the decrease in membrane potential the permeability to sodium rises and sodium ions enter, making the inside of the fiber electrically positive. In this way a waver of internal positivity and of increased sodium permeability spreads along the nerve fiber. The propagating agent is the electric current which is generated by the change in permeability.

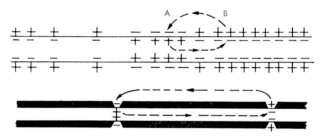

Figure 8. The upper sketch represents an unmyelinated nerve fiber, the lower a myelinated nerve fiber. (From Hodgkin, *The Conduction of the Nervous Impulse*, p. 32.)

The existence of a transient action potential and the possibility of sending trains of impulses is explained by the observations which show that the rise in sodium permeability is short-lived and that the potassium permeability increases during the latter part of the action potential. The effect of these changes is that after about 0.3 msec potassium ions leave the fiber faster than sodium ions enter. The outward migration of potassium ions restores the original potential difference across the membrane capacity and after a brief period the fiber is once more in a condition in which it can again conduct an impulse.*

Another example comes by increasing intensity of stimulation which leads to more frequent nerve discharges. When a single fiber is involved, an increase in intensity of stimulation can produce only a change in frequency of discharge. Under normal

*Hodgkin, A.L.: *The Conduction of the Nervous Impulses*. Thomas, Springfield, 1964, pp. 30-32.

circumstances, however, where bundles of fibers are stimulated, a more intense stimulus activates more fibers. Thus, increasing the intensity of stimulation does two things neurologically: (1) It increases the frequency of response in each fiber, and (2) activates more fibers. The effect, in each instance, is that more impulses reach the synapse, muscle, cerebral cortex, or whatever the terminal point happens to be.

The membrane theory of excitation has been worked out in great detail on nerve, and it is from nerve physiology that most of its support is derived. It is probable, nonetheless, that something like this occurs in excitation of other tissues as well. The finding of currents of injury and action potentials in glands, skeletal muscles, and the heart, exactly as in nerve, suggests that in excitation of all these tissues fundamentally the same changes in polarized surface membranes are taking place.*

CHANGE IN BODY HOMEOSTASIS

Here we are speaking of the equilibrium of fluid content, chemical reaction and temperature within the body. These are the physiological "drives" for survival of the organism and are often referred to as compensatory units. Ego-defensive functions are similar, on a psychological level, to the compensatory reactions referred to in physiology as homeostatic.

The way we are supplied with oxygen is interesting. We live in an ocean of air which is one-fifth oxygen. If deprived of it for even a few minutes one dies. While there is certain evidence of the physiological need, curiously enough, the need is not the basis of any strong physiological drive. The reason that man can continue to exist without such a drive is that under normal circumstances the need for oxygen is completely satisfied as a consequence of the satisfaction of a different need—the need to eliminate carbon dioxide.

---

*Portions of the foregoing material may be found between pages 393 and 396, *Machinery of the Body,* 4th ed., by Anton J. Carlson and Victor Johnson. Reprinted by permission of the University of Chicago Press. (Copyright 1937, 1941, 1948, 1953 by the University of Chicago. All rights reserved. Published 1937. 4th ed. 1953. Third Impression 1956. Composed and Printed by the University of Chicago Press.)

Among the blood's numerous functions is the chemical and thermal coordination of the body which is composed of 22% solids and 78% water. Life itself depends upon a great variety of intermittent or continuous chemical reactions between protoplasmic ingredients. These are made possible, then, partly by the dissolved state in which many of the reacting agents are held in the cell and its immediate environment.

Many of the important properties of cells, such as permeability, irritability, and nerve conduction, appear to be related to the presence of electrical charges upon cell membranes which depend upon the presence of electrolytes in and about the cells. Finally, water can absorb more heat from warm surroundings with less change in its own temperature than almost any other known substance. This is important in living systems because temperature changes markedly influence chemical reactions and, therefore, physiological reactions as well.

Of first importance in protoplasm are the protein compounds which are more intimately bound up with cell life than any other ingredient. Its coordinates which comprise the great bulk of materials in cells are carbohydrates and fats. Enzymes put these constituents together and place them in activity, even though the enzymes themselves are nonliving cellular products. In the state of the proteins and protoplasm lies a secret of protoplasmic organization. Protein is present in what is called a "colloidal suspension." Colloidal states are not peculiar to proteins, or even to living systems. They do have many properties in common with true solutions. These suspended colloidal particles are distributed homogeneously throughout the water. Within the cell there is a tremendously large total surface area of colloidal particles. Consequently the distribution of the cell proteins into these tiny particles and the multiplication of reactive surface area thereby plays a significant role in determining the rapid rate at which intracellular reactions are known to occur.

And so we see that the metabolic processes can be divided into two main categories: those in which the compounds of cells are synthesized, or built up, called anabolism; and those in which the chemical breakdown or decomposition occurs, called catabolism. Both usually proceed at all times.*

By following the condensed material aforegoing, we can readily imagine how both pathological and psychological disturbances in the body's homeostasis results in immediate changes in sweat gland activity, thus creating positive fluctuations in the polygraph instrument's galvanometer tracings.

A metabolism imbalance automatically changes the polarization and electrical conducting ability of the nerve tissue. A similar imbalance affects the rate of the heart volume and pressure of arterial blood, temperature of the capillaries and secretions of the sweat glands themselves.

THE NERVOUS SYSTEM

Both psychologists and physiologists refer to the brain and spinal cord as the main center of operations in the human body. In other words, after information is received at operations center via the peripheral afferent nerves from all parts of the body, "orders" are sent out along the efferent nerves, causing various body parts to make the appropriate adjustments.

It is largely through the agency of the central nervous system that all the various tissues and systems of the body are integrated into a smoothly operating unit. However, although we learn much about the heart by isolating it from the body, our information about heart action is woefully incomplete unless the data so collected are regarded as only a beginning. A clear picture emerges only when the heart is considered in relation to the rest of the body—to the blood it pumps; to the machinery of breathing, which depends upon the pump; to the glands of internal secretion, the blood vessels, the skeletal muscles, the digestive apparatus.

The nervous system is not the only integrating machinery of the body. Many chemical correlations supplement the nervous mechanisms.

---

*Portions of the foregoing material may be found on pages 47, 48, *Machinery of the Body*, 4th ed., by Anton J. Carlson and Victor Johnson. Reprinted by permission of the University of Chicago Press. (Copyright 1937, 1941, 1948, 1953, by the University of Chicago. All rights reserved. Published 1937. 4th ed. 1953. Third Impression 1956. Composed and printed by the University of Chicago Press.)

Even the most complex activities of the brain-conscious pro-cesses—emotions, thinking, reasoning—are interwoven with the functions of the lowliest of internal organs. A beautiful symphonic theme may quicken the pulse; anticipation of an examination may flood the blood with sugar. On the other hand, the state of the stomach may effect one's "state of mind."

When an event occurring internally or externally affects the nervous system, that event is said to be a stimulus. A stimulus re-ceived outside the body is called exteroceptive; one received from within the body is called interoceptive. Interoceptive stimuli may originate in the muscles, tendons and joints and give informa-tion as to their states of tension and position; such are also called proprioceptive. Similar stimuli may originate in the organs (vis-cera) and give information as to their activities. Such are called visceroceptive.

Responses thus appropriate to the nature of stimulation appear in animals having what is known as a "synaptic" nervous system. In this system, of which our own is a highly complicated form, there are relatively discrete nervous units known as neurons. Each neuron has a cell body and nerve fibers. Conduction through the neuron is normally in only one direction—from the dendrites through the cell body and along the axon. The junctions where nerve impulses pass from one neuron to another are known as synapses, hence the term "synaptic nervous system."

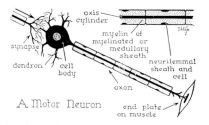

Figure 9. Schema of a (motor) neuron (greatly magnified). Inset shows part of axon for detail. (From Basmajian, *Primary Anatomy*, p. 271.)

Synapses slow down the passage of nerve impulses from one neuron to another and often block passage of an impulse com-

pletely. Interaction between neurons is possible at synapses and here the impulses of several neurons may combine to inhibit or facilitate further transmission. It is because we possess this type of nervous system that we do not, like the jelly fish, have to respond all over when stimulated. Impulses follow pathways which are more or less specific, allowing us to make partial responses. The nerves are such specific pathways, as noted in the following schematic.

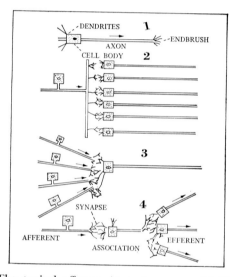

Figure 10. (1) The typical efferent (motor) neuron. (2) Here impulses are shown as coming along an afferent (sensory) axon into a synaptic junction involving several efferent neurons. (3) Several afferent neurons converging upon a single efferent neuron. (4) Association neuron in synaptic conjunction with an afferent and several efferent neurons. (After Munn, *Psychology*, p. 48.)

Impulses coming from the skin enter the spinal cord over afferent neurons and, at the same level, make synaptic connections with association and efferent neurons. When this circuit (the reflex arc) is completed, the muscles respond. As impulses come in over the afferent neuron, they not only travel around the arc but also ascend the cord. At the upper end of the cord, in lower brain centers, other circuits may be made, carrying the im-

pulses back to efferent neurons at the level of stimulation.* In the diagram below we visualize motor neurons in ventral horns and some of the connections between sense organs and muscles throughout the cord and brain.

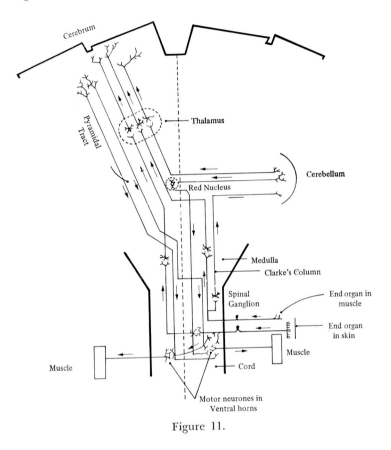

Figure 11.

THE AUTONOMIC NERVOUS SYSTEM

While a basic understanding of the central (cerebral) nervous system is necessary in polygraphy, the polygraphist must give more serious attention to functions of the autonomic (a motor system)

---

*Munn, Norman L., *Psychology*, 2nd ed., Houghton Mifflin, Boston, 1951, pp. 46, 48.

with emphasis on the sympathetic and parasympathetic sub-divisions.

It is the sympathetic division that takes charge in an emergency, and the parasympathetic that is in abeyance.

It is primarily due to the actions of this motor system that polygraph chart tracings are produced and graphically recorded.

A special division of the peripheral nervous system, the autonomics contain efferent fibers and nerves which supply the innervation of internal or visceral structures such as the alimentary canal, blood vessels, lungs, heart, bladder and other glands.

Voluntary or conscious control of the autonomic nerves is virtually absent. We cannot voluntarily slow the heart rate by activation of the vagus nerve, or cause the sweat glands to secrete by activation of their efferents, in the same direct way that we can voluntarily contract skeletal muscles.

Although the autonomic nerves are efferents, it is important to note that there are also afferent nerve fibers included in the autonomic nerve trunks. These visceral afferent fibers have only very indirect connections with the conscious centers of the brain. Normal stimulation of these afferent fibers, therefore, does not usually cause sensations, as contrasted with stimulation of such afferents as those mediating the sense of pain, touch, temperature, or pressure from the skin. We are totally unconscious of the stimulation of the afferent fibers in the lungs which occurs at the end of each normal inspiratory movement in breathing or of the fibers in the arch of the aorta occurring with each beat of the heart.

In a word, the autonomic nervous system and the visceral afferents carry out their functions mainly reflexly and automatically, without its manifold activities reaching consciousness in most cases, or without the possibility of direct voluntary intervention or modification of its activities.*

While both divisions, sympathetic and parasympathetic, are characterized by requiring two peripheral neurons for the con-

---

*Portions of the foregoing material may be found on pages 406, 407, *Machinery of the Body*, 4th ed., by Anton J. Carlson and Victor Johnson. Reprinted by permission of the University of Chicago Press. (Copyright 1937, 1941, 1948, 1953 by the University of Chicago. All rights reserved. Published 1937. 4th ed. 1953. Third Impression 1956. Composed and printed by the University of Chicago Press.)

duction of the efferent impulse, in each case the axon of the first neuron comes from the cell in a central nervous system; it is known as the preganglionic fiber, and it resembles an ordinary motor nerve. It ends by synapsing with a neuron entirely outside the central nervous system. The axon of this second cell is known as the postganglionic fiber and it is the final pathway of the autonomic nervous system since it activates smooth muscle, cardiac muscle, or gland.

Sympathetic Division

Cell bodies of the first neurons of the sympathetic division are found only in the spinal cord and only in a region of it restricted to an area between the first thoracic and third lumbar segments. They are small cells lying a little lateral to the anterior horn cells in a special column of cells (the intermediolateral cell mass).

These cells are often referred to as the lateral horn cells. The preganglionic fibers issuing from these cells, because of the restricted area of the cord from which they come, are sometimes referred to as the thoracolumbar outflow. Lying a little lateral to the vertebral bodies is a chain of ganglia connected by fibers. It extends from the level of the first cervical vertebra down to the coccyx. The (paired) chain is known as the sympathetic trunk and its ganglia are called the paravertebral ganglia.*

---

*Cates, H.A.; Basmajian, J.V., *Primary Anatomy*, 3rd ed. Williams & Wilkins, Baltimore, 1955, pp. 289-90.

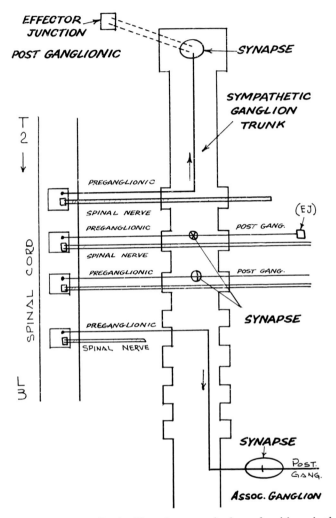

Figure 12. The preganglionic fiber leaves spinal cord with spinal nerve, enters sympathetic trunk where it may either synapse or pass through to a preaortic or associated ganglion before synapsing. Postganglionic fibers run to effector junctions (EJ) and thence to effector organs.

The sympathetic division of the autonomic nervous system, as diagramed below, acts as an efferent accelerator upon the heart; dialates the iris of the eye; constricts the salivary gland; inhibits activity of the stomach and small intestine and relaxes the rectum and bladder.

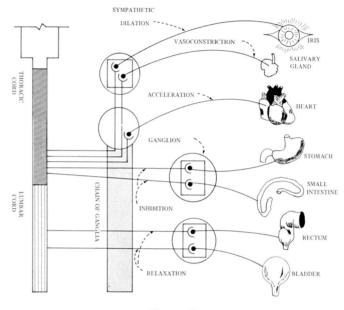

Figure 13.

To summarize, the sympathetic system is composed of a special set of nerves and ganglia uniting all parts of the body and subjecting them to a common involuntary nerve impulse. It consists of a pair of ganglionated cords, one on each side of the entire vertebral column, connected with the thoracic and lumbar parts of the spinal cord by means of ramicommunicantes, communicating visceral, sensory and preganglionic fibers, distributing to the viscera of the abdomen and pelvis, the heart and lungs, the peripheral blood vessels, glands and smooth muscles of the skin. Stimulation causes reflex dilatation of the pupil, arterioles, bronchioles, relaxation of the smooth muscle of the stomach, and intestines, and acceleration of the heart. Normally, there is a delicate balance between the divisions of the autonomic nervous system so that the insides of the body function well.

The sympathetic system is brought into action by certain stimuli or emotions, such as rage and fear, sensations or other emotions of the body's fight or flight mechanism. When it is brought into action it is able to overwhelm almost any action of the cranial division. With it in operation, as an emergency system, from a polygraph standpoint, it controls, regulates and handles nerve impulses to the eyes; increases, decreases or modifies respiration; increases the rate and force of the heart as it pumps blood into the circulatory system.

When protecting the body the sympathetic system also results in an increase in the secretion of adrenalin, increased sweat gland activity (however, the sweat glands per se are not immediately stimulated by adrenalin) ; produces a slight dilatation of blood vessels going to the brain and lungs, to the skeletal muscles and sweat glands, and a constriction of arteries and arterioles. Such a multiple process is one of the main causes for a sharp rise in blood pressure.

Upon facing a critical situation, sometimes fear and the desire for fight or flight develops. Through the sympathetic nervous system the body prepares for this situation. Since there are differences in brain energy reserves for each person, in glandular function, in character structure and in personality, the intensity of the stimulus may vary in the manner in which it is reproduced on a polygraph chart.

The Parasympathetic Division

When in action, this system causes constriction of the pupil, the arterioles and bronchioles; contraction of the smooth muscle in the stomach and intestines; slowing up of the heart; and stimulates secretions of many glands in the body. It controls certain aspects of cranial and sacral flow with a separateness between the two. Three of the most important functions in cranial outflow of the parasympathetic are control of

1. Facial: The 7th pair of cranial nerves affecting the great motor nerve of face and muscles; exclusively motor at its origin, but it subsequently receives fibers from the (5th) trigeminus which give it some sensory function.

2. Glossopharyngeal: The 9th pair, in part a special nerve of taste, a nerve of sensation, and also contains motor fibers (a) a sensory nerve of the mucuous membrane of the pharanyx, (b) a small branch of the carotid nerve carrying impulses dealing with blood pressure from the carotid sinus to the medulla.

3. Vagus nerve: 10th cranial nerve (pneumogastric); a mixed nerve having motor and sensory functions and a wider distribution than any of the other cranial nerves. It distributes motor inhibitor fibers to the heart. It also has constrictor fibers to the bronchi, stomach, small bowel and ascending colon, and secretory motor fibers to the digestive glands. It contains sensory fibers from the stomach and small intestines. It acts as a brake on the heart.

As we note, the sympathetic and parasympathetic are functionally antagonistic. For example, the sympathetic accelerates the heart action while the parasympathetic slows it down. On the other hand, the parasympathetic accelerates stomach activity, which is checked by the sympathetic. Most of the visceral and other internal structures have these dual connections working in opposition so that one accelerates while the other inhibits. The schematic below shows the two systems combined.

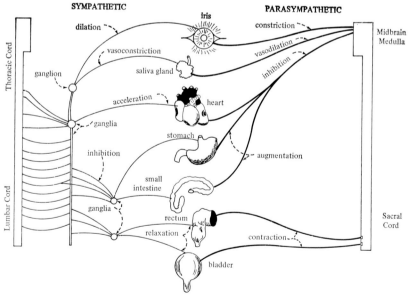

Figure 14.

We can readily draw a conclusion, therefore, that emotion is characterized by autonomic function rather than by sympathetic action alone.

The Emotional Aspect

In considering the role of the cerebral cortex in emotion, which transfers the emotion via nerve pathways to one division or another in the autonomic nervous system, four facts stand out: (1) Most emotion-provoking stituations cannot be perceived without a cortex. (2) The cortex plays a major role in adjustment to emotion-provoking situations. (3) Another contribution of the cortex is the sustaining of emotional behavior after the emotion-provoking stimulus has gone. (4) Removal of the cerebral cortex increases the intensity of emotional expression.

This widely accepted observation is consistent with the well-known fact that the cerebrum exerts an inhibiting influence over other neural mechanisms, including the hypothalamus.*

THE EFFECTS OF DRUGS UPON THE NERVOUS SYSTEM

Drugs can stimulate, depress or irritate.

A stimulant drug increases physiological activity; a depressant decreases physiological activity, and an irritant drug affects the cell nutrition and growth. Since irritant drugs are of no real concern to the polygraphist, only stimulant and depressant drugs will be touched upon.

Stimulant Drugs

These are the drugs that stimulate cells into greater activity. Two types of importance are central nervous system and cardiac.

The central nervous system stimulant drugs include amphetamines (bennies), antidepressants (such as Parnate®), and caffeine (coffee, No-Doz®).

The cardiac stimulant drugs include adrenalin, digitoxin, and nitroglycerin.

---

*For a survey of relevant studies on neurological aspects of emotion see Morgan, C.T., and Stellar, E.: *Physiological Psychology*, 2nd ed. McGraw-Hill, New York, 1950, Chapter XVI.

Both types of stimulant drugs can affect polygraph charts in the following ways:

1. Breathing.
    a. Decreased amplitude.
    b. Increased rate.
2. Galvanic Skin Response.
    a. Faster reactions.
    b. Greater reactions.
3. Cardiovascular.
    a. Increased pulse rate.
    b. Faster and greater reactions.

Depressant Drugs

The more widely known depressant drugs include

1. Alcohol.
2. Anticonvulsants.
    a. Dilantin®.
    b. Mesantoin®.

3. Antihistamines (over-the-counter).
    a. Anahist®.
    b. Contac®.
    c. Dristan®.
    d. Nytol®.
    e. Sominex®.
    f. Tri-Span®.

4. Antihistamines (prescription).
    a. Benadryl®.
    b. Chlor-trimeton®.
    c. Phenergan®.

5. Barbiturates ("goof-balls").
    a. Amytal®.
    b. Nembutal® ("yellow jackets").
    c. Phenobarbital.
    d. Seconal® ("red jackets").
    e. Tuinal®.

6. Narcotics.
   a. Codeine.
   b. Demerol® (Meperadine).
   c. Dilaudid®.
   d. Hycondan.
   e. LSD.
   f. Marihuana.
   g. Opium (includes heroin and morphine).
   h. Pantopon®.
7. Tranquilizers.
   a. Librium®.
   b. Meprobamate (Equanil®, Miltown®).
   c. Ultran®.

Depressant drugs can affect polygraph tracings in the following ways:

1. Breathing.
   a. Increased amplitude.
   c. Decreased rate.
2. Galvanic Skin Response.
   a. Slower reactions.
   b. Lesser reactions.
3. Cardiovascular.
   a. Decreased pulse rate.
   b. Slower and lesser reactions.

Every day most of us become "medicated" without our realizing it. Therefore, even a true denial to the standard pretest data sheet question: "Have you taken any pills, medicines or drugs today?" can be somewhat misleading.

For example, coffee can produce the same effect as a stimulant drug, especially if the coffee is strong or several cups are drunk just prior to the start of the pretest. This is because a strong cup of coffee can contain as much caffeine as the average caffeine pill.

The same stimulant effect can be obtained from most of the popular nasal sprays such as Sinex®, and inhalers, which contain one or more stimulants. The larger the dose the greater the stimulation.

There are two main depressants which are generally not considered to be drugs. Aspirin in large doses (6 or more tablets in a 3-hour period or less) produces depressant symptoms. Since almost all cough syrups contain either alcohol, an antihistamine, and/or codeine, they can also produce depressant effects.*

*Berman, Milton A.: Drugs versus the polygraph. *The Journal of Polygraph Studies*, Vol. 1, No. 4, Jan.-Feb. 1967.

Chapter 9

THE PHYSIOLOGY OF SUBJECT MOVEMENT

THE MERE KNOWLEDGE of how to activate a polygraph instrument, ask a series of questions and note some kind of response on a moving chart can be taught any dolt. But, the complicated psychophysiological phenomena taking place within the brain and the separate nervous systems requires acute and constant study.

A successful test conclusion, based on fairness, impartiality and objectivity cannot be obtained without a clear understanding of what must be realized to separate tracing changes caused by physical movement, voluntarily or involuntarily, from chart tracing changes caused by the emotional aspect.

As already noted, the kymograph pulls the chart paper under the pens at the testing rate of six inches per minute. Our first illustration below shows all three sections of the polygraph instru-

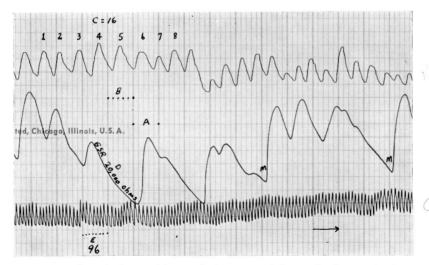

Normal tracing. A, 5-second intervals. B, 1-second intervals. C, Respiration—rate per minute. D, Normal GSR at 20,000 ohms. E, Cardio tracing—rate per minute.

ment recording a subject's physiological norm on a chart without question insertion. (The chart paper used is distributed by Associated Research, Inc., Chicago.) As we progress through this chapter we hope the reader will become aware of some rather startling psychophysiological-polygraph correlations which have heretofore been denied the general and professional public because of unconcern, "lie-detector" witch hunts, skepticism, misconception, and misinformation.

We shall now begin taking up general deviations from norm in all three sections, introducing sensitivity of the instrument's role followed by physiological explanation where possible or applicable. We shall see that subject movement or conduct while on the chart is instantly recorded in one, two, or all three tracing components.

In this particular, we shall consider audible sigh, cough, yawn, clearing the throat, sniff or snort, swallowing, subject talking other than yes or no, belch, where yes or no is recorded in the pneumograph tracing, gritting the teeth, contraction of the anal sphincter, wiggling toes, pressure on fingers where electrodes are attached, tightening leg muscles, and voluntary holding of the breath.

Whether or not these subject actions become indicative of attempted deception will depend to a great extent on where they take place during chart time, and their repetition, if any.

When the young subject, whose body produced the tracing example shown on page 235, was asked to submit to this simple experiment he was told that no questions of any nature would be asked. However, when "I" was inserted after a period of fourteen seconds, we note that some five seconds later there was a slight reduction in respiratory amplitude, though not in width. Normally this is indicative of anticipation. In other words, a slight emotion (perhaps apprehension) was generated.

Therefore, in A1, we see what may be termed subject's pretest norm without stimulus. The verbal stimulus, with respect to test commencement, results in a slight change which is shown at A, although both A1 and A cardio areas are still functioning at about eighty-four per minute. The emotional factor and the diminishing amplitude suggest a slight imbalance in oxygen intake and

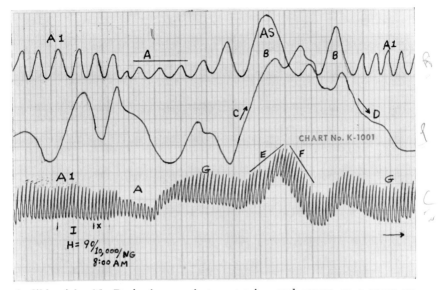

Audible sigh. A1, Beginning respiratory tracing and return to a more acceptable "resting norm." AS, Audible sigh. (Note change in tracing amplitude.) B, Physiological recovery period during return. (Note change in width of tracing as compared to A widths.) C-D, Rise and fall of galvo pen (GSR). E-F, Rise and fall of both systolic and diastolic pressures in cardio tracing. G, Normal cardio and return to norm. H, 90 mm of mercury pressure shown on sphyg dial, 10,000 ohms, electrical instrument constant (sensitivity setting). NG indicates normal galvo operation. I, Stimulus marks and "x" indicate subject was told the following: "Sit perfectly still. Do not move. The test is about to begin. Answer the questions yes or no only."

carbon dioxide outgo. As a result, we see the materialization of AS.

AS is the body's way of overcoming this imbalance and returning itself to resting norm. An increase of the chest size is effected by a contraction of the diaphragm and by the external intercostal muscles which lift the ventral ends of the ribs and increase the dorsoventral dimensions of the chest cavity. The diaphragm descends. A corresponding volume of air is drawn into the lungs. Thus, the inspiratory phase (ascending limb of the pneumo tracing). Elastic contraction and gravity brings about the expiratory phase, expelling the air (descending limb of the pneumo tracing).

In B we see a longer expiration period, the whole cycle of AS taking some eight seconds. The recovery period takes some ten seconds before A1 is reestablished. In B we note a change in the width and height of each segment of the tracing as it returns to its A1 status.

C-D presents us with a rise and fall—or a decrease and increase in subject's galvanic skin response—of the galvo pen. In other words, a change and return to norm. The time involved is about thirty-two seconds.

E-F introduces a rise and fall (elevation and decline in blood pressure) in both systolic and diastolic pressures without change in amplitude or position of the dicrotic notch.

G gives us the resting norm and return to cardiac (heart rate and pulse pressure as recorded through the brachial artery) normality as noted before AS. (Perhaps we should say here that an audible sigh or deep breath of the same duration generally affects all 3 tracings in a similar manner. There are, however, exceptions to this generality.)

H indicates that cardio instrument pressure over the brachial artery is set at about 90 mm. Ten thousand ohms signifies that an instrument constant of this degree was necessary to match subject's own electrically generating norm in order to provide a recording of decreases or increases therein. NG, as previously noted, indicates the galvanometer is operating in normal galvo, rather than in electrically controlled self-centering.

I is the verbal stimulus which generated our whole change from respiratory resting norm. This chart illustration was taken at 8 AM when subject was rested and suffering from no known physical defects or psychological abnormalities.

PHYSIOLOGICALLY SPEAKING

We have already learned that all muscles of breathing contract in a harmonious manner, most likely because the cells of the respiratory center resemble the tissue of the pacemaker of the heart and possess an intrinsic rhythmicity which is not dependent entirely on nervous influences.

At A1 we see this intrinsic rhythmicity which we have casually referred to as resting norm. With the introduction of stimulus

I, we observe a slight suppression. Here we might say that an emotional factor has created one or a series of nerve impulses in the cerebrum, sent it to the respiratory control center in the medulla with this type of message: "Watch it! We're getting too much vagus inhibition and an imbalance of oxygen and carbon dioxide!" Immediately an efferent nerve impulse hits the vagus center and decreases inhibition. The slight excess of carbon dioxide becomes a stimulant of sorts. Nerve endings near the carotid sinus and in the aorta are chemically stimulated, effecting a reflex acceleration, or AS. By or before the time the pneumograph pen reaches its maximum height (ascending limb peak), we have a slight overabundance of oxygen but maintain the same amount, plus, of unexpired carbon dioxide. Intercostals are stimulated efferently. Expiration takes place.

At the same time, during this afferent-efferent reflex, the cardio regulatory center in the medulla sends an efferent dilatory sympathetic nerve impulse to the sinus node. Vagus tonic inhibition is relaxed. Acceleration creates a momentary increase of the heart rate. More blood is pumped into the aorta, distending it, which in turn brings about a rise in blood pressure. Vasoconstriction shoots the increase into systemic circulation as compared to a wave rolling along the artery.

Immediately, the depressor nerve inhibits the vasoconstrictor center and restimulates the vagus center. A parasympathetic vagus impulse again inhibits the heart, restoring it to its normal tonic function. Hence, a fall in blood pressure.

To summarize, when the heart rate accelerates (sympathetic dilatation) more blood will be forced into the aorta and its branches, including the carotid artery and sinus. This distends and stimulates the aortic depressor and sinus nerves, which in turn stimulate the vagus center (parasympathetic), slowing the heart to its former rate. Likewise, if the heart should tend to slow down, the pressure would fall in these sensitive vascular areas. Both the tonic action of the nerves and the vagus inhibition would be reduced. Very soon the slowing heart would increase to its former rate.

We should also include here that B, the recovery period, shows a different depth with each phase of inspiration and expiration until resting norm is regained. This, perhaps, is due not only to nerve inertia, but also the time it takes for the respiratory and cardiac reflex nerve actions to readjust and correct themselves.

In the meantime, simultaneously with the foregoing, we see that GSR has been affected. We have previously established that the temperature (sweat gland activity) regulating center is in the thalamus. We saw earlier that, although respiration is controlled in part reflexly through the respiratory center (the medulla), conditions in the region of the center itself, namely the carbon dioxide concentration, also determined the activity of the center and, therefore, of the efferent systems leading from it to the breathing muscles. Similarly, in the case of the temperature-regulating center, nervous discharges through the appropriate efferent systems can occur reflexly. But they can also occur as a result of changes locally in the center itself. There is almost no lag between skeletal muscle activity and added heat production. A vasodilitation of skin vessels which brings more warm blood to the surface of the body also creates almost immediate changes, even though minute, in sweat gland activity. There is another factor which could be remotely included herein. Not only is there a definite quantity of heat liberated by the burning of a gram of carbohydrate, for example, but also this combustion always involves the consumption of the same volume of oxygen. Practically, this means that heat liberation can be measured indirectly simply by measuring the volume of oxygen used*

In polygraph language we now see a clearer picture of the following: (1) We have a certain element of skeletal activity in inspiration and expiration, initiated by a sudden intake of a large amount of oxygen; (2) We have the heat producing effect of a slight excess of carbon dioxide which has given us another heat-producing element, through dilitation, in increased blood pressure. Therefore, we picture galvo activity in the form of afferent

---

*Portions of the foregoing physiological material may be found on pages 322, 333, 336, *Machinery of the Body*, 4th ed., by Anton J. Carlson and Victor Johnson. Reprinted by permission of the University of Chicago Press. (Copyright 1937, 1941, 1948, and 1953 by the University of Chicago. All rights reserved. Published 1937. 4th ed. 1953. Third Impression 1956. Composed and printed by the University of Chicago Press.)

impulses to the thalamus, its efferent orders to the peripheral nervous system, resulting in a change in sweat gland activity.

While there may be many areas of the body secreting a certain amount of perspiration as a result of the foregoing physiological phenomena, finger electrodes of the polygraph instrument pick up this change within seconds after the verbal stimulus ended and reached the seat of consciousness and meaning in the appropriate brain centers. With the increase in sweat gland activity we see the production of the ascending portion of the galvanometer tracing and the descending limb which indicates a return to the existing status prior to verbal stimulus insertion.

In addition, with respect to sweat gland activity, many of the neurons susceptible to rising blood temperature are located in the anterior part of the hypothalamus, perhaps extending into the preoptic area. Their descending pathways pass down the brain stem and set connections with respiratory and cardiovascular mechanisms of the brain stem and spinal cord.* (2) When the blood temperature changes (or blood pressure in many cases), discharges evoked through these neurones set into play the peripheral processes which contribute to heat loss (respiratory changes, increased peripheral blood flow and perspiration). It is also possible that heat production may be somewhat inhibited.

Since peripheral vasodilation and perspiration are cholinergically regulated functions, some authorities have ascribed primarily parasympathetic activity to the anterior hypothalamus. The "neurones affected by falling blood pressure" are scattered in the hypothalamus, mostly below the supraoptic region, and have descending pathways similar to others. These cells set in motion the complex processes whereby the body temperature is maintained or elevated, including increased production of heat within the body and also conservation of heat by reducing radiation. The latter is accompanied by peripheral vasoconstriction. It is also believed that mechanisms in the midbrain take part. Heat production is also stepped up by a general metabolic speed-up, brought about by increased hypothalamic activity when an individual is exposed to cold. Again we stress the importance of maintaining an even examining room temperature of about 70 to 72 degrees.

*Ranson, S.W.: *A. Research Nerv. & Ment. Dis., Proc.,* 20:342, 1940.

COUGHING

For illustration purposes, the chart below shows the effect of a cough on all three tracing components.

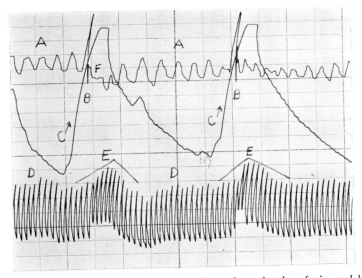

A, Respiratory norm. B, Subject coughs. (Note sharp intake of air, and break in pneumo tracing.) Five to 10 seconds elapse before a return to norm. C, Immediate rise in galvanometer tracing (sweat gland activity changes), lasting 2 to 3 seconds before a shaky return on the descending limb of the tracing. D, Normal cardiovascular rate. E, Rise and fall in blood pressure immediately following the cough. F, At the base of the forceful expulsion, the cough, subject swallowed. (The chart paper used here is lined in 5-second intervals and is distributed by the C.H. Stoelting Co. of Chicago, Illinois.)

Usually, coughing results from irritation of the linings of the respiratory passages. (There are occasions when a subject will deliberately force a cough at one or more key relevant questions of importance to himself in an effort to beat the test.) Essentially, these are modified respiratory act; in which at first a strong forced expiratory movement is started with the vocal cords tightly apposed (i.e. with the glottis closed). This greatly elevates the pressure within the lungs, so that when suddenly the glottis is opened, a blast of air is abruptly forced from the lungs through

the mouth in a cough, or through the nose in a sneeze, tending to expel the irritating object from the breathing passages. Yawning, snoring and hiccoughing are all modifications of the respiratory movements whose mechanisms are imperfectly understood and whose adaptive significance is even less clear.

YAWNING

Most yawns involve numerous facial, throat and tongue muscles as well as, in many cases, muscles of the neck whenever the head is moved. Any muscle movement expends energy, thereby creating a minute change in sweat gland activity and a deflection of the galvanometer pen.

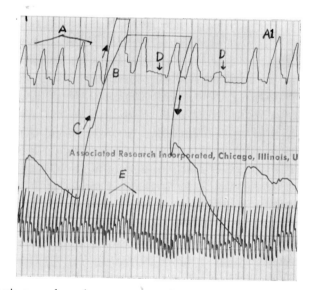

A, Subject's normal respiratory pattern. B, Here we see the deep breath associated with a yawn. C, Muscle contraction expends energy, creating a rise in the galvo pen which held aga⁺ st the top pen stop for some 12 seconds before the examiner mechanically returned it to center of the chart. D, Presents alternating deviations as the body overcomes an imbalance of oxygen and carbon dioxide and returns to normal respiration at A1. E, We see a rather minute deviation in the cardio tracing, created primarily by the deep breath commencing the yawn.

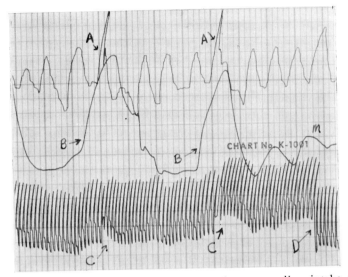

CLEARING THE THROAT. A, We see a sharp ascending intake and a break on the descending limb of the pneumo tracing when glottis closure combined with a tightening of stomach muscles momentarily stops all breathing. B, muscle contraction of the diaphragm with an elevation of the rib cage expends additional energy, thus imbalancing the preactive electrical energy "norm," resulting in a decrease in subject's resistance and immediate galvo deflection which lasts some 8 seconds before a return to the preestablished base line. C, Because of the sudden intake of air, along with elevation of the rib cage and the "forceful" clearing of the throat, we first see a minute break in the cardio tracing followed by a 5-second rise and fall in blood pressure. D, Some 13 seconds later subject flexed his right arm muscle which caused a sudden downward break in the cardio tracing.

Necessity for clearing the throat may frequently be associated with the same physiological purpose of coughing, e.g. to eliminate a foreign or irritating substance. The effect on all three tracings is clearly shown above.

SNIFFING

Sniffing may be caused by any number of things, e.g. fever, cold, irritation due to wet or dry mucous membranes, as well as foreign particles lodged in the nasal passage. In the illustration on page 243 we see the effects of sniffing on all three chart tracings.

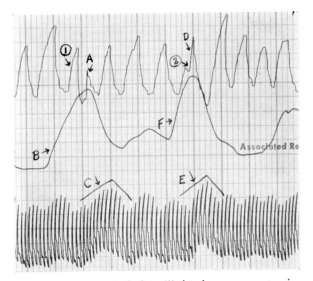

A, Just prior to A we see a deviation (1) in the pneumo tracing signifying the "need to sniff." At A, the short sharp sniff takes place. B, The need to sniff creates the generated nerve impulse as shown by galvo activity, prior to the actual sniff itself, lasting some 12 seconds before the galvo pen returns to its base line. C, Noted here is a slight rise and fall in blood pressure lasting some 8 seconds. D, Our second sniff takes place about half way up the ascending stroke of the pneumo tracing. Note the brief break (2) as the glottis closes and then opens to create the pointed tracing itself. E, Again we see a sharp 6-second rise and fall in blood pressure. F, Galvo activity this time runs about 5 seconds (because the galvo pen is longer) behind the pneumo recording pen.

Ciliated cells, which are end organs of nerve fibers, pierce the skull and pass back to the brain as the olfactory nerve or tract. Like the peripheral neuron system, the olfactory nerve is also composed of a series of neurons and is not entirely a true nerve but partly a fiber tract of the brain. The olfactory epithelium is bathed in liquid, and stimulation depends upon solution of the chemicals in this fluid. The moist receptors lie in the upper portion of the cavity, off the direct pathway of the stream of respired air. This tends to prevent drying of the surface and is responsible for the necessity of "sniffing" to bring a maximal concentration of chemicals in the air into contact with the sensitive cells.*

SWALLOWING

The tracing segment below was taken from a "live" test, an eighteen-year-old boy, 145 lbs., five feet four inches, blind in his right eye; inherently nervous and somewhat afraid of anything which might mean harm to his well-being; a psychiatric patient.

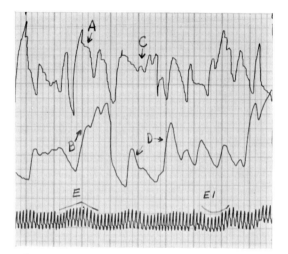

A, We note a sharp intake of air with a swallow on the descending stroke. B, Indicates immediate galvo activity created by a minute bombardment of nerve impulses, generated by action of those various muscles necessary to effect a swallow, in turn causing an increase in perspiration. C, A second swallow occurs almost at the top of inspiration, followed by a sharp expiration. D, Galvo activity caused by both events contained in C. E, The first "need" to swallow creates a minute rise in both systolic and diastolic pressure. However, at E-1, the swallowing itself produces only a minute decrease in systolic pressure.

---

*Portions of the foregoing physiological material may be found on page 497, *Machinery of the Body*, 4th ed., by Anton J. Carlson and Victor Johnson. Reprinted by permission of the University of Chicago Press. (Copyright 1937, 1941, 1948, and 1953 by the University of Chicago. All rights reserved. Published 1937. Fourth ed. 1953. Third Impression 1956. Composed and printed by the University of Chicago Press.)

Even with the raggedness of subject's respiratory tracing, the actual "swallowing" is clearly discernible.

The swallowing act is entirely dependent on nerves and is reflex in nature. Only the initial part of the act is voluntary. We are quite unable to stop the act of swallowing once saliva or materials in the mouth have reached the pharnyx.

There is a sharp contraction of the muscles comprising the walls of the pharynx, which moves the saliva or food downward. In this reflex the afferent side of the reflex arc is made up of certain of the cranial nerves, trigeminal and glossopharyngeal, and the superior laryngeal branch of the vagus which innervate the mucosa of the back of the mouth, the pharynx and the laryngeal region. Besides the afferent nerves mentioned, sensory fibers in the vagi, innervating the mucosa of the esophagus itself, are also capable of initiating reflex esophageal peristalsis. In swallowing, all possible pathways for food except the normal one are closed off by muscular contractions. The tongue muscles, pressing that organ of the muscle against the roof of the mouth and fitting against the cheeks on both sides, close off the anterior portion of the mouth cavity. Other muscles elevate the roof of the mouth and prevent passage of substances into the nasal cavity.

Considering the fact that breathing goes on at all times, it would seem that it would be very easy to aspirate particles into the lungs if an inspiration should occur just at the time of swallowing. But this is virtually impossible, because those same sensory nerves whose stimulation reflexly causes the swallowing movements at the same time transmit impulses to the respiratory center and inhibit it.* The schematic below illustrates.

The autonomic nervous system controls secretion of the salivary gland via sympathetic vasoconstriction and parasympathetic vasodilitation.

---

*Portions of the foregoing physiological material may be found on pages 291, 292, *Machinery of the Body*, 4th ed., by Anton J. Carlson and Victor Johnson. Reprinted by permission of the University of Chicago Press. (Copyright 1937, 1941, 1948, and 1953 by the University of Chicago. All rights reserved. Published 1937. Fourth ed. 1953. Third Impression 1956. Composed and printed by the University of Chicago Press.)

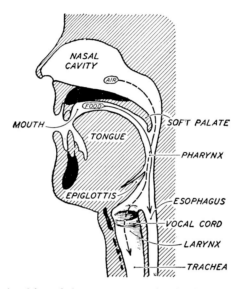

Figure 15. Relationships of the passageways for food and air. (From Carlson & Johnson, *Machinery of the Body*, Fig. 106, p. 293.)

TALKING (Other than Yes or No)

In most cases, talking, other than yes or no, depending on the force, meaning and intensity of the words uttered, along with what they mean to the person who utters them, will cause a deviation in both respiratory and galvo tracings. Movement at the same time will often cause a deviation in the cardio tracing. The illustration on page 247 covers both areas.

The breathing movements serve a number of useful functions besides the chief one of providing an exchange of the respiratory gases between the lungs and outside air. Vocalizaton of any kind—talking, singing, laughing—is a complex of muscular movements involving not only the lips, tongue, jaws and mouth but the breathing machinery as well. Sound production is a modification of breathing in which currents of air set the vocal cords into vibration. The pitch of the sound is regulated by the tautness of the vocal cords, which can be modified voluntarily. The volume of sound, its intensity, can also be varied at will by changing the

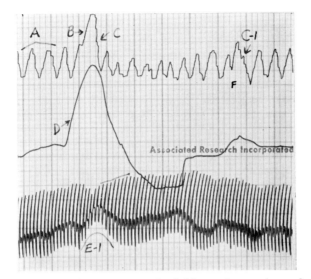

A, Uninterrupted respiratory norm. B, Subject takes a sharp deep breath and opens his mouth. C, We see the jagged-like serrations on the descending limb of the pneumo tracing as he speaks. D, Because of elevation of the rib cage at B, momentary closure of the glottis before talking commences, expended energy to do so results in a sharp rise of the galvo pen. E, The effects of B create a marked change in diastolic pressure, E-1, and a slight increase in both systolic and diastolic pressures. F, Again subject talks, at C-1, but this time at the top and on the descending stroke of a normal breath. There is no undue movement or sudden imbalance of oxygen and carbon dioxide, hence little to no galvo or cardio deviation.

force of the air current. Speech as we know it depends upon a degree of voluntary control of the breathing machinery—upon a limited control of the respiratory center by the higher conscious centers of the brain. Vocalization is limited ordinarily to the expiratory phase of respiration.*

*Portions of the foregoing physiological material may be found on page 247, *Machinery of the Body*, 4th ed., by Anton J. Carlson and Victor Johnson. Reprinted by permission of the University of Chicago Press. (Copyright 1937, 1941, 1948, and 1953 by the University of Chicago. All rights reserved. Published 1937. Fourth ed. 1953. Third Impression 1956. Composed and printed by the University of Chicago Press.)

BELCHING

Belching is seldom encountered during polygraph testing but it has been known to occur, either deliberately at relevant questions having some importance to the subject, or from strictly an involuntary standpoint.

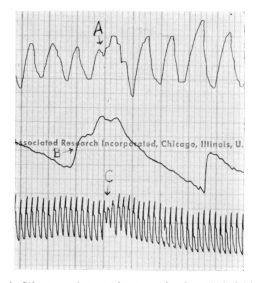

Belch tracing. A, We note that at the top of a breath belching takes place. Breathing is momentarily stopped, until the expulsion is concluded. B, Straining of abdominal muscles forcing the belch creates a deflection upward in the galvo tracing. C, Reflex sympathetic and parasympathetic action, caused by the forceful expulsion, and momentary holding of the breath, results in a brief cardio tracing change.

The act of belching indicates a momentary holding of the breath and a straining of certain abdominal muscles. The act itself may force out gastric fermentation, excessive air built up by continuous swallowing, or gases caused by foods or drinks containing acid and alkaline substances. In the straining associated with belching there is a sharp contraction of the skeletal muscles of the abdominal wall which serves to elevate pressure within the abdomen. The glottis is temporarily closed. As pressure builds up and the gaseous substance starts upward, the diaphragm relaxes and a forced expiration is effected. We might say this process is similar to the activity required for defecation and elimination of urine, except in this case there is no relaxation of the anus or urinal spincters.

The belch requires smooth muscular effort. Even some striated muscle is often put into motion, particularly in the shoulder and upper arm areas. Energy is consumed. A deep breath usually preceeds the actual expulsion, thus creating a momentary imbalance in oxygen and carbon dioxide. As a result, we see a break in the cardio tracing and a rise and return in the galvo tracing (sweat gland activity) .

ANSWER OF YES OR NO RECORDED

Arrows in the pneumograph tracing below point to instrument recording sensitivity each time the subject says yes or no.

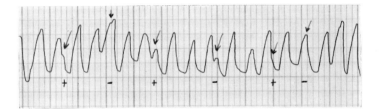

The simple yes or no, though consuming only perhaps one second, is immediately recorded. It is interesting to note that nearly all answers are recorded at the top, part way down, or near the bottom of the descending limb of the tracing. Rarely will a person answer on the ascending limb, primarily because it is habitual to speak or talk during the expiratory phase of respiration, then take another breath before talking again.

Answering yes or no is not the response-producing agent in the other two sections, any more than it is in the pneumograph tracing; it is what the question and the answer means to the subject.

GRITTING THE TEETH.

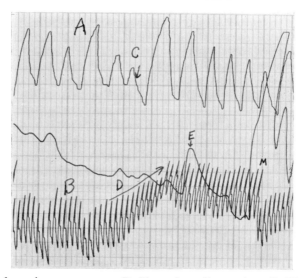

A, Normal respiratory pattern. B, Normal cardio tracing. C, Here we see "gritting the teeth" commence and continue for a full 8 seconds through a deep breath. As jaw muscle tension relaxes, a second deep breath follows. D, The combination of the 2 deep breaths develops a sharp rise in blood pressure which lasts some 10 seconds before it levels off or returns to norm. E, The deep breaths, change in blood pressure, and expended muscle energy create changes in sweat gland activity. (It should be noted that self-centering galvo was used during this tracing. This is about 80% of normal galvo sensitivity.)

Generally, gritting the teeth consumes energy via tightening of the jaw muscles and tensing of the tongue muscles. For this reason we see proprioceptive nerve impulses creating certain changes in sweat gland secretion. These impulses, generated from gritting the teeth or from stretching the muscles of mastication, reach the mesencephalic root whose fibers are the only sensory fibers of the somesthetic system which do not arise within ganglia but from cells within the central nervous system. Often times, if we grit the teeth hard enough, we will hear a type of "popping," or feel a "hollowness" in the ears. The drawing below gives us a deeper insight into this subject matter.

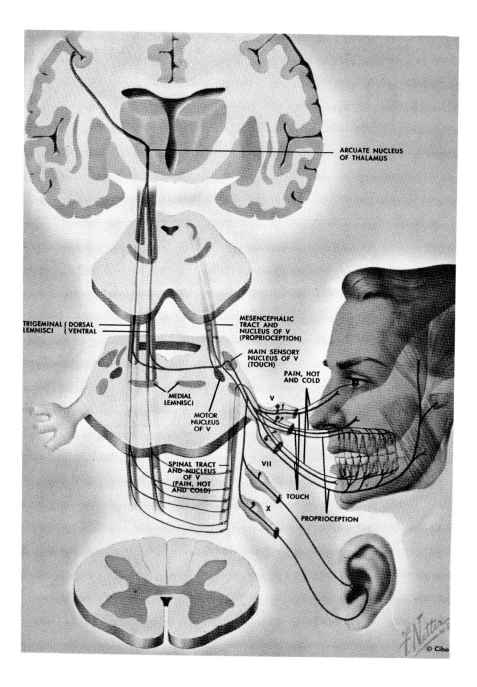

Color Plate II. Somesthetic System Head. The face is supplied with sensory nerves by the trigeminus (V), the facial (VII) and the vagus (X) nerves. The trigeminus and cervical nerves overlap. Roughly, only that part of the face which is not bearded in the male is exclusively innervated by the trigeminus. The ophthalmic and the maxillary divisions of this nerve are purely sensory, the mandibular division contains also motor fibers to the muscles of mastication. Just as in the rest of the body, dichotomy of lemniscus and spinothalamic system is present—touch is conducted over myelinated fibers to the main sensory nucleus in the pons, while pain is conducted over unmyelinated fibers to the spinal nucleus of the trigeminus. This nucleus extends from the pons down to the uppermost cervical levels of the cord where it merges into the gelatinous substance of Rolando. For a short space below the pons the spinal tract of the trigeminus lies directly at the surface of the brain stem; elsewhere it is covered by the dorsal spinocerebellar tract (Sjöqvist). Many fibers turn ventral without bifurcating into the spinal tract, others bifurcate and thus supply both nuclei (Gerard).

The facial (VII) sends sensory fibers (nervus intermedius) to a small patch in the anterior wall of the external auditory meatus, while the vagus (X) sends sensory branches to a small patch on the posterior wall of that meatus. The central processes of these sensory neurons feed into the main and spinal trigeminal nuclei respectively (Brodal).

The neurons in the main sensory nucleus and in the spinal nucleus send their axons to the opposite side where they ascend in either of two bundles known as the dorsal and ventral trigeminal lemnisci. They end in the arcuate nucleus of the thalamus, just medial to the ventrolateral nucleus. The thalamic cells send their axons to the face, field of the somesthetic area in the postcentral gyrus.

Proprioceptive impulses, evoked by stretching the muscles of mastication or by pressure on the teeth (Corbin and Harrison), reach the mesencephalic root. These fibers are the only sensory fibers of the somesthetic system which do not arise within ganglia but from cell bodies within the central nervous system.

The further course of impulses arriving at the mesencephalic nucleus is not known. References:
Brodal, A.: *Arch. Neurol. & Psychiat.* 57:292-306, 1947.
Corbin, K. B., and Harrison, F.: *J. Neurophysiol.* 3:423-435, 1940.
Gerald, M. W.: *Arch. Neurol & Psychiat.* 9:306-338, 1923.
Sjöqvist, Olaf: *Zentralbl. f. Neurochir.* 2:274-281, 1937.
Copyright *The CIBA Collection of Medical Illustrations* by Frank H. Netter, M.D. Plate 34, p. 59. (By permission of CIBA.)

CONTRACTION OF ANAL SPHINCTER

The following tracing segment was obtained from live preemployment testing and, while somewhat amusing in one sense, illustrates very definitely the polygraph instrument's physiological recording sensitivity.

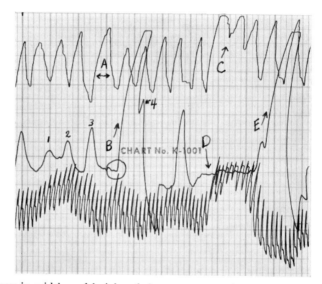

A, Change in width and height of the pneumo tracing indicates that further internal physiological phenomena is occurring. B, Here we see a sudden rise in the galvo pen indicating muscle contraction. This is confirmed by the sharpness (encircled) of the ascending stroke. On the descending galvo tracing (4) the break indicates a finger movement of the hand to which the galvo electrodes were attached. C, A deep breath, broken twice at the top, as a little air is let out and sucked in, lasting some 8 seconds, creates a sudden imbalance of oxygen and carbon dioxide. D, There is a sharp break in the cardio tracing, accompanied by a quick rise in blood pressure, lasting some 6 seconds before the pressure declines and seeks its previous norm. E, The sudden changes aforegoing have obviously created some effect on the body's temperature-regulating center, and peripheral resistance. E is significant of this physiological phenomena.

Prior to 1-2-3, operating in self-centering galvo (electrically controlled), this particular tracing was rather smooth, or fluid, with some change in sweat gland activity at every stimulus. However, commencing at 1-2-3, we see small but sudden sharp appearances of galvo deflection and a rise and fall in blood pressure. All question formulation ceased for the balance of the chart.

After the instrument was deactivated, subject was asked to explain what he was experiencing internally the last forty-five seconds. He replied: "I took a laxative last night and it suddenly hit me. Will you please get these attachments off and let me use your toilet?"

The parasympathetic innervation of the distal portion of the transverse colon probably involves preganglionic components of the sacral outflow. The parasympathetic innervation of the descending colon and the rectum is derived through the sacral outflow. The sympathetic innervation of the descending colon and the rectum is derived through the inferior mesenteric, the hypogastric and the pelvic plexuses. The fibers which arise in the inferior mesenteric ganglion are distributed mainly through the nerves which accompany the inferior mesenteric artery and its branches. The external anal sphincter is innervated through the pudendal nerves. These nerves are essentially somatic and include both efferent and afferent components. The afferent components of the vagus and the pelvic nerves which are distributed to the gastrointestinal tract subserve reflex activity. They probably play no part in conduction of impulses which reach the sensory level.

Collateral with contracting the anal muscles are two considerations. First, it can be done deliberately—and a few subjects have tried this in an effort to beat their test. Secondly, if pneumo and galvo activity of this nature occurs periodically, or is somewhat consistent, it might be well to ask a male subject if he would like to use the toilet. Urinal and other waste pressures create discomfort and can have considerable effect upon pneumo and galvo tracings. Certainly these pressures can have a mentally distracting effect.

WIGGLING THE TOES

Wiggling the toes, as noted below, is a rather common proprioceptive occurrence found during polygraph testing. Sometimes it is done deliberately but most of the time subject does this unconsciously.

Ingredients in the foregoing illustration somewhat contra-

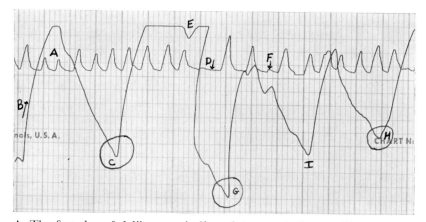

A, The first clue of deliberate wiggling of the toes is shown with a pneumo amplitude reduction. One might say the subject was "getting ready to wiggle his toes." B, A sudden sharp rise of the galvo pen to the top pen stop. C, Another wiggling of the toes shows a sharp "V" (encircled) as the galvo tracing ascends. D, Concentration on wiggling the toes produces a holding of the breath while energy to wiggle is expended. E, The results of D. F, Again a concentration respiratory deviation. G, The results of F. Note the sharp "V" effect, (encircled). H, Another wiggling of the toes. I, Normal galvo response.

dicts psychology's past assertions of not being able to differentiate between emotion and work. Most physical movements by a subject during a test produces the "V" as the descending limb of the galvo tracing sharply commences ascent. Normal galvo response, from emotion provoking sources, will show the descending limb curl upward with either a narrow or wide "U" effect.

When wiggling of the toes is done deliberately we might picture the following: At the seat of consciousness we see a message formulating, such as, "wiggle the toes." The steering of voluntary movements by the cortex involves at least three types of signals, perhaps even more. First, the cerebellum, the great regulator of the extrapyramidal system, has to be attuned. The parieto-temporo-pontine fibers, arising in the vicinity of the cortical area concerned with the body scheme, as well as the frontopontine fibers, arising from cortical areas concerned with biological intelligence, carry such signals. Then, the extrapyramidal system proper has to be informed of what is about to happen. Cortico-pallidal and corticorubral fibers arising from the premotor area or near it carry these signals. Lastly, pyramidal fibers carry messages toward the final common pathway as depicted in the following drawing on page 256.

Finally our message gets to the sciatic nerve, dividing into the medial and lateral popliteal nerves. The medial becomes the posterior tibial which ends in the sole as medial plantar and lateral plantar nerves. The sural nerve and the communicating sural nerve are cutaneous branches of the popliteal nerves and they supply the back of the leg and the lateral margin of the foot. Nerve stimulus here at the periphery of the central nervous system causes a contraction of long flexor tendons to the toes. These lie along the shafts of the metatarsals.

We have stressed herein the basics of a voluntary movement, not one which is reflex in nature. Once the proprioceptive wiggling of the toes takes place, the illustration below shows us how the message, "it has been done," gets back to the brain.

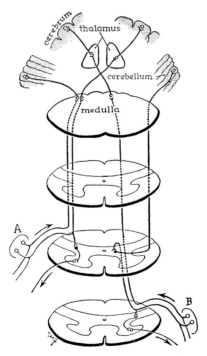

Figure 16. Proprioceptive pathway to cerebrum and to cerebellum; A, from upper limb, B, from lower limb of opposite side. (From *Primary Anatomy,* p. 289, by permission of Dr. J. V. Basmajian.)

Color Plate III. Pyramidal System. The pyramidal tracts connect the cortical motor area, shown in the upper right-hand corner, with the final common pathway in the spinal cord. In the cortex of the precentral gyrus the parts of the body are arranged topographically, roughly as the caricature sprawling over the cross section of the hemisphere indicates. The center for the larynx is close to the Sylvian fissure and may even extend into "Broca's area."

Proceeding upward will be found the center for the face, a large region for the fingers and hand, and a much smaller one for the elbow, shoulder, trunk and hip.

Most of the centers for the foot are on the medial side where the motor area stops about halfway between the dorsal margin and the corpus callosum. In the figure the extent of this area is exaggerated for the sake of clarity.

The pyramidal fibers take their origin from the large pyramidal cells in the fifth layer of the cortex, some of which attain in the motor cortex a length of over 0.1 mm. These are known as giant pyramidal cells of Betz. The pyramidal fibers twist in their course through the white matter of the hemisphere in such a way that fibers for the leg (shown in brown) are most posterior in the internal capsule. The fibers for the face, which are shown in red, pass through the knee of the internal capsule (see sketch at right side of illustration).

Descending toward the cerebral peduncle, the twisting continues so that in the pedunculi the fibers for the leg are lateral. The corticobulbar fibers, coming from the area for face and larynx, stream to the motor nuclei of the brain stem of which III (which is symbolic for III, IV and VI) is shown in the basis pedunculi. Nuclei V (mastication), VII (mimetic musculature), IX, X (larynx), XI (trapezius and sternocleidomastoid), and XII (tongue) are shown schematically above the decussation of the pyramids.

Of the pyramidal fibers proper, the corticospinal fibers, about 80 per cent cross over to the opposite lateral funiculus of the spinal cord at the border between brain stem and spinal cord, while about 20 per cent enter the anterior funiculus on the same side. The lateral pyramidal tract ends in the internuncial pool of the posterior horn and thus acts indirectly on the motor neurons, principally on those of the hand and foot. The anterior pyramidal tract ends on the anterior horn, mostly on the motor neurons innervating the musculature of the trunk. Whether these cross over at lower levels of the spinal cord is not certain. References:

Bucy, P. C.: *The Precentral Motor Cortex,* 2nd ed. Urbana, Univ. of Illinois Press, 1949.

Penfield, W., and Rasmussen, T.: *The Cerebral Cortex of Man.* New York, Macmillan, 1950, 248 pp.

Copyright *The CIBA Collection of Medical Illustrations* by Frank H. Netter, M.D. Plate 43, p. 68. (By permission of CIBA.)

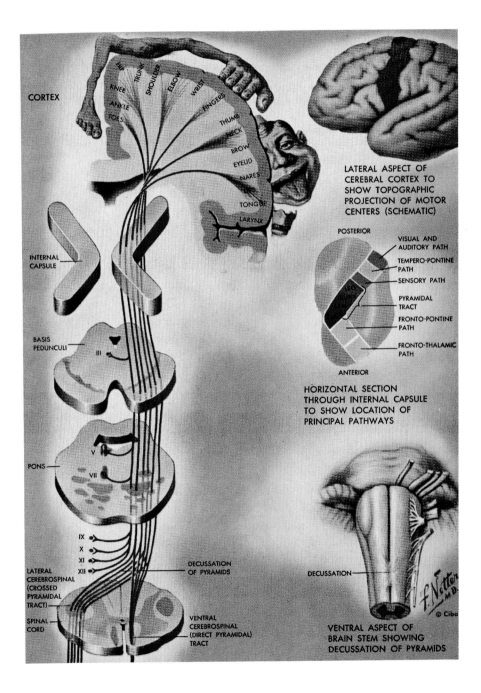

CORTEX

LATERAL ASPECT OF
CEREBRAL CORTEX TO
SHOW TOPOGRAPHIC
PROJECTION OF MOTOR
CENTERS (SCHEMATIC)

POSTERIOR

VISUAL AND
AUDITORY PATH

TEMPERO-PONTINE
PATH

SENSORY PATH

PYRAMIDAL
TRACT

FRONTO-PONTINE
PATH

FRONTO-THALAMIC
PATH

ANTERIOR

HORIZONTAL SECTION
THROUGH INTERNAL CAPSULE
TO SHOW LOCATION OF
PRINCIPAL PATHWAYS

INTERNAL
CAPSULE

BASIS
PEDUNCULI

PONS

LATERAL
CEREBROSPINAL
(CROSSED
PYRAMIDAL
TRACT)

SPINAL
CORD

DECUSSATION
OF PYRAMIDS

VENTRAL
CEREBROSPINAL
(DIRECT PYRAMIDAL)
TRACT

DECUSSATION

VENTRAL ASPECT OF
BRAIN STEM SHOWING
DECUSSATION OF PYRAMIDS

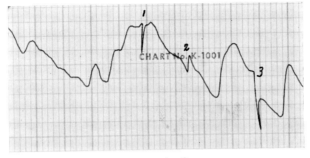

Pressure on the fingers.

PRESSURE ON FINGERS

Above we see the smooth or "fluidness" of a normal galvo tracing sharply broken at 1-2-3. Galvanometer sensitivity is quite acute. Even the slightest pressure or movement of the electrode fingers is instantly recorded in the form of a sharp break in the tracing.

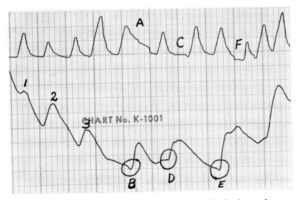

FLEXING LEG MUSCLES. A, Concentration deviation shown in respiration as straining to contract an upper leg muscle occurs. B, The sharp "V" results. C, Again a strain deviation in respiratory. D, The results of C, E, The "V" break caused by a strain shown at F.

The first clue to deliberate movement by the subject appeared at 1-2-3, above. We see a descending galvo tracing suddenly being interrupted three times for no apparent reason.

In further support of instrument sensitivity to differentiating between emotion and work, the cardio tracing example below shows the results when a person attempts to flex his right arm muscle or move the fingers of his right hand during a test.

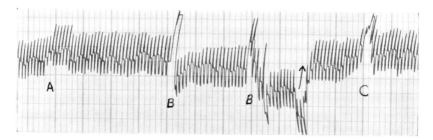

A, Pressure on fingertips of right hand causes a slight upward break in the cardio tracing. In this instance the pressure applied was very light. However, note sharpness of the break from norm. B, Slight flexing of the right arm muscle is very prominent. The tracing break is generally more pronounced and disrupts pulse tonicity to a considerable extent. The arrow indicates examiner made an upward mechanical adjustment, returning the tracing to a preestablished base line. C, More pressure (than at B) was exerted on the fingertips. While the tracing break is clearly discernible, we notice a ready return to preestablished base line norm within about 4 seconds.

Flexing of the right arm muscle is generally caused by (1) discomfort due to lengthy arm cuff pressure and, (2) subject trying to "foul up" his tracing, or attempting deception in itself.

Fingertip movement usually falls into three categories: (1) deliberate attempt at deception during key questions only, (2) unconsciously done during brief periods of heavy concentration on abstract thinking immediately following a crucial question (deception criteria is present), and (3) discomfort due to arm cuff band pressure.

Certain types of leg movements, "shivering" due to cold temperature of examining room and "jerking" at an unexpected or relevant stimulus can also cause cardio tracing breaks.

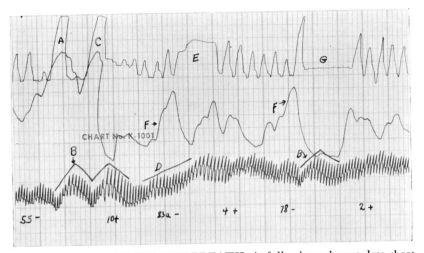

VOLUNTARY HOLDING THE BREATH. A, following relevant data sheet question 55 (Have you ever suffered a back injury?) subject takes his first deep breath. B, Immediately there is a rise and fall in blood pressure with a slight change in cardio amplitude and width. C, Another deep breath compounds the reflex nerve impulse bombardment with another sharp rise and fall in blood pressure. Irrelevant data sheet question 10 is answered on the descending limb of the pnuemo tracing about three-fourths of the way down. Some suppression follows as a return to norm commences. D, At relevant data sheet question 83a (Have you been arrested for anything besides what you've told me?) we see nerve stimulus create a steady rise in blood pressure. E, Another deep breath and suppression lasting some 8 seconds again causes a change in cardio amplitude and width. F, In each instance, sweat gland activity is accelerated by both the momentary cardio and respiratory imbalances. Irrelevant question 4 permits a return to norm. G, Relevant data sheet question 78 (Have you ever stolen money from a place where you have worked?) is immediately followed by a sharp deep breath and expiratory suppression lasting some 10 seconds. Repeating itself is B. Irrelevant question 2, permits a return to norm.

The tracing above has been segmented from an actual pre-employment test and illustrates two things, (1) the effect of nerve impulses producing deviations at relevant questions which mean something to the subject and, (2) a deliberate attempt at deception by voluntarily holding the breath following a relevant question.

In the foregoing we sense an imbalance of oxygen and carbon dioxide playing conflicting roles. On one hand each is a stimulant and, on the other, each a depressor of sorts. Sympathetic acceleration and parasympathetic inhibition are quite clear. In turn, vasoconstriction and vasodilatation is rather prominent.

An important part of the polygraph technique is maintaining a tight psychological control of the subject. The subject is instructed as to what is expected of him during every part of the test, including chart production. No part of the entire test procedure can be of any more importance, as an individual test component, than the examiner's last-minute instruction to the subject. These instructions specifically set forth the "do's" and "don'ts" while the chart is underway. After all attachments are secured to the subject's body, the examiner stands in front of him and says:

> Mr. Smith, please listen carefully. These last-minute instructions are for your benefit. You will be producing this chart for some two to four minutes. During this brief period your right arm will become a little uncomfortable due to continued arm cuff pressure. You may have a tendency to flex the right arm muscle, but try not to. The pressure will not hurt you. If you are not comfortable in the chair, please adjust your sitting position now. Place both feet flat on the floor.
>
> Now, it is very important that you do not wiggle your toes, move your feet, tighten up on leg muscles, press or squeeze on your fingers, hands, or arms. Try to sit still and relax. This instrument is very sensitive, and every time you wiggle, squeeze, squirm, press or tighten up, you will be creating on your chart what we call false responses. If you produce too many of these false responses there is no way you can clear your test.
>
> When a question is asked, answer it with a simple yes or no. However, if you do not understand a question, or if you do not hear the question, remain silent, forget that question entirely, and let it go by. But, no talking during the test for any reason except yes or no. Do you understand? Is everything clear?

The examiner carefully observes the subject and rechecks position of instrument attachments. The instrument is activated and the chart set into motion. Pen tracings are adjusted. If the subject is violating any of the pretest instructions he is corrected thus: "Quit gritting your teeth, breathe normally, try to relax, quit moving, hold your head still, quit pressing on your fingers, blink your eyes normally, quit looking at the floor."

A subject is never allowed to chew gum during the actual chart production. Such has adverse effect on the galvo tracing.

A further safeguard takes place just before question formulation commences when the examiner says: "Sit perfectly still. Do Not move. The test is about to begin. Answer the questions yes or no, only."

In view of the foregoing, it becomes rather simple for the qualified examiner to differentiate between nerve response deviations and those deviations deliberately created by the subject. Their individual makeup, how and when they occur, are the keys to chart interpretation as well as a conclusive opinion containing reliability and accuracy within the immediate realm of truth verification.

Chapter 10

AUTONOMIC CARDIOVASCULAR TRACINGS

Scientific research considers any environmental energy change to be a stimulus. However, the stimulus must be strong enough to reach threshold intensity before it can cause nerve impulses to reach organ destination and subsequently be recorded on a moving polygraph chart.

Nervous activity is invariably accompanied by electrical changes. When a sense organ is active or when the brain issues an order, impulses can be detected in the appropriate nerve fiber. Experiments have revealed that the nervous impulse in one fiber is of constant amplitude and shape and that its characteristics cannot be altered by changing the strength or quality of the stimulus. The quality of a sensation does not depend upon changes in individual messages but upon alterations in the type of nerve fibers which are active. Although nerves normally conduct impulses in one direction—towards the central nervous system in sensory fibers, away from it in motor fibers—all nerves can conduct impulses in both directions and the velocity at which the impulse propagates is independent of the direction in which it is traveling.*

The polygraphist is more concerned with nerve impulses which are handled by the autonomic nervous system where voluntary or conscious control is virtually absent.

Autonomic efferents and visceral afferents carry out their functions mainly reflexly and automatically, one set of nerves exciting and another set inhibiting. The only exception of further concern to the polygraphist is a subject's deliberate or voluntary movements.

Our primary pursuit henceforth lies in what a relevant question means to the person receiving it. The question is the stim-

---

*Hodgkin, A.L.: *The Conduction of the Nervous Impulse.* Thomas, Springfield, 1964, pp. 13-15.

ulus which we follow through the ear to the cerebral cortex, down to the medulla and thence to organ destination.

First we follow the verbal stimulus afferently through the ear. Since a large part of each temporal lobe appears to be concerned with hearing, physiologists have found that impulses initiated in stimulation of the cochlea of the internal ear by sound are transmitted to this area of the brain via the auditory nerve and nerve pathways, e.g. ventral cochlear nucleus, dorsal nucleus, superior olivary complex, up through nuclei of the lateral lemnisci and thence via the medial geniculate body on into the supratemporal plane. There is a point-to-point correspondence between the cochlea and the acoustic area of the cortex.

To what part of the cerebral cortex the individual stimulus may go will, again, depend on what the stimulus means to the subject receiving it. Certainly the associational areas must digest it to some extent. The outflow toward the lower centers can be followed anatomically through the dorsal longitudinal fasciculus which consists of thin unmyelinated fibers within the central gray. It influences, as its origin from the parasympathetic mammillary body would suggest, the parasympathetic centers in the brain stem. It may be supposed also to influence the sacral parasympathetic center. Its play on the sympathetic centers in the intermediolateral column of the thoracolumbar cord is not so clearly understood.

Now, we shall move into actual "live" polygraph chart examples for physiological correlation.

Whether the tracings are taken from private industry or criminal charts is of little import. The basis for accurate chart interpretation is strictly dependent on what the question means to the person receiving it with respect to ascertaining truth or deception. For example, theft, dishonesty, or deceit in private industry, though not prosecuted, is no different from the same acts wherein police investigation results in prosecution.

CARDIOVASCULAR DEVIATIONS
Example I: Preemployment

Subject is W/M/A, age twenty-five. He is applying for a laborer's job. His application contains no obvious irregularities. The pretest interview and data sheet questions are completed. Instrument attachments have been secured to his body. The chart is underway. (Questions numbers shown on a chart will correspond with those found on the data sheet utilized.)

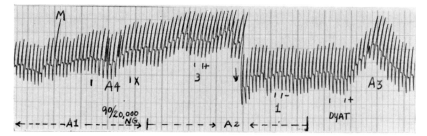

A1, Subject's norm cardio tracing without stimulus. Heart rate is 96 (MBP) per minute. Dicrotic notch is in center of descending stroke. A2, Norm tracing with insertion of irrelevant stimulus, (data sheet questions 3 and 1). A3, (DYAT) "Do you intend to answer the questions truthfully?" Note slight rise in both systolic and diastolic pressures. This puts the examiner on guard. A4, Examiner's remarks: "Sit perfectly still. Do not move. The test is about to begin. Answer the questions yes or no only." Immediately following we note a slow tension rise in the cardio tracing which had to be mechanically returned by the examiner to the tracing's former base line, as signified by the arrow pointing downward. A1, 2, 3, May be considered subject's physiological norm at the time of this test. The response at DYAT (A3) is initially referred to as his "minimum response producing capability."

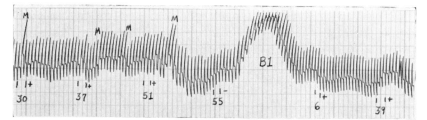

B1, Data sheet question 55: "Have you ever suffered a back injury?" Here we note a considerable change from norm in both systolic and diastolic pressures, and a return to norm. This response lasts some 11 seconds before norm base line is reestablished. If we look at the stimulus marks we also see that it took 2 seconds to say the question and approximately 3 seconds for the stimulus to go through the ear to the brain, generate a nerve impulse which was sent to the cardio acceleration and inhibitory centers in the medulla, commencing the deviation recorded via the brachial artery.

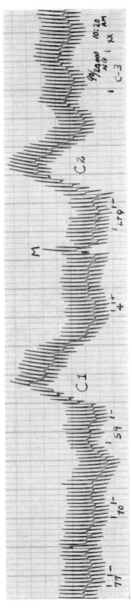

C1, Data sheet question 59: "Have you ever filed for or collected workman's compensation insurance from an on-the-job injury?" Ordinarily, in a first preemployment chart, this question is not used, but in this case, we used it as a probing follow-up of question 55, and it "paid off." Again we see a sharp deviation from norm lasting 12 seconds before a return to norm, noting 7 seconds elapsed from the time subject understood the full meaning of the question and answered it until his physiological reaction to it was recorded on the chart. C2, LTQ means, "Have you deliberately lied to any question I've asked you during this test?" As previously, we see a clear-cut change in systolic and diastolic pressures. The nervous inertia involved to turn the question stimulus into a chart response consumes approximately 9 seconds until norm reestablishes itself. C3, This is the time necessary (7 seconds) to begin and conclude: "Sit perfectly still. Do not move. The test is about to end. I will release pressure in the arm cuff in just one moment." The XX signifies end of the test; 90 indicates the cardio sphygomanometer dial read 90 mm of mercury at test conclusion; 20,000 is the amount of galvanometer sensitivity (ohms) matching subject's resistance. NG indicates the test concluded in normal galvo operation, 10:20 shows the actual time the instrument was deactivated. We also note subject's heart rate still at about 96 per minute.

Between Chart Probe

The responses in the foregoing cardio tracings are obvious. We know that something about questions DYAT, 55, 59, and substantially LTQ stimulated subject enough to cause the deviations from norm. While we may surmise, we still do not actually know the direct cause and will never know it unless the subject decides to tell us. At the same time, we know that no response can appear without a cause. By comparison, it also appears that none of the other questions were of sufficient concern to the subject to result in chart response.

Interrogative Results

Subject admitted a back injury on job number 3, as listed on his employment application. He was off work two months, drew W.C.I., saw an attorney, filed suit, settled out of court for a gross of $1,800. Further, he jokingly agreed that all his alleged back problems suddenly vanished with the money settlement and assured the examiner he had absolutely no back problems at the time.

Summation

Under normal circumstances a person suffering a severe back injury, as subject initially claimed when he filed his suit, is out of work more than two months, is frequently confined, and is not able to do heavy labor, as this subject had been doing in the meantime. Usually, according to insurance statistics, when such an injury is bonafide and is put in the hands of an ethical attorney, it is worth trial unless a sizeable and equitable out of court settlement is agreed upon. Of course, there are exceptions in every case.

Example II: Preemployment

Subject is W/M/A, forty-three. He is applying for a retail liquor store clerk's job. During the data sheet interview he admitted being fired from his last job because of a "personality clash" with his immediate supervisor, and to having been fired from three other jobs in the past for the same reason. He also admitted being arrested one time in 1943 for being drunk, and again for the same offense in 1955.

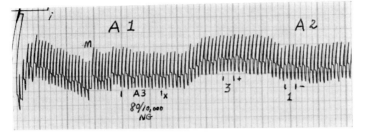

A1, 2, 3, These are the same as in Example I. Heart rate for this subject is approximately 96 (MBP) per minute.

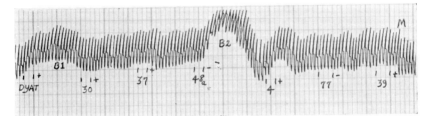

B1, We note a slight deviation (BP increase and fall) from physiological norm at DYAT, which lasts some 11 seconds. B2, Here we note a strong deviation, or response, at question 48a: "Have you been fired from more jobs than what you've told me?" Between 15 and 20 seconds elapse, even encompassing irrelevant question 4, before impact of the stimulus declines and the cardiac cycle returns to norm.

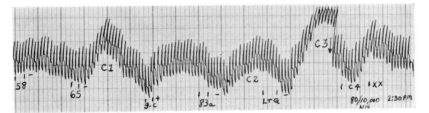

C1, The obvious response at question 65: "Did you ever drink beer, wine, or whiskey on the job?" consumes some 14 seconds. C2, A mild response at question 83a: "Have you been arrested for anything besides what you've told me?" Response time consumes a good 10 seconds. C3, LTQ stimulus produces a sharp response which hits the top cardio pen stop. The arrow indicates examiner has reestablished base line by mechanical adjustment. The impact of this question on subject's autonomic nervous system consumes at least a full 10 seconds. C4, Same ending as in Example I. Heart rate is still at approximately 96 per minute.

Between Chart Probe

If we evaluate subject's previous admissions to specific question areas during the data sheet interview we automatically sense a tie-in with chart responses. Again, there seems to be nothing about the other chart questions which stimulates his autonomic nervous system. But, the relevant questions which apparently had some meaning to the subject brought about the obvious systolic and diastolic blood pressure changes.

Interrogative Results

A probe of the foregoing chart responses developed further admissions, i.e. that subject was fired from his last two jobs for drinking on one and coming to work with liquor on his breath at the other. Therefore, responses at questions 48a and 65 are confirmed as relevant. The response at 83a resulted in subject admitting he had been arrested four times in the past year for common drunk. His own substantiation, of course, proves response relevancy. The deviation at LTQ is simply subject's reaction to being aware of his own attempts at deception.

Summation

While we can certainly sympathize with subject's desire, and perhaps need, for employment in this capacity, his admissions project a long-standing drink problem which has already affected his employment competency and, possibly, his on-the-job productivity. Of course, in all these cases it is the employer's decision as to whether or not he will hire subject, irrespective of the polygraph test results.

Example III: Preemployment—"Association"

Subject is W/F/A, age twenty-one, as listed on her employment application. She is applying for a cocktail hostess job. The pretest interview and data sheet probe turned up no unusual irregularities. The instrument has been activated and we pick up the chart at question 37.

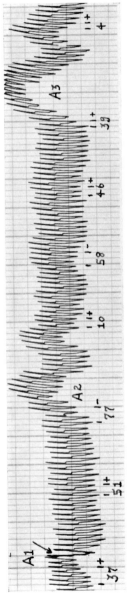

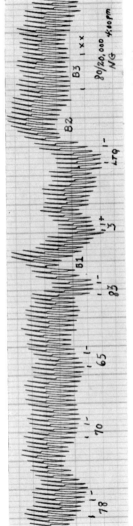

A1, Here we see an extra systole (skip beat) at question 37: "Did you tell the truth on your employment application?" A2, The deviation at question 77: "Have you ever stolen merchandise from a place where you've worked?" is quite clear with a "double bounce" contained therein and lasts for some 14 seconds. We see subject's heart rate at about 72 (MBP) per minute. (However, it is interesting to note no change in position of the dicrotic notch.) A3, Response at question 39: "Have you given us your correct age?" consumes a total of 15 seconds, also containing a double bounce.

B1, Again we see a response but no change in position of the dicrotic notch. This appears more like a smooth rise and fall in both systolic and diastolic pressures. It is somewhat compared to A2. B1 consumes 8 seconds of chart time. B2, At LTQ we see a clear-cut response, with just a minute change in position of the dicrotic notch, consuming some 7 seconds. B3, We note no change in mm of mercury as shown on the sphyg dial.

Between Chart Probe

Subject emphatically denies theft of merchandise from a previous employer. She insists she has given her true and correct age, and that she has never been arrested and placed in jail.

Interrogative Results

Subject still denies theft of either money or merchandise from a previous employer. She does, however, admit that she and her girl friend have shoplifted some $800 worth of jewelry and clothing items from local stores during the past year. Her girl friend was prematurely stopped by a store detective recently and both girls were questioned by police but released due to lack of evidence. She does admit being nineteen years old instead of twenty-one as previously claimed.

Example III—Second Chart

We pick up the question formulation and cardio pattern at question 55:

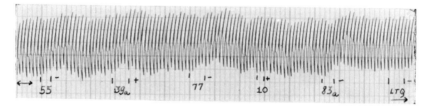

Chart Evaluation

Question 77 was repeated as it appears on the data sheet and produced no response. Question 39a was asked: "Have you now given us your correct age?" We see no response. Question 83a was worded: "Besides what we've already discussed, have you actually been arrested and placed in jail?" Again we see no response and an absence of deviation at LTQ.

Summation

We now more clearly see the response-producing capabilities of mental association with something irrelevant to the immediate issue or question, but similar through sensitivity. In this case subject was not old enough, under state law, to work as a cocktail hostess. Other than question 39, we can safely assume subject answered the questions truthfully on Chart I, confirmed by lack of response in the second chart.

Example IV: Problem—Peak of Tension

Subject is W/M/A, age twenty-eight. He is under suspect, along with three others, of stealing a metal cash box containing $650 which had been secretly hidden behind a medicine cabinet in Mr. Smith's office yesterday. Mr. Smith has not mentioned the theft or the amount of money missing to any of the employees. Therefore, only the guilty party would actually know how much money was in the cash box, and where it was located. At this point, we might interject that the two other suspects have "cleared" the test satisfactorily.

In this case we have already completed three charts which probed subject's presence in Smith's office yesterday at the specified time, knowledge of location of the box, along with theft of a metal cash box from a list of other possibilities, and see sufficient deceptive criteria which warrants the present approach. We shall use a series of seven questions as follows: (1) Did you steal a metal cash box containing $300 in bills from behind the medicine cabinet in Mr. Smith's office yesterday? (2) Did you steal a metal cash box containing $400 in bills from behind the medicine cabinet in Mr. Smith's office yesterday? (3) Did you steal a metal cash box containing $500 in bills from behind the medicine cabinet in Mr. Smith's offices yesterday? (4) *Did you steal a metal cash box containing $650 in bills from behind the medicine cabinet in Mr. Smith's office yesterday?* (5) Did you steal a metal cash box containing $700 in bills from behind the medicine cabinet in Mr. Smith's office yesterday? (6) Did you steal a metal cash box containing $800 in bills from behind the medicine cabinet in Mr. Smith's office yesterday? (7) Did you steal a metal cash box containing $900 in bills from behind the medicine cabinet in Mr. Smith's office yesterday?

All questions were read to the subject. Then they were handed to him and he was asked to read each question to himself. He was told the questions would be asked in exactly the same order as they appeared on the paper. Further, subject was instructed to answer all questions in the negative.

EXAMPLE IV – CHART IV

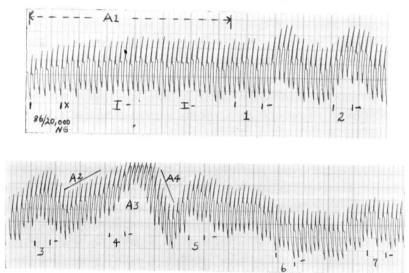

A1, This is subject's norm. Heart rate is about 72 per minute. A2, Here we see a slow tension rise consuming some 13 seconds. A3, Impact of the crucial question which consumes some 6 seconds. A4, This is an interesting "fall off" or reduction of tension and the heart's return to norm. At questions 1 and 2 we note a minor "nervous" rise in blood pressure. Following question 3, we see an immediate "anticipatory" rise, followed by the physiological impact of question 4. However, the reader will see no deviations at questions 5, 6, 7. Not shown in the above segmentations was an increase of 2mm on the sphygmomanometer dial (from 86 to 88 mm).

Summation

In this instance chart interpretation is self-explanatory. We have also seen how this sensitive instrument records the physiological buildup to and through the crucial question, with relief taking place thereafter as the heart output returns to its preestablished norm. This particular subject subsequently confessed his guilt, gave his employer a promissory note, and was quietly discharged. He was not prosecuted.

Illustration Chart

For more comprehensive and comparative reader understanding we have isolated the cardio tracing from one of the other Example IV employee's charts (equally under suspicion) to illustrate the difference contained in the innocent person's tracing. Relevant PTA questions only are shown.

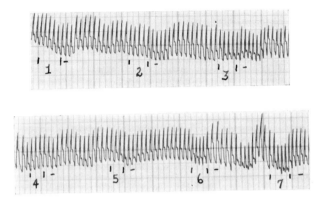

Reference

While there is a normal amount of nervousness or apprehension shown through slight rises and returns in both systolic and diastolic pressures at each question—with a steady heart rate of 72 beats per minute—there is no deviation from norm which contains potential deception criteria.

Example V: Problem—Different Type Peak of Tension

Subject is W/M/A, age forty. He was a stock manager and open-up man for a grocery chain. Early on the day in question he opened the store, then reported an $8,000 safe burglary. Investigation indeed revealed an open safe. In the stockroom several empty money bags were found next to the exit door. All doors to the store were covered by an audible burglar alarm system. The burglar alarm company was immediately called. Their check showed no damage to, tampering with, or breaks in the alarm circuit. A spare set of safe keys, which usually hung out of sight in the office, were found on the floor some ten feet from the safe.

However, the interlocking top to the inside safe well had been replaced and locked. The top well was still open. Subject stated he came by the store at 5:30 AM, drove slowly through the lot, then went some eight blocks for a cup of coffee. He came back at 6:20 AM, secured the front door burglar alarm, opened the store and went inside. He noticed the safe was open and completely empty. He started turning on store lights. In the back room he found the exit door ajar, then noticed empty money bags on the floor. He called police, then his store manager. Subject readily agreed to submit to polygraphy.

Three polygraph charts contained deception criteria. Subject steadfastly denied any complicity or any knowledge thereof. The following chart is but one example of the Peak of Tension "B" theory in application. It is a "search" for whereabouts of the missing money.

A series of seven relevant questions were prepared from a list of possibles, their contents dictated by investigative experience obtained in similar such incidents. As in the Peak of Tension "A" test previously illustrated, all questions were read to the subject. He was instructed to answer each question in the negative. The questions were worded: (1) Did you hide any of the missing money in a bank account? (2) Did you hide any of the missing money on the store premises? (3) Did you hide any of the missing money in your car? (4) Do you have any of the missing money on your person now? (5) Did you hide any of the missing money in your home? (6) Did you hide any of the missing money within a three-block radius of the store property? (7) Did you hide any of the missing money in the back room of the store?

Example V—Chart IV

Summation

We have seen several big loopholes in subject's story. When he came back from having coffee, why wasn't the burglar alarm ringing? A thief ordinarily doesn't open a safe's inner compartment, take out money, carefully lock it again, then leave the top wide open. This is more habitual—via company policy—for the employee who does this every day. When an actual burglary occurs,

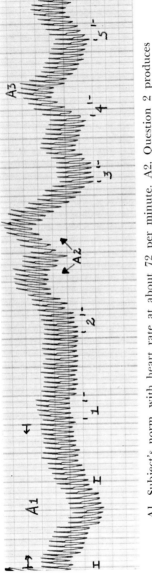

A1, Subject's norm, with heart rate at about 72 per minute. A2, Question 2 produces quite a change. This type of response is called a double bounce and consumes some 20 seconds. A3, A sharp rise in blood pressure lasting 5 seconds before the "fall-off" indicates that question 4, meant something to this subject. Question 5 is even interfered with due to a physiological carry-over from the preceding question.

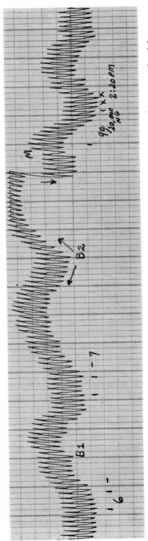

B1, Impact of this question and what it meant to the subject again produces a double bounce consuming some 10 seconds. B2, Here we note a type of sustained rise of short duration, about 8 seconds, an attempt at return to norm, and then an aftermath nerve impulse bombardment which sees question 7 produce a sharp rise in blood pressure. Finally the cardio pen is driven against its pen stop and brought down by mechanical adjustment. The whole response consumes 30 seconds. M indicates subject slightly flexed his right arm muscle.

an employee doesn't ordinarily spend time turning on the back room lights before reporting same to police. When, as he said, he drove through the lot and checked the store at a glance, he had to drive right by the exit door. Ironic that he didn't notice it open at that time, because if it had been open he couldn't keep from hearing the burglar alarm. If the burglary actually took place between 5:30 and 6:30 AM, the alarm would have been ringing when he returned.

Investigative Results

On the strength of chart responses, investigating police officers and store employees began a search of the store and found $7,000 in a paper sack above the main freezer. Subject was taken into custody and searched. In his right shoe officers found $1,000 in hundred dollar bills. Two days later subject admitted guilt.

Example VI: Problem—Relevant-Irrelevant

Subject is W/F/A, age thirty-one. She and three other girls are under suspect for theft of $21 from a finance company's petty cash box. All are aware of the amount which the branch manager reported as missing.

The questions asked were worded as follows: (1) Do you drink water? (2) Is today Sunday? (3) Do you intend to answer the questions truthfully? (4) Do you actually know what happened to the $21 in question? (5) Are you sitting in a chair? (6) Did you take the $21 in question? (7) Are you wearing shoes? (8) Do you know where any of the missing money is now? (9) Were you in collusion with any other person to take the $21 in question? (10) Have you ever stolen cash money in any manner from this company? (11) Do you ever drink coffee? (12) Do you suspect another employee of taking the $21 in question? (13) Did you, yourself, take the $21 in question? (14) Are you married? (15) Are you wearing a watch? (16) Have you deliberately lied to any question I've asked you during this test?

Summation

Between chart probes resulted in subject's admission that not only had she taken the $21 in question but also had stolen about $400, a little at a time, during the past year of employment. An-

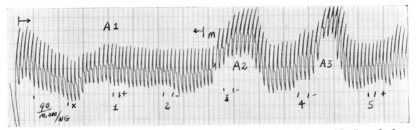

A1, Subject's norm, with heart rate at about 72 per minute. A2, Just before question 3 we see a movement which actually caused a higher tracing than normally might have occurred. Even so, the response is there, consuming some 6 seconds with a fall-off following. A3, This is a sharp, rather obvious response showing the impact of question 4 on subject's autonomic nervous system, and consumes about 7 seconds.

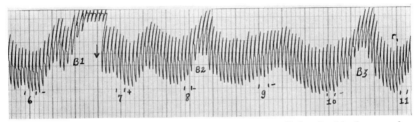

B1, Question 6 "hits home" hard. Again we see a slight double bounce before the cardio pen hits the top pen stop. The arrow indicates mechanical readjustment by the examiner. B2, From question 7 on we see autonomic control more clearly, with sympathetic acceleration and parasympathetic inhibition. The sharp stimulus impact at question 8 lasts about 5 seconds. B3, This is quite a significant response consuming some 7 seconds with a sharp fall-off.

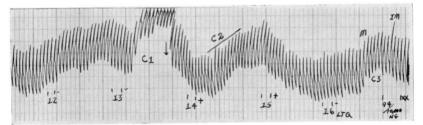

C1, Here we see almost a duplication of B1, which consumes some 8 seconds, and again requires a downward mechanical adjustment. C2, Actually this 15-second rise and fall in blood pressure could be referred to as sensitivity or projection by association. C3, The quick blood pressure rise which started is somewhat broken by a movement and then compounded by an involuntary movement (IM—a slight jerk). The deviation is still apparent. It is interesting to note that blood pressure fluctuations, reflecting on minute output and volume of the heart, has increased the MBP some 4 mm of mercury on the sphyg dial.

other interesting factor in this case should be presented rather briefly. This female subject was married and the mother of two children. Her husband held a responsible position locally. When she knew she had caught herself by her own atempts at deception (the association referred to at question 14) she became quite tearful and distraught. It was only after she was assured by her employer that her discharge would be listed as "for other reasons," and the promise that her husband would not be notified, did she sign a statement and promissory note.

This is quite a common occurrence amongst married women who have succumbed to temptation on the job. They are frequently not so concerned with losing their job as they are with having to face their husband and family with the embarrassing truth. Perhaps this is one of the reasons why history dictates that when women do turn bad they become the most prolific liars and often times nothing, even severe punishment of innocent persons as a result thereof, will make them confess the truth.

Example VII: Problem—Special "Yes Test"

Subject is W/M/A, age nineteen, employed in a large department store. Internal security officers have uncovered an employee theft ring involving men's suits, hardware items and electrical appliances, along with some musical instruments. Subject is under suspect.

Thus far, three charts have been completed which contained deception criteria. At this point subject has made no admissions. It was noted, however, that prior chart responses were more prominent at, "Do you actually know who," and "collusion," rather than at the question, "Did you personally remove . . . from the store?" The special Yes Test is designed to assist the examiner in eliminating association or knowledge from the deliberate personal act of theft. When this is successfully accomplished it affords the examiner a tremendous psychological interrogative wedge.

In this actual case, subject was advised to answer all questions, no matter what the wording, in the affirmative. It was explained to him that deliberately being forced to lie goes "against the grain," and that this test would be used for comparison purposes only. Question formulation went as follows: (1) Are you sitting in a chair? (2) Is this the month of January? (3) Did you kill Mary Jane Doe in Waco last night? (4) Do you actually know the names of employees who have been stealing merchandise from this store? (5) Do you live in Texas? (6) Have you personally stolen any items of merchandise from this store? (7) Do you ever drink water? (8) Have you seen stolen company merchandise in another employee's home? (9) Are you wearing a shirt? (10) Have you ever helped another employee steal merchandise from this company? (11) Are you nineteen years old? (12) Do you know where and merchandise stolen from this company is being sold in this area? (13) Are you wearing a watch? (14) Have you stolen any merchandise from this company in the past six months?

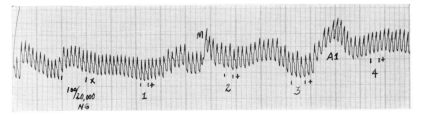

A1, At question 3 we see a response lasting some 7 seconds.

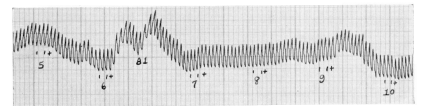

B1, This response lasts for some 13 seconds.

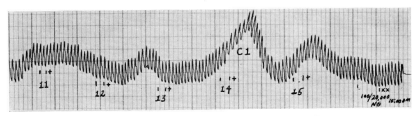

C1, Response here consumes some 8 seconds.

Example VII—Fourth Chart

Considerations

The special Yes Test reverses itself psychologically. Since psychologists have fairly well established that, inherently, a person does not like being forced to lie, we reason that deliberate lying to a relevant question invariably generates a nerve impulse to the autonomic center. However, theoretically, when a person does answer a question truthfully, there is a reduction of tension which results in very little to no change in physiological norm.

Summation

We see this clearly demonstrated at question 3. The subject knows he did not kill Mary Jane Doe. The response follows a psychological rebellion of sorts at being forced to admit he did. The same applies at questions 6 and 14. But we should carefully note the absence of response at the other key relevant questions. By comparison, let's look at irrelevant questions 1, 2, 5, 7, 9, 11, 13. It is obvious that subject answered these truthfully. He would have no reason not to. Therefore, we may also presume that he answered truthfully at questions 4, 8, 10, 12, since there is no response forthcoming.

This chart confirmed deviations noted in the first three charts and subsequently brought considerable admissions with respect to questions 4, 8, 10, 12.

He was the "lookout" on occasion while others did the stealing.

Example VIII: (PE—Extra Systoles—Consistent)

Subject is W/M/A, age forty-two. He is applying for a sales job. His employment application evidences an employment background suggesting job stability. He presents himself in a complimentary manner. Data sheet admissions are not significant.

First Chart

The tracing below has been segmented from an actual pre-employment chart.

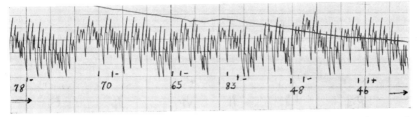

Herein we see the extra systole (skip beat) occurring every 2 to 4 seconds with uninterrupted systolic and diastolic function between.

Summation

Since there is no deviation from norm at any of the questions, not only can we safely assume subject has answered the questions truthfully but also that these consistent extra systoles are his norm. And, since the dicrotic notch is so pronounced we may fairly well assume that there is no pathological malfunction newly associated with the valves of the heart. Subject confirmed our probe in this area. He said such was the aftermath of a rheumatic fever seige between ages eight and twelve, and that his doctor had told him that while his heart was strong, this "norm" would be with him the rest of his life.

Example IX: Problem—Vagus Roll

Our subject is W/M/A, age twenty-two. He is employed in a wholesale liquor warehouse as a forklift operator, truck loader and part-time outgoing dock checker. He and a truck driver are under suspect for overloading the outgoing trucks and keeping or selling the overloads for personal gain. A good customer reported the driver had tried to sell him a case of I.W. Harper pints at half price. The driver was questioned and admitted his complicity and involved subject as an accomplice. Interrogation thus far has developed no admissions from the warehouse man. Prior to the polygraph examination an office girl said subject bragged to her that he had "beat the test before, and, I can beat it any time."

Considerations

Our first relevant-irrelevant chart produced no deviation in the cardio norm. However, there appeared a good response in the respiratory pattern at key relevant questions. Subject remained extremely polite during the between chart probe, repeatedly accusing the driver of lying about subject's alleged complicity. A card test was conducted. Strong galvo response indicated the card subject had concealed under his leg. He shrugged it off, apparently unconcerned. However, certain physical manifestations began to appear. He began to lick his lips, swallow more frequently, fidgeted in his chair, crossed and uncrossed his legs. His posture went from straight and proper into a semi-slump. At any rate, he maintained his innocence and fell back on the old subterfuge of saying he knew that "machine isn't always conclusive anyhow."

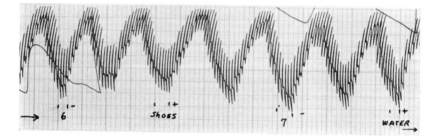

We see in the above tracing almost uncontrolled response to every question, even the two irrelevant ones. Notice how each deviation in both systolic and diastolic pressures rises to the top cardio pen stop, bangs away there for some three to four seconds before returning to about the same baseline, and then commencing all over again. Interesting here is heart rate, calculated at about 108 per minute.

Summation

Experience dictates two primary ingredients which initiate a vagus roll tracing: (1) extreme fear and guilt complex, and (2) deception in itself. When this chart was concluded, subject confessed his part in the problem at hand.

Again we can fairly well isolate the "fear emotion" (the fear of being found out).

Not shown in this tracing was subject's violent and expansive breathing which coincided dramatically with his cardio pattern and, of course, was collaterally responsible physiologically therefore.

Example X: Problem PTB—Changes in Rate

Our subject is W/M/A, age thirty-three, a bookkeeper in a new car agency. He is under suspect for embezzlement. At the time of his polygraph test auditors reported no accurate loss figure had as yet been established. Subject was aware that the auditors had discovered some shortages. One relevant-irrelevant chart indicated subject's knowledge of record discrepancies. However, at this point he has maintained his innocence. He was shown the PTB question order and instructed to answer all questions in the negative. All irrelevant questions were worded so they could easily be answered in the negative without response producing potential.

The questions used were as follows: (1) Do you live in Washington? (2) Is this the month of December? (3) Have you knowingly embezzled as much as $200 from Blank Company? (4) Have you embezzled as much as $400 from Blank Company? (5) Have you embezzled as much as $600 from Blank Company? (6) Have you embezzled as much as $800 from Blank Company? (7) Have you embezzled as much as $1000 from Blank Company? (8) Have you embezzled as much as $1200 from Blank Company? (9) Have you embezzled as much as $1400 from Blank Company? (10) Is today Sunday?

Example X—Second Chart—PTB

Summation

Between charts the examiner was called out of the room and informed that at least a $700 discrepancy had been found and definitely traced to the subject. On return to the examining room, a probe brought a series of admissions totaling $600 in record falsifications during the past year. Subject insisted he had taken no more. Therefore, a PTA test was conducted with all relevant questions worded, "Have you stolen as much as . . . at one single time from Blank Company during the past year?" Following this chart subject admitted the $700. The final relevant-irrelevent chart which contained the basic question pattern of,

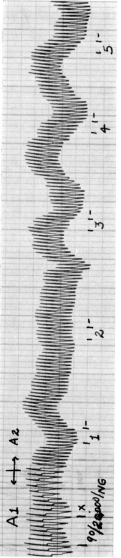

A1, In the beginning we see a norm tracing of some 72 heartbeats per minute. A2, When the examiner said, "Sit perfectly still. Do not move. The test is about to begin. Answer all questions with a simple no only," we note that after about 4 seconds norm suddenly changes into a rate of 96 heartbeats per minute. This signifys a "fear emotion" has been generated in the cerebral cortex and is already being handled by the autonomic nervous system. At questions 3, 4, 5, 6 we see the increased pulse rate continuing with rather uniform rises and falls in both systolic and diastolic pressures.

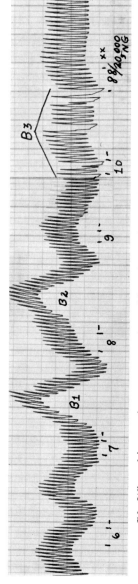

B1, What this question meant to the subject drove the cardio pen against its top pen stop for some 2 seconds before sharp relief and fall-off sets in. B2, At question 8, impact reproduces itself in somewhat of a classical manner. B3, Following question 10 (the subject knows the test is about to end) we see a return to norm with 4 strong extra systoles. Heart rate has returned to about 72 beats per minute.

"Have you knowingly stolen more money than what you've told me from Blank Company," contained no further deceptive criteria. Subject signed a statement for $1300.

ILLUSTRATED TRACINGS (CARDIOPATHOLOGICAL)

While the segmented chart portions below were produced by "live" subject during an actual preemployment or problem test,

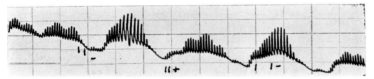

Subject said his doctor told him in 1965 that he had an enlarged heart artery. (No confirmation obtained.)

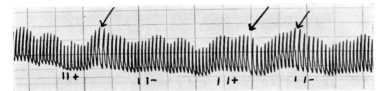

(Note spacing of pulse pressure as signified by arrows.) To a probe of this unusual phenomenon, subject stated he was in a hospital from Feb. 25, 1966, to March 18, 1966, for a heart infection (endocarditis, he believed his doctor said). He was a truck driver and as of this test, subject said the I.C.C. doctor would not give him a medical clearance to get his commercial driving license renewed. (Confirmation obtained.)

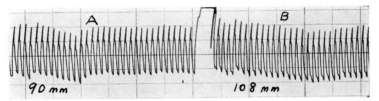

Subject was WMA, age 61, overweight. At A we first note spacing width between strokes with suggestion of a second dicrotic notch at the bottom. Sphyg dial pressure was increased at B, which brought out the second dicrotic notch. However, there is no change in tonicity or position of the upper dicrotic notch. Subject said he previously suffered from sugar diabetis and stomach ulcers. At test time he said he was under a doctor's care for high cholesterol content and hardening of the arteries. (No confirmation obtained.)

they are introduced here only for the purpose of illustrating the instrument's sensitivity in recording heart malfunctions, rather than diagnosing or ascertaining deception in itself. Our last chart in this area is not a malfunction, pathologically. It is what is known as a "feinting tracing," rarely occurring.

Feinting Tracing

Subject was W/M/A, age seventeen. He was applying for a part-time after school job in a theater. He had no employment background to go on. Apparently he had led a very sheltered life, appeared unsure of himself, and quite frightened at the thought of the test itself.

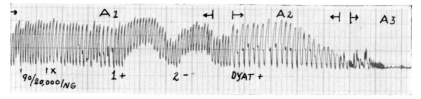

A1, Heart rate is about 96 per minute, fluctuating. A2, Here we note a sudden drop in heart rate to about 60 per minute with wide spacing between systolic and diastolic strokes, plus a diminishing amplitude. A3, A momentary increase in amplitude and then literally nothing at all.

Observation of subject revealed his face quite pale, mouth slack, eyes almost closed and head falling forward. Instrument attachments were immediately removed from his body.

There are many other cardio tracing examples which could be included but space prohibits. The ones we have illustrated are, perhaps, some of the more common. We must emphasize that no interpretative "scale of accuracy" can be attributed to a specific chart response or tracing. While a subject may produce a similar type of response, duplicating, he will not produce the same response to the same question each time it is asked.

In the cases we have gone through the same reaction has taken place to varying degrees in all tracings, with exception as we shall note. We say this because the heart confirms the "all-or-none" principle. Weak stimuli fail to generate little or no response. By increasing the strength of the stimulus, a point is reached where the irritability threshold is exceeded, and each stimulus will induce a response of specific magnitude. However, even though the strength of the stimulus is increased beyond the irritability the amplitude of contractions will not increase. In general, then, when contraction heart tissue becomes active, it becomes electrically negative to adjacent inactive portions. During the activity the muscle fiber becomes somewhat of a minute battery, with positive and negative poles. Physiologists have established that the electrical negativity commences at the sinus node. Under all normal conditions, heart rate can be changed only by stimulating or inhibiting the sinus node or the "pacemaker" of the heart.

In the atria, the activation appears to spread directly through the muscle fibers. The only means available for the stimulus to pass from atria to ventricles is through the atrioventricular bundle. This systole function is illustrated thus:*

a. Beat initiated at sinus node.

b. Adjacent atrial muscle excited; impulse spreads to all of atrial muscle, which contracts as it is stimulated.

c. A-V node and bundle stimulated.

d. Impulse rapidly transmitted to all parts of ventricles via nodal tissue.

e. Entire ventricular muscle mass contracts practically at once.

Relaxation of each chamber follows immediately upon completion of the contractions, so that the atria are already relaxing at about the time the ventricles have begun contracting.

The electrical charges (action potentials) developed by each beat of the heart can be demonstrated (or recorded) even at the surface of the body. At that instant of the cardiac cycle when the upper portion of the heart is active, either of the hands will be at a lower potential (more negative) than either foot because the

---

*Portions of the foregoing physiological material may be found on pages 144, 145, 148, 157, *Machinery of the Body*, 4th ed., by Anton J. Carlson and Victor Johnson. Reprinted by permission of the University of Chicago Press. (Copyright 1937, 1941, 1948, and 1953 by the University of Chicago. All rights reserved. Published 1937. Fourth ed. 1953. Third Impression 1956. Composed and printed by the University of Chicago Press.)

hands are relatively closer to the active negative region of the heart than are the feet. The extremities of the body becomes the poles of a temporary true electrical battery. Both the electrocardiogram and the polygraph instrument can record, to varying degrees, this physiological phenomena.

Nerve impulses from the autonomics do not act upon the cardiac muscle, causing it to contract, but upon the pacemaker, stimulating it to act at an accelerated tempo. The beat is accelerated because successive activations of the cardiac muscle by the pacemaker now occur at shorter intervals than before.

The vagus fibers also terminate in the sinus node and exert their inhibitory effect upon the heart rate by slowing the rate at which the sinus node activates the heart.

We repeat that accelerator nerves arise in the spinal cord. The inhibitory nerves arise in the medulla of the brain.

In our previous examples, then, we have seen a nerve stimulus go afferently into the cerebral cortex, generate an emotion provoking nerve impulse which has been "lit and gun-powdered" under sympathetic control, causing a lessening of tonic vagus inhibition. In the reflex action here we see more blood volume leaving the heart and being forced into systemic circulation. As this occurs we see a stretching of the aortic wall, a stimulation of the depressor nerve and an afferent vagus inhibition returning the heart rate to its previous status.

Once the increased blood volume leaves the aorta and commences its journey towards the brachial artery we see sympathetic vasodilatation of the blood vessels commence a similar reflex. The walls of blood vessels are distended and give rise to the traveling pulse wave. Even during diastole the blood is kept moving forward. At this time, however, smooth muscles are stimulated, sending afferent impulses back through the central nervous system to the vagus center in the medulla and are thence relayed back to skin vessels by way of vasoconstrictor efferents. These are called pressor and depressor nerves.

In previous examples, I through VII we see this combination reflex activity occurring at every response. It is interesting to note the "double bounce" leading up to B1 in Example VI. Here, the impact of a nerve impulse raises both systolic and diastolic pressures. Then, vagus inhibition commences, interrupted by another nerve impulse which creates further acceleration on the sympathetic side. In effect, we are sensing a sort of momentary "nerve impulse bombardment" finally overcome by the vagus and vasoconstrictor medullary centers.

The extra systole at A1 in Example III, at question 37, is also significant in correlation with the final test results. Here, a nerve impulse has reached the heart during diastole and produced a fleeting premature contraction. However, had the stimulus reached the heart during early systole there would have been no disturbance in spontaneous rhythm. The extra systole here is a form of, or degree of, "fibrillation," and is not pathological.

The illustration chart in Example IV verifies the general tonicity of vagus constriction. In Example VIII we see the consistent extra systoles, no doubt pathological in origin, which has become subject's norm. The heart is subject to a number of disorders. The contractile power of the muscle itself may be reduced by damage to the muscle from bacteria, chemical agents, or a diminution of the blood supply. The muscle may also be damaged by certain infections such as, perhaps, rheumatic fever. The germs of scarlet fever or diptheria, though they do not grow in the heart, produce toxins which reach the heart through the blood stream and are injurious to the heart tissues. In thyroid malfunction, also, an excessive production of thyroid harmone may be injurious to the heart muscle. Defects of valves such as a leakage from aorta into ventricles may occur during diastole.

These, plus strength of stimulus (the number of nerve fibers actually activated by a relevant question) along with the condition of the heart muscle affects minute output and stroke volume. When the ventricles contract more forcibly and eject a greater quantity of blood, we cannot ascribe this to a more intense stimulation of the ventricular muscle, via the A-V bundle. It is due to modifications within the heart muscle itself, e.g. effect of stretch, distention, presence of abnormal amounts of oxygen or carbon dioxide, temperature, certain chemicals and other things.* However, along with emotion, all these factors play a role in creating rhythmic interruption and irregular cardio patterns evidenced on a chart.

In the vagus role tracing, Example IX, aforegoing, we see the automatic reflex action of the respiratory regulating center in clear contrast to the cardio acceleration and inhibitory centers. Emotion has generated sort of a constant bombardment of these centers. Deep gasping breaths, not shown here, offset the balance of oxygen and carbon dioxide. As one nerve impulse hits the sinus node we have an increase in systolic pressure (or blood volume being ejected) and a vagus nerve inhibitive attempt to bring the heart's activity back to norm. Again we have sympathetic acceleration and parasympathetic inhibition. With continued heavy inspiration and expiration accompanying each rise and fall in the cardio tracing, we also well sense a stimulation of the carotid sinus and general blood flow. Excess carbon dioxide is the primary stimulating agent.

Example X, at A1 and B3, containing cardio rate changes from slow to fast and vice versa, is a rather obvious verification of the roles emotion and fear can play in this particular type of tracing. We have seen that certain activities of the cerebral cortex influence certain centers through nervous channels inside the brain. Excitement may lead to a rapid heart rate. Fear (of being caught or found out in this instance) may cause cardiac slowing. The pertinent relevant questions in example X trace the nerve impulse from the brain to the medulla. Vagus constriction is lessened by sympathetic acceleration. The reflex action shows distention of the aortic nerves, with an impulse being relayed afferently back to the vagus center, and then efferently to the sinus node, resulting in a slowing down. A2 illustrates rather clearly the excitement level present (the emotional aspect) commencing at

---

*Portions of the foregoing physiological material may be found on pages 150, 151, *Machinery of the Body*, 4th ed., by Anton J. Carlson and Victor Johnson. Reprinted by permission of the University of Chicago Press. (Copyright 1937, 1941, 1948, 1953 by the University of Chicago. All rights reesrved. Published 1937. Fourth ed. 1953. Third Impression 1956. Composed and printed by the University of Chicago Press.)

questions 1 thru 9. Thereafter, at B1 and Bs, we see specific response in both systolic and diastolic, with heart rate suddenly returned to A1 normal at B3. The sharp vagus inhibition here (pressor and depressor reflex) evidences five extra systoles (often times considered a phenomena evolved from emotional relief) before full norm is reestablished.

The authors hope that the foregoing cardio tracing briefs will stimulate further professional exploration into the all important physiological correlates, and associated body phemomena, which see themselves recorded on a moving chart during application of the polygraph technique.

Chapter 11

AUTONOMIC PNEUMOGRAPH TRACINGS

WITH THE respiratory control center located in the medulla, we again note that the phrenic nerves innervate the diaphragm while the intercostal nerves innervate the muscles whose contractions elevate the ribs. The phrenic nerves arise from the neck (cervical) region of the spinal cord and pass downward through the thorax, one on each side of the heart. The intercostal nerves arise at various levels of the thoracic region of the spinal cord. At this point we might add that the vagus nerve is both a sensory and a parasympathetic nerve for the heart, respiratory tract, digestive tract, also being the motor nerve to the pharyngeal and laryngeal muscles. Numerous afferent nerve systems play upon the respiratory center and stimulate or inhibit it.

Efferent nerve impulses leave the emotion-provoking centers in the cerebral cortex and, when they do stimulate the vagus fibers in the respiratory center, breathing movements may temporarily cease or be curtailed to one degree or another. The pneumograph component of the polygraph instrument instantly records any changes from norm in subject's respiration.

It should have become clear that breathing and circulation are intimately related physiologically. In the exchange of gasses between cells and external air, the breathing movements and the circulation of the blood are successive stages in the same process. Also, there are instances where factors controlling blood flow simultaneously influence breathing. In general, these two physiological processes are attuned to the rate of tissue and organ activity, and the rate of breathing and blood flow vary in parallel fashion.* When circulatory adjustments produce a greater blood

*Portions of the foregoing physiological material may be found on page 261, *Machinery of the Body*, 4th ed., by Anton J. Carlson and Victor Johnson. Reprinted by permission of the University of Chicago Press. (Copyright 1937, 1941, 1948, and 1953 by the University of Chicago. All rights reserved. Published 1937. Fourth ed. 1953. Third Impression 1956. Composed and printed by the University of Chicago Press.)

flow, breathing is also accelerated by carbon dioxide stimulation, and vice versa in somewhat of a different sense.

Before we illustrate norm and deviations from norm as recorded by the polygraph's pneumograph section, perhaps it would be apropos to study some of the main nerve controlling pathways. Dr. Netter's magnificant drawing opens the doors.

Color Plate IV. Control of Respiration. Through the solitary nucleus is concerned with taste, control of respiration appears to be its primary function, for it is present even in animals which have no tastebuds, such as birds.

At least three stimuli are effective in respiratory control and are indicated in the illustration: (1) CO_2, bathing the respiratory center directly (and acting, perhaps, by influencing the actual reaction of the blood), (2) the chemical composition of the circulating blood, acting on the chemoreceptors in the carotid and aortic bodies, and (3) the degree to which the lung is distended.

The motor neurons to the phrenic nerve (in C4 and C5), to the intercostal muscles (in the thoracic segments, particularly the upper half) and presumably those to the auxiliary muscles of respiration are under the control of an expiratory and an inspiratory center in the medulla oblongata, approximately at the level of the inferior olive. These centers are in the "reticular substance" and appear to be a part of the inhibitory and the facilitatory centers recently described by Magoun and Rhines. These two respiratory centers, in their turn, receive afferent fibers from the pneumotaxic center near the hypothalamus and from the solitary nucleus. The latter is under the influence of the messages sent by the chemoreceptors of the carotid body over the glossopharyngeus (IX) and vagus (X) and by the stretch receptors in the lung sent over the vagus. When the lung is collapsed (expiration, left half), impulses traveling from stretch receptors over the vagus to the solitary nucleus have a low frequency. They are picked up by the inferior portion of the solitary nucleus and are relayed, probably via the reticulospinal tract and motor neurons in the spinal cord, to the inspiratory center which then causes the diaphragm and external intercostal muscles to contract. Expansion of the lung in inspiration (right half) stimulates the stretch receptors, and impulses are sent along the vagus at high frequency. They are now picked up by a more superior portion of the solitary nucleus which relays impulses to the expiratory center; the latter inhibits the inspiratory muscles and may, in exceptional circumstances, also stimulate the expiratory muscles.

This mechanism (Wyss) appears sufficient in itself to insure the play of alternate inspiration and expiration. Chemoreceptors and CO_2 provide additional security, perhaps by changing the threshold of response of the neurons composing the respiratory centers. References:

Magoun, H. W., and Rhines, R.: *Spasticity. Springfield,* Thomas, 1948.
Wyss, O. A. M.: *J. Neurophysiol. 10:*315-320, 1947.

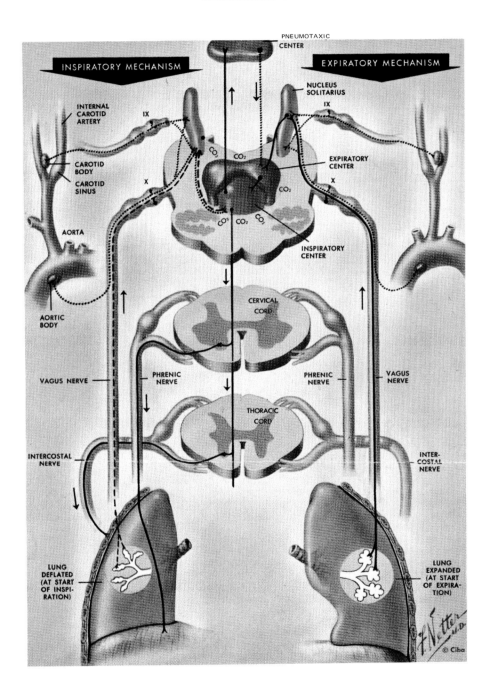

ILLUSTRATED NORM TRACINGS

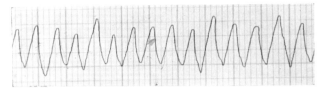

We note the respiratory rate of 8 breaths in a 30-second period, which gives us 16 per minute. From the beginning of inspiration through the end (or descending stroke base) of expiration we count an average of 3 to 4 seconds.

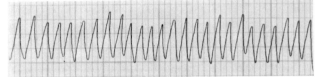

The respiratory rate is 15 in a 30-second period, or 30 per minute. Each inspiration-expiration cycle lasts about 2 seconds.

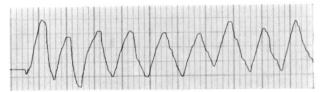

Respiratory rate is 5 in 30 seconds, or an average of 10 per minute. Each inspiration-expiration cycle lasts some 5 seconds.

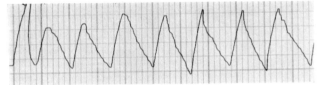

This tracing is somewhat interesting as inspiration takes only about 2 seconds while expiration consumes some 5 seconds. Rate is about 10 per minute.

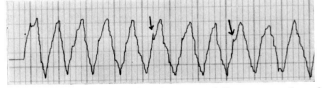

Rate is about 12 per minute. Notice the serrated "nervousness" on both the ascending and descending limbs. Arrows indicate a slight "catch" in the breath.

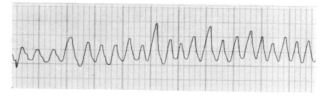

Rate is rapid here, about 26 per minute, and quite shallow. The average inspiration-expiration cycle consumes only 2 to 3 seconds.

DECEPTIVE CRITERIA TRACINGS
Example I—Preemployment

Subject is W/M/A, age twenty-eight, applying for a truck driver's job. The standard data sheet questions used are the same as those illustrated in the preceeding chapter. We use them by number. The reader merely has to refer to the full data sheet on pages 320 and 321 to find the question wording which matches the number.

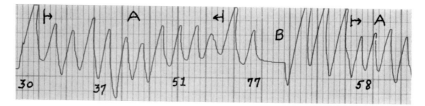

A, Subject's respiratory norm is recorded at about 18 breaths per minute. B, At question 77 (Have you ever stolen merchandise from a place where you've worked?) we see an obvious change from norm. Subject stops breathing for some 4 seconds, momentarily goes into supplemental air reserve, and then takes 3 deep breaths. This B response is referred to as "blocking," or apnea, in polygraph language. Nerve stimulus from the cerebral cortex has shuttled down thalamic relays efferently to the respiration center in the medulla, thence parasympathetically via the phrenic nerve to inhibition of the diaphragm. During intensity of the nerve impulse, and a holding of the breath involuntarily, we consider an imbalance of normal oxygen and carbon dioxide concentration. Therefore, a nerve stimulus is sent afferently to the carotid sinus, or nerve center, thence efferently to respiratory acceleration. The 11 seconds consumed by the 3 deep breaths is the body's way of compensating for the apnea. Vagus nerves again efferently inhibit, and a return to normal respiratory rhythmicity is seen following question 58.

Example II: Preemployment

Subject is W/F/A, age forty, as listed on her employment application.

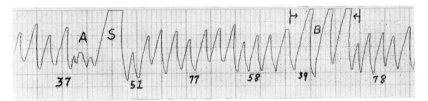

Norm here is about 22 per minute at approximately the same amplitude until we come to question 37 (Did you tell the complete truth on your employment application?). At A we see a considerable reduction in amplitude, with a deep sigh immediately following, then a return to norm until we finish question 39 (Have you given us your true and correct age?). The B deviation is quite prominent. Amplitude and respiratory rate increases considerably above norm. We know that something about question 39 generated enough nerve impulse intensity to cross the "threshold" and cause the change. Within 11 seconds norm is reestablished.

A post-chart probe confirms a correlation between questions 37 and 39. Subject falsified her application as to age, subsequently admitting she was forty-seven years old.

Physiologically we see a suppression at 37 not sufficient to be classified as apnea, but coming close. Vagus stimulation through the medullary respiratory center has inhibited via the phrenic nerve. However, at 39, we may visualize a stimulation of nerve endings near the carotid sinus, and perhaps in the aorta, effecting a reflex acceleration of respiration through a lessening of vagus inhibition. The return to norm sees the same reflex action in reverse.

Example III: Problem

Subject is W/M/A, age thirty. He is under suspect for theft of a case of cigarettes from Blank Warehouse.

Physiologically, at A, we sense a stimulation of the intercostal nerves, and a stimulus closure of the glottis. Suddenly we have too much oxygen and no escape for carbon dioxide. Again the

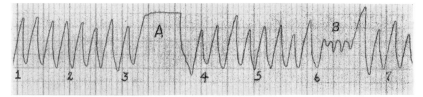

Respiratory norm is about 20 per minute and goes through questions 1, 2, 4, 5, 7. In area A, question 3 (Do you actually know who stole the case of cigarettes in question?), we again see apnea, this time at the top of the ascending stroke, lasting some 7 seconds. At question 6 (Did you steal the case of cigarettes in question?), area B, we see a suppression in amplitude lasting some 5 seconds.

reflex afferent stimulation of the carotid sinus, and a distention of the aorta efferently releases vagus inhibition. Area B is unconscious control from the higher brain centers. It is involuntarily a mild form of "panting" and effected reflexly through vagus inhibition. Carbon dioxide stimulation releases vagus control and we visualize a stimulation of chemical receptors coming from the pneumotaxic center through the solitary nucleus and relayed via the reticulospinal tract and motor neurons in the spinal cord to the inspiratory center. The diaphragm and the external intercostals contract. We follow with a deep breath, new vagus control, and a return to norm.

Example IV: Problem—Voluntary Subject Activity

Subject is W/M/A, age thirty-six. He is under suspect for theft of $450 from his employer's petty cash box.

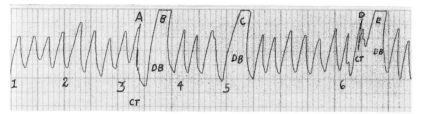

Area A, at question 3 (Do you actually know who stole the $450 in question?), is where subject first clears his throat and then takes a deep breath at B. Area C, at question 5 (Did you get all or part of the $450 in question?), produces another deep breath. At D, question 6 (Do you know where any of the missing money is now?), subject again clears his throat and takes a deep breath at E.

The questions were worded: (1) Do you live in Tucson? (2) Do you ever drink water? (3) Were you involved in the death of Mary Jane Doe in Wickenburg last Friday? (4) Did you steal the $450 in question? (5) Did you burglarize Jake's Pharmacy in Phoenix day before yesterday? (6) Do you actually know what happened to the $450 in question?

Again, there is no unusual subject activity or voluntary movement at any of the questions except A4 and B6, where he repeats clearing his throat and breathing deeply.

Summation

Obviously, subject was deliberately attempting to beat the test. Subsequently he confessed. Coughing and sniffing, or talking, are other very common subject performances while attempting deception. Invariably this conduct is seen at key relevant issue questions but not so at any of the others.

GENERALIZED DECEPTION CRITERIA TRACINGS

Deviations from norm in the tracings below follow a crucial question, or a question which means something to the subject.

A.

B.

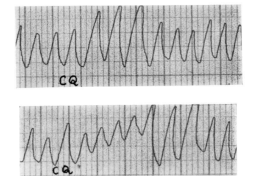

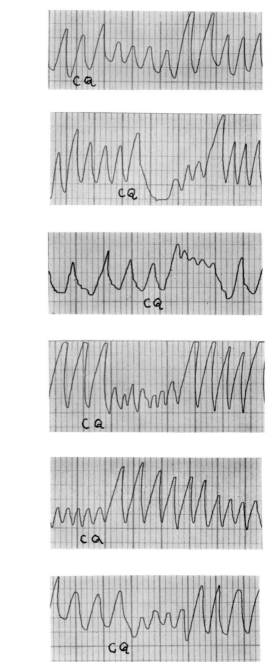

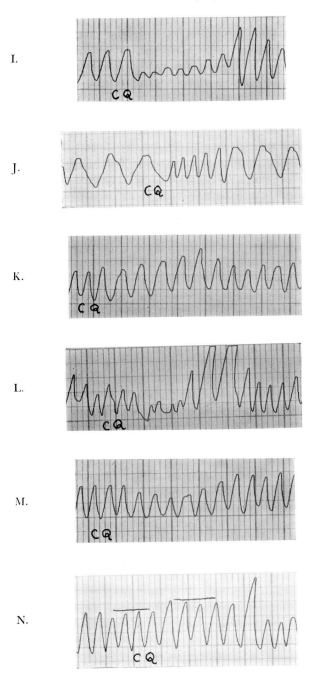

O.

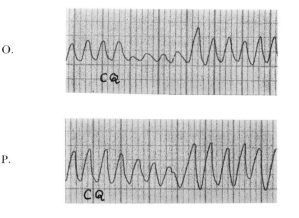

P.

Pneumograph tracings A through H may be considered the result of strong nerve impulse impact upon the medullary breathing center, effecting deviation from respiratory norm. These types of tracings will appear more often in charts conducted during problem or criminal cases where the outcome of the test is of paramount importance to the subject.

Examples I through P are more frequently found in preemployment testing where a known lie, or association with something similar, has generated a series of nerve impulses sufficiently strong enough to cause the deviation. In other words, while the subject knows he has not been truthful, he may not consider such of great importance to his own well-being.

However, any of the foregoing examples can appear in any type of testing. Generally, accurate chart interpretation in preemployment requires far more attention to the minute deviations than it does in criminal testing since question stimulus is frequently less potent.

We must not forget that in all deviations from respiratory norm, again with respect to the amount of emotional energy expended, the body's temperature-regulating center also plays a vital role in harmony with the carotid sinus, aortic sensory nerves and, specifically, the medullary respiratory control center itself.

Chapter 12

GALVANIC SKIN RESPONSE TRACINGS

W<small>E BELIEVE</small> that activity of all major systems of the body directly contributes to changes in sweat gland secretion, particularly when these systems are stimulated by emotion-provoking causes.

The examples set forth herein support, confirm, and perhaps surpass all previous theories with respect to changes affecting sweat gland activity. We feel this phase of physiological research, based on actual cases, will result in further exploration and additional interpretation of GSR phenomenon.

This chapter is quite simply based on "energy expended," consciously or unconsciously. The energy consumed may be voluntary or involuntary. It may also be referred to as subject "emotion" or "work."

If the temperature-regulating center in the thalamus is stimulated by environmental changes, so also it must be stimulated by various degrees of enteroceptive, visceroceptive and proprioceptive activity.

Whenever a subject wiggles his toes, grits his teeth, voluntarily contracts inner sphincters, a change in sweat gland secretion is instantly recorded by the polygraph's sensitive galvanometer.

In conjunction herewith we may safely say—as in the cardio and respiratory areas—that sweat gland activity has its own type of "norm." Sweat secretion also "commences to function" at one pace. Whether the examining room is too hot or too cold, whether the subject is rested, feeling well, excited or tired, he still produces his norm of the moment.

This norm is increased or decreased by internal mental, chemical and electrical energies, governed by the temperature-regulating center, and somewhat moderated by external environmental conditions. Dilatation produces more heat. Vasoconstriction reduces heat. Physical exercise increases friction (heat) ; inactivity lessens friction.

When a person is rested and feeling well, there is less bodily friction, therefore less heat. When a person has been through the ordeals of a tough day, all systems of the body are forced to work a little harder in maintaining functional homeostasis, resulting in more internal friction and more heat. Obviously, the foregoing establishes the fundamental causes for changes in sweat gland activity.

The polygraph galvanometer generates against a given area of a person's sweat glands a current of 50 microamperes at 500 mv. The current is connected to the grid of a detector and transmitted through two primary legs of a bridged circuit which contains an established constant. Sensitivity of the galvanometer circuit may be adjusted from 1 to 800,000 ohms. The lower the amount of ohms in the system, the higher the power of electricity.

As the body functions, it generates its own peculiar form of electrical energy. By using the ohm sensitivity dial the polygraphist attempts to instrumentally match a machine constant with the body's electrical output. When this is accomplished, pen excursion on the chart should be about one inch for every 10,000 ohms. Again, this will vary due to subject's resistance, physical condition, as previously noted. The conducting agent is the bodily compounds which create the beads of sweat oozing outwardly to the surface of the skin.

A decrease in subject's resistance will momentarily imbalance the machine constant and the galvo pen will rise on the chart. An increase in subject's resistance results in the opposite, or a return to machine constant and a downward movement of the galvo pen. A 250,000 ohms galvanometer circuit used in the standard Stoelting #22500 Deceptograph through 1966 is schematically illustrated in Fig. 17.

EXPERIMENTAL RESULTS FROM NEW GALVO THEORY

For some time the authors have been experimenting with galvanometer responses. Quite frequently a relevant question stimulus will produce no deviation in the cardio or pneumo tracings but does so in the galvo. Therefore, we asked 100 subjects to volunteer for a "thought" experiment. Each person was balanced

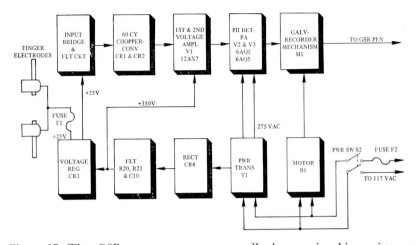

Figure 17. The GSR components sense small changes in skin resistance (from subject's general resistance level) when subject is under test. A simple wheatstone bridge circuit uses the finger electrodes and compensating resistances in one arm, and is so arranged that the subject's general resistance level, across the electrode plate, can be balanced against the other bridge arms. The subject's emotional response to stimuli introduced by the polygraph examiner will trigger small changes in subject's general resistance level, causing a positive or negative imbalance. This imbalance is picked up by the chopper converter, fed as a rectilinear wave into the first and second voltage amplifier stages, and transmitter to the power and phase detector stage, which receives signal greatly magnified and translates it as an output signal, according to polarity and magnitude. The recording galvanometer will receive the signal, and its pen will swing from the zero reference base line, depending on polarity and magnitude of signal. The size of any input signal to the cathode connected galvanometer is proportioned to the imbalance existing at the input bridge output. The intensity of subject's response to stimulus (as transmitted by the electrodes from general resistance level) can normally be measured by the arc of the GSR pen swing from the zero reference base line of chart. The recording galvanometer is electrically connected into both cathodes of the GSR amplifier system. Its coil resistance makes up the cathode resistances. The galvanometer section consists of a strong magnet with a coil of wire suspended in the field of the magnet. When a current from the amplifier goes through the coil, it turns on its axis. The degree of the turn depends on the amount of current going through the coil. (From the C.H. Stoelting Emotional Stress Monitor Polygraph operating manual).

into the galvanometer circuit and simply asked to think of something which was considered extremely repugnant to them. In 95 percent of these cases an upswing of the galvo pen was noted. For the 5 percent who did not respond we merely asked them to change their concentration to another subject matter considered equally repugnant. The whole 5 percent produced a galvo response on the chart.

It seems apparent that any mental activity also utilizes energy, in turn stimulating to some degree the function of the temperature-regulating center and thereby producing minute changes in sweat gland activity.

The next experiment involved word association tests. All kinds of words were used, such as love, hate, murder, theft, narcotics, church, God, robbery, mother, father, husband, wife, money credit, health, employment, crimes, sickness. All of the 100 subjects responded to one or more words, but with different degrees of intensity.

While we somewhat confirm that specific mental activity creates the capability to generate enough nerve impulse intensity to produce a change in sweat gland activity, we must remember that the degree of intensity depends on what the particular word projected meant to the person receiving it.

Our third experiment was conducted on ten men and ten women, all between the ages of eighteen and thirty. With proper galvo sensitivity established, an assistant projected the picture of a mutilated child upon a screen. Only one subject was tested at a time, in complete privacy, and was not permitted to discuss the experiment with any of the others awaiting. All twenty subjects responded with varying degrees of intensity, women more so.

Then the men were separated into one group and individually tested. Without warning each subject was shown a picture of an attractive nude woman. Some responded with considerable galvo activity; others only mildly. However, when a picture of a voluptuous woman wearing panties and a bra was projected on the screen, each subject responded by sending the galvo pen against its top pen stop.

In the foregoing we see that sensory impressions along with imagination, are digested in the cerebral cortex and provoke nerve impulses sufficient in intensity to produce a change in sweat gland activity, again confirming that the amplitude of galvo pen excursion is primarily governed by what the stimulus means to the subject who receives it.

Our last experiment on five men was rather interesting. We took three galvanometers and placed conducting electrodes on both hands, under the arm pits, and to their foreheads. All three instruments were activated and balance obtained at 20,000 ohms of sensitivity. Each subject was barefooted. The stimuli utilized were quite simple: words, touch, sound, and requesting subject to wiggle his toes. In all five cases, mild to excessive galvanometer recordings were obtained from all instrument attachment points simultaneously.

In normal live polygraph testing, galvo electrodes are placed on the finger tips or in the palm of the hand because of the ease, accessibility, and for the purpose of eliminating any psychological adversity.

Work or Emotion

Work, in this instance, is usually referred to as any galvo deviation caused by muscular activity or movement. However, there is another classification of work which must be given serious consideration. This is the "work" of involuntary contraction of smooth and even striated muscles originating from normal physiological phenomena or as a result of some emotion provoking stimuli.

The previous conflict between work and emotion is also considered in the light of meaning, conscious understanding of meaning and what associational effects evolve therefrom. The following galvo tracings more or less separate the two for purposes of chart interpretation.

Work—Example I

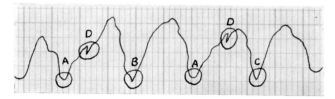

A—Here we see a smooth "U" as the galvo pen dips and starts upward, normal function.

B—The sharp "V" occurred, indicating a voluntary movement,
after subject was instructed to bite his tongue.

C—Again the sharp "V" when subject was asked to wiggle his toes.

D—This sharp downward break in the tracing, forming a thin
"V", specifically is finger movement of the hand to which the
galvo electrodes are attached.

Work—Example II

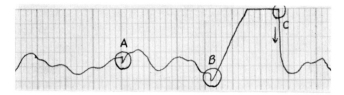

A—Repeated are the effects of finger movement.

B—Subject was asked to contract his anus sphincter. Note the
narrowness of the "U", preceeded by a sharp break, indicative
of movement interruption of normal galvo pen flow, with the
pen hitting the top pen stop and staying there.

C—Indicates a mechanical readjustment by the examiner which
returns the galvo pen back to center of the chart. Arrow denotes.

As aforementioned, the galvo pen is longer than both the
cardio and pneumo pens in order that it may have a greater area

of excursion potential and not collide with the other two. For this reason, a Stoelting galvo pen is about seven inches long and records some four to five seconds behind the other two, as noted below.

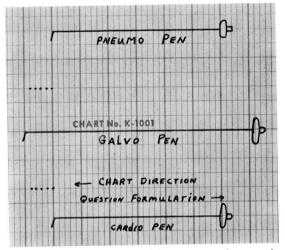

When the galvo pen rises to either extremity, entirely or partially, the five-second lag diminishes, as illustrated below:

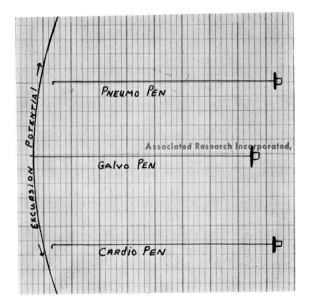

In galvo chart interpretation, an emotion-producing response will usually occur during the middle or at the end of question stimulus; it will commence as soon as subject's brain has understood the meaning of the question and can get the generated nerve impulse under way. This will generally take some two to three seconds from the first audible word of the question until the tracing change starts. There are times, however, when galvo response will be seen some four to five seconds after subject has answered the question. Two reasons for this are: (1) some association of the past, or just remembering something else, and (2) subject first answered the question without really comprehending its full meaning and then suddenly does understand its meaning. We illustrate:

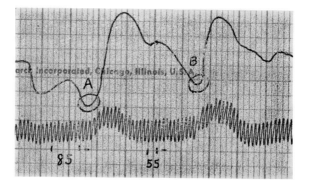

A—To data sheet question #85 (Do you know any employee presently working for this company who has been stealing money or merchandise?) we see the response in galvo occurring just as the subject answers. We also see some cardio deviation which verifies both responses to specifically be the result of an emotional aspect, clearly separating itself from "work".

B—Here we see galvo response coming some five seconds after subject answered in the negative at Question #55 (Have you ever had a back injury?) and is again supported by a slight rise and fall in cardio systolic and diastolic pressures.

Summation

A between chart probe revealed that a former employee of this particular company once told subject he had stolen a small set of socket wrenches. The A response is, therefore, confirmed as emotional. With respect to the delayed reaction at B, subject said that after he answered the question he suddenly remembered falling out of a tree when a boy and slightly injuring his back. Again, we have a confirmed separation of emotion from work. The smooth "U," encircled, at A and B supports this.

Spacing between questions of not less than ten seconds is most important. It permits a response rise and return to norm and prevents one question interrupting the response potential of another. Therefore, we might say that the rhythm of question formulation is some ten seconds. The subject quickly senses this and he often anticipates the next question just before its first word is uttered. Anticipation is far more prevalent in PTA problem tests because the subject is aware of question sequence and knows exactly where the crucial question will fall, if he is so involved. We first illustrate with preemployment data sheet questions and then with a PTA test:

EMOTION—Example II (Preemployment)

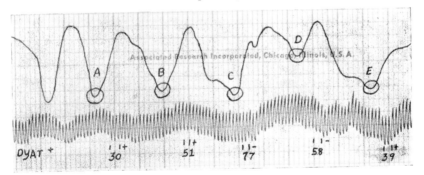

Reference: At A-B-C-D-E we see anticipation in the form of galvo pen excursion upwards before the first word of each data sheet question was uttered. The encircled "u"s indicate emotion instead of work.

EMOTION—Example III (PTA)

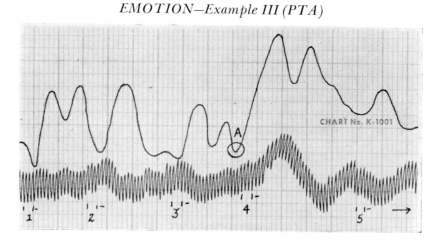

CHART No. K-1001

Reference: Between questions 1 and 4, we see "tension" responses in the galvo. As we approach the crucial question, #4, we see a rise in the cardio tracing. Exactly
five seconds behind subject's negative answer at #4,
we note the sharp galvo excursion upwards supported
by a twelve second cardio response. Once the crucial
question is past, galvo tension slacks off. Since there is
no indication of voluntary "work" here, we can safely
assume that responses in both tracings are emotional
in origin.

INVOLUNTARY WORK

There are times when internal happenings of the body, involuntary in origin, can have specific effect upon galvanometer
tracings. We may say that such activity, when involuntary, is an
enteroceptive reflex. More directly, we are referring to the unconscious contraction of certain areas of smooth muscle and
sphincters. While a person can voluntarily contract bladder and
anal sphincters almost at will, cerebral centers of awareness are
constantly bombarding all portions of the body with numerous
control-type reflex nerve impulses. This is one way mother nature
helps us to keep from involuntarily urinating or defecating.

One of the most common physiological phenomena having

considerable bearing on galvo tracings occurs when a woman is in her menstrual period. In comparison, her cardio tracings will either be to the extreme in fluctuation (nervous tension or fear of the test itself, which aggravates the physiological abnormalities occurring during the menstrual cycle) or will be completely flat with no fluctuating tonicity—rhythmicity—observed in either systolic or diastolic pressures. Her pneumograph tracings will generally be quite erratic, ordinarily with no maintenance of a respiratory base line. Inspiration and expiration will appear somewhat "ragged." In many instances galvanometer tracings will repeatedly occur without rhyme or reason, with or without verbal stimulus.

Menstruation is brought about by hormones originating in the anterior pituitary body. The blood originates in the endometrium where definite cyclic changes can be noted. These are post-menstrual, about five days; proliferative or estrogen phase, some fourteen days; premenstrual of about five days, when the mucous membrane becomes congested with blood and thickens. The actual menstruation period lasts about four days, during which capillary hemorrhage takes place and epithelium of the mucous membrane is expelled. During this period one-half to two-thirds of the endometrium is extruded. Usually during menstruation, most women undergo a feeling of fullness in the pelvis, bearing down sensations, fullness in the breasts, slight nausea and headache. The total amount of blood lost in a normal period is about two ounces. This is a mild form of hemorrhage, and the physiological constant of the body is therefore upset.

We might attribute a portion of the irregular respiratory tracing to a slight reduction in red blood cell count, during part of the menstrual period, since the red cells are the body's oxygen-carrying agents, although oxygen lack is not a general cell stimulant. However, other cells do respond to oxygen deficiency, such as certain nerve endings. Lowered oxygen content of the blood stimulates the red bone marrow. Often, if the blood loss or destruction is not too excessive the bone marrow is able to cope with the menstrual situation. In fact, normal menstruation may so stimulate the bone marrow that the moderate deficiency is more than compensated for. If a female subject is having a "bad time" of it during her menstrual period (flowing heavily and cramping), the red blood cell deficiency impairs the oxygen balance, cell oxidations are hampered, energy liberation inadequate, and nerves controlling both smooth and striated muscles lose a portion of their ability to maintain a strict vessel tonicity.

During menstruation, there is a constant two- to three-second involuntary contraction of muscles supplying the endometrium and the uterus as blood is ejected. This in itself expends a certain amount of energy. Particularly during the more severe menstrual muscle contractions, or the cramping period, effecting oxygen imbalance, the temperature-regulating center is bombarded by reflex nerve impulses, and as a result there are changes in sweat gland activity which are recorded by the polygraph instrument's galvanometer section.

Example I

Subject is W/F/A, age twenty-three, married. She was applying for a secretarial job. In the pretest interview, to data sheet question 34, (Do you feel well today?) she replied in the negative, stating that she was menstruating and had been experiencing mild cramps. Her doctor had prescribed some medicine to help "ease her through" but she did not know what it was.

The tracing below was merely conducted for illustration purposes. Although no questions were asked, they are hypothetically
inserted about every ten seconds to emphasize the erratic galvo
tracing.

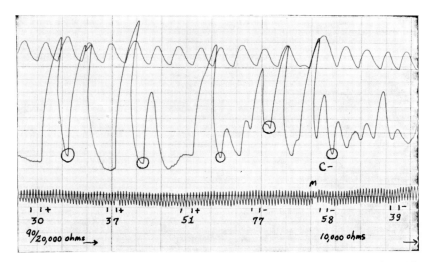

The encircled "V" again verifies the difference between work, which this
clearly is, and emotion. The flatness of the cardio pattern is quite obvious.
The condition is, no doubt, more prevalent when medications containing
sedative and pain-reducing ingredients are present. Note the 3-to 5-second
sharpness of galvo amplitude. At question 58, we reduced instrument sensitivity to 10,000 ohms. This merely curtailed amplitude. At every third or
fourth breath in the pneumo tracing there is also slight change in amplitude.

Example II

Subject is W/F/A, age thirty-eight. She was taking a loyalty
test for promotion. To question 51 (Are you in good health now?)
she answered in the affirmative but added she was just finishing
her period; she was not experiencing any cramps or unusual discomfort. A slightly different pneumo tracing and a considerable
change in the cardio tracing is noted as compared to the foregoing
one in Example I.

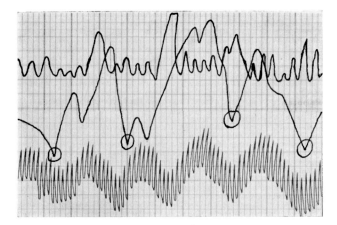

In the pneumo tracing we see what appears to be the beginning of a norm tracing suddenly suppressed without question stimulus. Normally, the deeper breaths should produe galvo fluctuation of the "U" nature, but here we see (encircled) sharp "V"s. These involuntary movements are appearing some 10 to 12 seconds apart. The rhythmic rise and fall in the cardio pattern makes no rhyme or reason and does not seem to be affected by the usual breathing pattern. Therefore, we see the physiological carry-over of the effects of subject's menstrual period. While there are still smooth muscle contractions ejecting small amounts of blood, the strength of these with respect to crossing the stimulus threshold is not now as frequent. Again, the emotional "fear of the test" aspect is seen in the intermittent rapidity of the respiratory pattern.

Example III

Earlier in this chapter we mentioned the involuntary "work" of smooth and striated muscles occurring in response to nerve impulse intensity. The degree of intensity and the amplitude of recorded response will, of course, depend on what the question stimulus means to the subject. In turn, this reflects on how many nerve fibers are activated in a given nerve pathway. The tonus of smooth muscle, with which the polygraph examiner is more concerned, is much more variable than that of striated muscle. We shall more or less confine our remarks to this area. In other words, the energy for conduction of the impulse comes from the nerve itself and not the stimulating agent, providing that the stimulus is of at least threshold strength.

However, as noted in galvanometer deflections, the foregoing is somewhat conditioned on whether or not the condition and the temperature of nerve fiber is unchanged. When stimuli producing a series, or volley, of impulses are used, it is found that graded intensities of stimuli lead to fewer or more impulses per volley. Stronger stimuli lead to more nerve impulses, each of which is maximal intensity. The effects of nerve stimulation, whether it be experimental or physiological, are dependent upon the destination of the nerve and the structures to which the impulses are carried and not upon any functional peculiarity of the nerve fibers or specificity of the nerve impulses.*

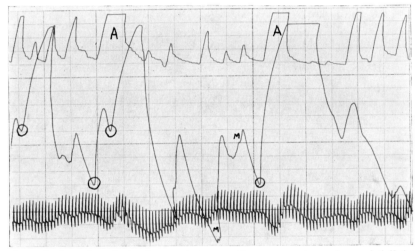

At each deep breath in the respiratory pattern we note a rise and fall in both cardiovascular systolic and diastolic pressures and in galvanometer tracings. Physiologically, this has already been explained in previous chapters and illustrations. At A, we see a "block" in respiratory and a coordinating galvo pen upswing as changes in sweat gland activity take place.

---

*Portions of the foregoing physiological material may be found on pages 389, 390, 391, *Machinery of the Body*, 4th ed., by Anton J. Carlson and Victor Johnson. Reprinted by permission of the University of Chicago Press. (Copyright 1937, 1941, 1948, and 1953 by the University of Chicago. All rights reserved. Published 1937. Fourth ed. 1953. Third Impression 1956. Composed and printed by the University of Chicago Press.)

Involuntary work of this type is illustrated in the next chart tracing.

There are two excellent physiological possibilities here. A contraction of the diaphragm through stimulation of the phrenic nerve is, in itself, action of striated muscle. We also see a nerve stimulus closure of the glottis. The oxygen-carbon dioxide imbalance reflexly stimulates the temperature-regulating center as well as both the cardio- and respiratory-regulating centers. Hence, the individual tracing deviations as noted on page 318. Electrical energies, combined with other bodily energies have been consumed.

While there are many other types of galvanometer tracings resulting from physiological phenomena, categorically separating "work" from "emotion," we trust the foregoing basic correlates will give the reader a deeper insight into sensitivity of the ingredients necessary for accurate chart interpretation.

From the New Testament, St. John, Chapter 8, Verse 32, we read:

> And ye shall know the truth and
> the truth shall make you free.

Portions of a Polygraph Testing Data Sheet Utilized by Texas Industrial Security, Inc., Forth Worth, Texas.

Has subject previous file? Yes _____ No _____   FILE No. _____

Booking Number _____   EXAMINER _____

ACCOUNT NAME _____ BUSINESS PHONE _____

APP'T BY _____ REPORT TO _____

APPT'T DATE _____ TIME _____ TEST GIVE: DATE _____ TIME _____

TYPE OF TEST: _____ PE _____ PC _____ S _____ POSITION _____

SUBJECT _____
     FIRST   MIDDLE   LAST   MAIDEN

ADDRESS _____ PHONE _____

_____ SEX _____ AGE _____ HT. _____ WT. _____ DOB _____ Place of Birth _____

WHERE REARED _____ TIME HERE _____ Location Before _____

DRIVERS LICENSE _____ Social Security No. _____ Draft Class. _____
     STATE   NUMBER   EXPIRES

EDUCATION _____

MARITAL STATUS: M _____ OTHER MARRIAGES _____ DIV. _____ SEP. _____ S _____
     DATE   PLACE   Spouse Employed   DATE   PLACE   DATE

CHILDREN _____ Spouse Employed _____ INCOME _____

CHILDREN BY _____ _____ CHILD SUPPORT _____
     NUMBER   AGE

PREV. MARRIAGE _____ _____ CHILD SUPPORT _____
     NUMBER   AGE   AMOUNT   PAST DUE

MILITARY RECORD BRANCH: _____ DATE OF ENTRY _____ DATE OF DISCHARGE _____ RANK _____

TYPE OF DISCHARGE _____ COURT MARTIALS _____ COMP. _____

FINANCIAL STATUS: HOME: _____ AUTO _____ OTHER DEBTS: _____

TOTAL OWED _____ MAKE _____ MODEL _____ OWE _____ STATUS OF ACCOUNTS _____
     RENT   BUY   PAYMENT   BAD DEBTS

JUDGEMENTS _____ BANK REFERENCE _____ CURRENT, BEHIND, ETC.
     CHECKING   SAVINGS   LOAN

FAVORITE HOBBY _____

INDEX DATA: _____ TOTAL _____ REPORT TO _____

TIME OUT: _____ TIME _____ BY _____

RESULTS: _____ TESTED BY: _____

DATE _____ PLACE _____

I, _____, by my signature below, acknowledge that I have voluntarily consented to submit to this polygraph test. The Polygraphist conducting this test has my permission to report the results of this examination to the party or parties directly concerned.

Polygraphist _____   Signature of Testee _____

TIS-11

GENERAL QUESTIONS

	Yes	No
30. HAVE YOU GIVEN US YOUR TRUE AND CORRECT NAME?		
31. HAVE YOU EVER TAKEN A POLYGRAPH TEST BEFORE?		
32. HAVE YOU TAKEN ANY PILLS OR MEDICINES TODAY?		
33. HAVE YOU DRANK ANY ALCOHOL TODAY?		
34. DO YOU FEEL WELL TODAY?		
35. HAVE YOU EVER BEEN EMPLOYED BY THIS COMPANY BEFORE?		
36. HAVE YOU EVER BEEN EMPLOYED BY A SIMILAR COMPANY BEFORE?		
37. DID YOU TELL THE COMPLETE TRUTH ON YOUR EMPLOYMENT APPLICATION?		
38. DID YOU LEAVE A FORMER EMPLOYER OFF YOUR APPLICATION? (HOW MANY?)		

JOB RESPONSIBILITY QUESTIONS:

	Yes	No
39. HAVE YOU GIVEN US YOUR TRUE AND CORRECT AGE?		
40. HAVE YOU TOLD THE TRUTH ABOUT YOUR EMPLOYMENT BACKGROUND?		
41. DID YOU TELL THE COMPLETE TRUTH TO THE PERSON WHO INTERVIEWED YOU FOR THIS JOB?		
42. DO YOU KNOW WHAT JOB YOU ARE APPLYING FOR?		
43. DO YOU FEEL QUALIFIED TO DO THIS TYPE OF WORK?		
44. DO YOU NEED TRAINING FOR THIS JOB?		
45. WILL YOU BE SATISFIED WITH THE STARTING SALARY?(WHAT IS IT?)		
46. ARE YOU SEEKING LONG TERM (TEMPORARY) EMPLOYMENT WITH THIS COMPANY?		
47. HAVE YOU EVER QUIT A JOB WITHOUT GIVING PROPER NOTICE? (HOW MANY?)		
48. HAVE YOU EVER BEEN FIRED FROM A JOB FOR ANY REASON? (HOW MANY?)		
1. _____ WHY?		
2. _____ WHY?		
3. _____ WHY?		

ACCIDENT PRONE QUESTIONS

	Yes	No
50. HAVE YOU HAD ANY MAJOR OPERATIONS WITHIN THE PAST TEN YEARS? _____ (DATE) (REMARKS)		
1.		
2.		
3.		
ARE YOU IN GOOD HEALTH NOW?		

GENERAL QUESTIONS

	Yes	No
66. HAVE YOU EVER BEEN ARRESTED FOR DRIVING WHILE INTOXICATED?		
67. HAVE YOU EVER HAD STOMACH ULCERS?		
68. HAVE YOU EVER THOUGHT YOU SHOULD TAKE THE CURE FOR ALCOHOLISM? (HAVE YOU?)		
69. HAVE YOU PADDED TICKETS, EXPENSE OR MILEAGE VOUCHERS? (TRUCK DRIVERS)		

SECURITY QUESTIONS:

	Yes	No
70. ARE YOU APPLYING FOR THIS JOB FOR ANY REASON OTHER THAN EMPLOYMENT?		
71. DO YOU WANT THIS JOB FOR ANY HARMFUL (BAD) OR DEVIOUS REASON?		
72. COULD YOUR EMPLOYMENT BE HARMFUL TO THIS COMPANY IN ANY PLANNED WAY?		
73. HAVE YOU EVER WORKED WITH (COLLUSION) ANYONE TO TAKE MONEY, MERCHANDISE, OR DEFRAUD AN EMPLOYER?		
74. HAVE YOU EVER "SHORT CHECKED" FRIENDS, RELATIVES OR OTHER EMPLOYERS? (UNAUTHORIZED DISCOUNTS?)		
75. HAVE YOU EVER TAKEN TRADING STAMPS, REDEMPTION COUPONS OR FALSELY EXCHANGED MERCHANDISE FROM AN EMPLOYER?		
76. HAVE YOU EVER INTENTIONALLY DAMAGED (OPENED) MERCHANDISE?		
77. HAVE YOU EVER STOLEN MERCHANDISE, TOOLS OR MATERIAL FROM A PLACE WHERE YOU HAVE WORKED?		
78. HAVE YOU EVER STOLEN MONEY FROM A PLACE WHERE YOU HAVE WORKED?		
79. ARE YOU WANTED BY THE POLICE ANYWHERE FOR ANY KIND OF A CRIME? (TRAFFIC TICKETS?)		
80. HAVE YOU EVER KNOWINGLY SOLD STOLEN MERCHANDISE?		
80a. HAVE YOU EVER KNOWINGLY BOUGHT STOLEN MERCHANDISE?		

52. HAVE YOU BEEN TREATED FOR DIZZY SPELLS, BLACKOUTS OR A NERVOUS BREAKDOWN?

53. HAVE YOU SOUGHT PSYCHIATRIC CONSULTATION OR BEEN A PATIENT IN A MENTAL HOSPITAL?

54. HAVE YOU BEEN TOLD YOU WILL NEED OR DO YOU ANTICIPATE SURGERY WITHIN THE NEXT 12 MONTHS?

55. HAVE YOU EVER HAD A BACK INJURY OR STRAIN?
1.
2.
DO YOU HAVE ANY CURRENT BACK PROBLEMS?

56. HAVE YOU EVER HAD A RUPTURE OR HERNIA?
1.
2.

57. HAS YOUR HERNIA (RUPTURE) BEEN REPAIRED (SURGERY)?
1.
2.

58. HAVE YOU BEEN INJURED ON ANY JOB WHERE YOU LOST TIME?
1.
2.

59. HAVE YOU EVER FILED FOR OR COLLECTED WORKMAN'S COMPENSATION INSURANCE FROM AN ON THE JOB INJURY?
1.
2.
3.

60. HAVE YOU HAD ANY AUTOMOBILE ACCIDENTS WHILE YOU WERE DRIVING?
(DATE)
1.
2.
3.

61. HAVE YOU EVER HAD A COMMERCIAL VEHICLE ACCIDENT WHILE YOU WERE DRIVING?
(HOW MANY TIMES?)

62. HAVE YOU RECEIVED ANY MOVING TRAFFIC CITATIONS IN THE PAST YEAR? (3 YEARS?)

63. HAVE YOU EVER HAD A DRIVER'S LICENSE REVOKED OR SUSPENDED?

64. HAS DRINKING EVER INTERFERRED WITH YOUR WORK?

65. DID YOU EVER DRINK ANY ALCOHOLIC BEVERAGES ON THE JOB?

83. HAVE YOU EVER BEEN ARRESTED AND PLACED IN JAIL?
1.
2.
3.
4.

84. HAVE YOU EVER SERVED TIME IN A REFORMATORY OR PENITENTIARY?

85. DO YOU KNOW ANY EMPLOYEE PRESENTLY WORKING FOR THIS COMPANY WHO HAS BEEN STEALING MONEY OR MERCHANDISE?

86. HAVE YOU EVER BEEN TURNED DOWN BY A BONDING COMPANY?

87. HAVE YOU EVER PAID A DEFAULT TO A BONDING COMPANY?

88. HAVE YOU WRITTEN ANY BAD CHECKS IN THE PAST YEAR? (ANY OUT NOW?)

89. HAVE YOU BEEN INVOLVED IN ANY UNDETECTED CRIMES IN THE PAST THREE YEARS?

90. HAVE YOU EVER FORGED ANOTHER PERSON'S NAME TO A CHECK?

91. HAVE YOU EVER USED OR SOLD NARCOTICS ILLEGALLY?

92. DID YOU EVER TRY MARIHUANA, ACID, LSD OR HEROIN?

93. DID YOU FALSIFY YOUR EMPLOYMENT APPLICATION IN ANY MANNER?

94. IS THERE ANYTHING IN YOUR PERSONAL LIFE THAT COULD DISCREDIT THIS COMPANY?

95. HAVE YOU EVER FOUND IT NECESSARY TO SUE A FORMER EMPLOYER FOR ANY REASON?

NOTES & REMARKS:

REFERENCES

Arther, Richard O.: *The Journal of Polygraph Studies,* Vol. 1, No. 3, 1966; Vol. 2, No. 1, 1967.

American Polygraph Association Newsletter, Vol. 3, No. 1, Jan.-Feb. 1969 (containing an address by F. Lee Bailey before the American Polygraph Association Seminar, Silver Spring, Maryland, 1968.)

Benussi, V.: Die Atmungssymptome der Luge. *Arch Gesamte Psychol., 31:* 244, 1914.

Breese, B.B.: *Psychology.* Scribner's Sons, New York, 1917.

Cates, H.A., Basmajian, J.V.: *Primary Anatomy,* 3rd ed., (also new 5th ed. by J. V. Basmajian). Williams & Wilkins, Baltimore, 1955.

Carlson, Anton J., Johnson, Victor: *Machinery of The Body,* 4th ed. The University of Chicago Press, Chicago, 1937, 1941, 1948, 1953.

Dienstein, William: *Are You Guilty?* Thomas, Springfield, 1954.

Erlanger, J.: *A New Instrument For Determining The Minimum and Maximum Blood Pressures in Man.* Johns Hopkins Hospital Report, 1904.

Fulton, John F., Wilson, Leonard C.: *Selected Readings in the History of Physiology,* 2nd ed, Thomas, Springfield, 1964.

Gardner, Ernest: *Fundamentals of Neurology.* Saunders, Philadelphia and London, 1947, 1952, 1958.

Gough, H.G.: Some common misconceptions about neuroticism. *J. Consult. Psychol.,* 1954.

Hilgard, E.R., Atkinson, R.C.: *Introduction To Psychology,* 4th ed. Harcourt, Brace & World, New York, 1967.

Marston, W.M.: Systolic blood pressure symptoms of deception. *J. Exp. Psychol., 2(2):* 117, 1917.

Morgan, C.T., Stellar, E.: *Physiological Psychology,* 2nd ed. McGraw-Hill, New York, 1950.

Munn, Norman L.: *Psychology,* 2nd ed. Houghton Mifflin, Boston, 1946, 1951.

Netter, Frank H.: *The CIBA Collection of Medical Illustrations,* Vol. I., CIBA Pharmaceutical Products, New Jersey, 1957.

Ranson, S.W.: *A. Research Nerv. and Ment. Dis., Proc., 20:*342, 1940.

Woodworth, R.S.: *Experimental Psychology.* New York, Holt, 1938.

INDEX

THE POLYGRAPH IN COURT